Citizens in the Making in Post-Soviet States

The political outlook of young people in the countries of the former Soviet Union is crucial to their countries' future political development. This is particularly relevant now as the first generation without firsthand experience of communism is approaching adulthood. Based on extensive original research and including new survey research amongst adolescents, this book examines adolescents' political outlook in countries of the former Soviet Union; it compares and contrasts Russia, where authoritarianism has begun to reassert itself, and Ukraine, which experienced a democratic breakthrough in the aftermath of the Orange Revolution.

The book examines questions such as: How supportive is this new generation of the new political order? What images of the Soviet Union prevail in the minds of young people? How much trust does youth place in current political and public institutions? Addressing these questions is crucial to understanding the extent to which the current regimes can survive on the wave of public support. The book argues that Russian adolescents tend to place more trust in the incumbent president and harbour more regrets about the disintegration of the Soviet Union than their peers in Ukraine; it demonstrates that young people distrust political parties and politicians, and that patriotic education shapes social and political values.

Olena Nikolayenko is an assistant professor in the Department of Political Science at Fordham University, New York, USA.

BASEES/Routledge Series on Russian and East European Studies

Series Editor:
Richard Sakwa, *Department of Politics and International Relations, University of Kent*

Editorial Committee:
Julian Cooper, *Centre for Russian and East European Studies, University of Birmingham*
Terry Cox, *Department of Central and East European Studies, University of Glasgow*
Rosalind Marsh, *Department of European Studies and Modern Languages, University of Bath*
David Moon, *Department of History, University of Durham*
Hilary Pilkington, *Department of Sociology, University of Warwick*
Graham Timmins, *Department of Politics, University of Stirling*
Stephen White, *Department of Politics, University of Glasgow*

Founding Editorial Committee Member:
George Blazyca, *Centre for Contemporary European Studies, University of Paisley*

This series is published on behalf of BASEES (the British Association for Slavonic and East European Studies). The series comprises original, high-quality, research-level work by both new and established scholars on all aspects of Russian, Soviet, post-Soviet and East European Studies in humanities and social science subjects.

1   Ukraine's Foreign and Security Policy, 1991–2000
    Roman Wolczuk

2   Political Parties in the Russian Regions
    Derek S. Hutcheson

3   Local Communities and Post-Communist Transformation
    Edited by Simon Smith

4   Repression and Resistance in Communist Europe
    J.C. Sharman

5   Political Elites and the New Russia
    Anton Steen

6   Dostoevsky and the Idea of Russianness
    Sarah Hudspith

7   Performing Russia
    Folk revival and Russian identity
    Laura J. Olson

8   Russian Transformations
    Edited by Leo McCann

9 **Soviet Music and Society under Lenin and Stalin**
The baton and sickle
Edited by Neil Edmunds

10 **State Building in Ukraine**
The Ukranian parliament, 1990–2003
Sarah Whitmore

11 **Defending Human Rights in Russia**
Sergei Kovalyov, dissident and Human Rights Commissioner, 1969–2003
Emma Gilligan

12 **Small-Town Russia**
Postcommunist livelihoods and identities: a portrait of the intelligentsia in Achit, Bednodemyanovsk and Zubtsov, 1999–2000
Anne White

13 **Russian Society and the Orthodox Church**
Religion in Russia after communism
Zoe Knox

14 **Russian Literary Culture in the Camera Age**
The word as image
Stephen Hutchings

15 **Between Stalin and Hitler**
Class war and race war on the Dvina, 1940–46
Geoffrey Swain

16 **Literature in Post-Communist Russia and Eastern Europe**
The Russian, Czech and Slovak fiction of the changes 1988–98
Rajendra A. Chitnis

17 **The Legacy of Soviet Dissent**
Dissidents, democratisation and radical nationalism in Russia
Robert Horvath

18 **Russian and Soviet Film Adaptations of Literature, 1900–2001**
Screening the word
Edited by Stephen Hutchings and Anat Vernitski

19 **Russia as a Great Power**
Dimensions of security under Putin
Edited by Jakob Hedenskog, Vilhelm Konnander, Bertil Nygren, Ingmar Oldberg and Christer Pursiainen

20 **Katyn and the Soviet Massacre of 1940**
Truth, justice and memory
George Sanford

21 **Conscience, Dissent and Reform in Soviet Russia**
Philip Boobbyer

22 **The Limits of Russian Democratisation**
Emergency powers and states of emergency
Alexander N. Domrin

23 **The Dilemmas of Destalinisation**
A social and cultural history of reform in the Khrushchev era
Edited by Polly Jones

24 **News Media and Power in Russia**
Olessia Koltsova

25 **Post-Soviet Civil Society**
Democratization in Russia and the Baltic States
Anders Uhlin

26 **The Collapse of Communist Power in Poland**
Jacqueline Hayden

27 **Television, Democracy and Elections in Russia**
Sarah Oates

28 **Russian Constitutionalism**
Historical and contemporary development
Andrey N. Medushevsky

29 **Late Stalinist Russia**
Society between reconstruction and reinvention
Edited by Juliane Fürst

30 **The Transformation of Urban Space in Post-Soviet Russia**
Konstantin Axenov, Isolde Brade and Evgenij Bondarchuk

31 **Western Intellectuals and the Soviet Union, 1920–40**
From Red Square to the Left Bank
Ludmila Stern

32 **The Germans of the Soviet Union**
Irina Mukhina

33 **Re-constructing the Post-Soviet Industrial Region**
The Donbas in transition
Edited by Adam Swain

34 **Chechnya**
Russia's "War on Terror"
John Russell

35 **The New Right in the New Europe**
Czech transformation and right-wing politics, 1989–2006
Seán Hanley

36 **Democracy and Myth in Russia and Eastern Europe**
Edited by Alexander Wöll and Harald Wydra

37 **Energy Dependency, Politics and Corruption in the Former Soviet Union**
Russia's power, oligarchs' profits and Ukraine's missing energy policy, 1995–2006
Margarita M. Balmaceda

38 **Peopling the Russian Periphery**
Borderland colonization in Eurasian history
Edited by Nicholas B. Breyfogle, Abby Schrader and Willard Sunderland

39 **Russian Legal Culture before and after Communism**
Criminal justice, politics and the public sphere
Frances Nethercott

40 **Political and Social Thought in Post-Communist Russia**
Axel Kaehne

41 **The Demise of the Soviet Communist Party**
Atsushi Ogushi

42 **Russian Policy towards China and Japan**
The El'tsin and Putin periods
Natasha Kuhrt

43 Soviet Karelia
Politics, planning and terror in Stalin's Russia, 1920–1939
Nick Baron

44 Reinventing Poland
Economic and political transformation and evolving national identity
Edited by Martin Myant and Terry Cox

45 The Russian Revolution in Retreat, 1920–24
Soviet workers and the new communist elite
Simon Pirani

46 Democratisation and Gender in Contemporary Russia
Suvi Salmenniemi

47 Narrating Post-Communism
Colonial discourse and Europe's borderline civilization
Nataša Kovačević

48 Globalization and the State in Central and Eastern Europe
The politics of foreign direct investment
Jan Drahokoupil

49 Local Politics and Democratisation in Russia
Cameron Ross

50 The Emancipation of the Serfs in Russia
Peace arbitrators and the development of civil society
Roxanne Easley

51 Federalism and Local Politics in Russia
Edited by Cameron Ross and Adrian Campbell

52 Transitional Justice in Eastern Europe and the former Soviet Union
Reckoning with the communist past
Edited by Lavinia Stan

53 The Post-Soviet Russian Media
Conflicting signals
Edited by Birgit Beumers, Stephen Hutchings and Natalia Rulyova

54 Minority Rights in Central and Eastern Europe
Edited by Bernd Rechel

55 Television and Culture in Putin's Russia
Remote control
Stephen Hutchings and Natalia Rulyova

56 The Making of Modern Lithuania
Tomas Balkelis

57 Soviet State and Society under Nikita Khrushchev
Melanie Ilic and Jeremy Smith

58 Communism, Nationalism and Ethnicity in Poland, 1944–1950
Michael Fleming

59 Democratic Elections in Poland, 1991–2007
Frances Millard

60 Critical Theory in Russia and the West
Alastair Renfrew and Galin Tihanov

61 Promoting Democracy and Human Rights in Russia
European organization and Russia's socialization
Sinikukka Saari

62 The Myth of the Russian Intelligentsia
Old intellectuals in the new Russia
Inna Kochetkova

63 Russia's Federal Relations
Putin's reforms and management of the regions
Elena A. Chebankova

64 Constitutional Bargaining in Russia 1990–93
Information and uncertainty
Edward Morgan-Jones

65 Building Big Business in Russia
The impact of informal corporate governance practices
Yuko Adachi

66 Russia and Islam
State, society and radicalism
Roland Dannreuther and Luke March

67 Celebrity and Glamour in Contemporary Russia
Shocking chic
Edited by Helena Goscilo and Vlad Strukov

68 The Socialist Alternative to Bolshevik Russia
The Socialist Revolutionary Party, 1917–1939
Elizabeth White

69 Learning to Labour in Post-Soviet Russia
Vocational youth in transition
Charles Walker

70 Television and Presidential Power in Putin's Russia
Tina Burrett

71 Political Theory and Community Building in Post-Soviet Russia
Edited by Oleg Kharkhordin and Risto Alapuro

72 Disease, Health Care and Government in Late Imperial Russia
Life and death on the Volga, 1823–1914
Charlotte E. Henze

73 Khrushchev in the Kremlin
Policy and government in the Soviet Union, 1953–1964
Edited by Melanie Ilic and Jeremy Smith

74 Citizens in the Making in Post-Soviet States
Olena Nikolayenko

Citizens in the Making in Post-Soviet States

Olena Nikolayenko

LONDON AND NEW YORK

First published 2011 by Routledge
2 Park Square, Milton Park, Abingdon, Oxfordshire OX14 4RN

Simultaneously published in the USA and Canada
by Routledge
711 Third Avenue, New York, NY 10017

First issued in paperback 2014

Routledge is an imprint of the Taylor & Francis Group, an informa business

© 2011 Olena Nikolayenko
The right of Olena Nikolayenko to be identified as author of this work has been asserted by her in accordance with the Copyright, Designs and Patent Act 1988.

Typeset in Sabon by Bookcraft Ltd, Stroud, Gloucestershire

All rights reserved. No part of this book may be reprinted or reproduced or utilised in any form or by any electronic, mechanical, or other means, now known or hereafter invented, including photocopying and recording, or in any information storage or retrieval system, without permission in writing from the publishers.

British Library Cataloguing in Publication Data
A catalogue record for this book is available from the British Library

Library of Congress Cataloging in Publication Data
Nikolayenko, Olena.
Citizens in the making in post-Soviet states / Olena Nikolayenko.
  p. cm. -- (BASEES/Routledge series on Russian and East European studies ; 74)
  Includes bibliographical references and index.
  1. Political participation--Russia (Federation) 2. Youth--Political activity--Russia (Federation) 3. Democratization--Russia (Federation) 4. Political participation--Ukraine. 5. Youth--Political activity--Ukraine. 6. Democratization--Ukraine.
  7. Russia (Federation)--Politics and government--1991-
  8. Ukraine--Politics and government--1991- I. Title.
  JN6699.A15N55 2011   323'.0420947--dc22
  2010034412

ISBN 13: 978-0-415-59604-6 (hbk)
ISBN 13: 978-1-138-81688-6 (pbk)

To my parents, Ludmila Grigorievna and
Vitaly Dmitrievich Nikolayenko

Contents

List of figures	xii
List of tables	xiii
Acknowledgments	xiv
Note on transliteration	xvii
1 Introduction	1
2 Attitudes toward democracy	17
3 Trust in authorities	34
4 Building the new political community, remembering the old one	51
5 Learning about politics	73
6 Construction of Soviet history in school textbooks	96
7 Growing up, but growing apart	116
Appendix A	124
Appendix B	127
Notes	129
Bibliography	136
Index	155

List of figures

2.1　Adolescents' support for democracy by conceptions of democracy　32
3.1　Adolescents' trust in authorities　36
3.2　Trust in authorities among the adult population　38
4.1　National pride among adolescents in Russia and Ukraine　53
4.2　National pride by Soviet nostalgia　71
5.1　Political discussions with parents　75
5.2　Political support and discussions with parents　76
5.3　Patterns of media news consumption among adolescents　81
5.4　Political support and media news consumption　85
5.5　Political discussions with teachers　93
5.6　Political support and discussions with teachers　94

List of tables

2.1	Adolescents' support for democracy: a cross-city comparison	19
2.2	Support for democracy: profiling don't knows	21
2.3	Adults' support for democracy, 1995–2006	23
2.4	Adolescents' evaluation of democracy	24
2.5	Adolescents' conceptions of democracy	26
2.6	Conceptions of democracy: profiling don't knows	30
4.1	National pride among adults in Russia and Ukraine	54
4.2	Adolescents' attitudes toward the dissolution of the Soviet Union	63
4.3	Adolescents' reasoning in evaluating the dissolution of the USSR	65
6.1	Textbook analysis: a summary	98
6.2	Pictorial analysis	108
6.3	Documentary analysis	112

Acknowledgments

This book has grown out of my personal fascination with political processes in post-communist societies and intellectual curiosity about political socialization in contemporary non-democracies. I am indebted to many people for their support and feedback at various points during the research project.

This book started as a dissertation project at the University of Toronto, and I am grateful to my dissertation committee for their helpful feedback and encouragement in undertaking this study. Neil Nevitte, my supervisor, provided outstanding support and valuable advice throughout my graduate studies. With his encouragement, I attended a summer session in quantitative research methods at the University of Michigan and then ventured to collect my own survey data in Eastern Europe. Other members of the dissertation committee were also remarkable in providing insightful comments on my research and reading drafts at short notice. Jeffrey Kopstein challenged me to develop my arguments and apply methodological rigor to the study of politics. Peter Solomon generously shared his expertise on Russian politics and offered an abundance of scholarly advice. At a later stage, Lucan Way and Brian Silver provided helpful feedback and constructive criticism. Valery Khmelko and Grigoriy Ketrman graciously commented upon the questionnaire design. For their insightful comments, I am also thankful to Kimitaka Matsuzato, Blair Ruble, Susan Solomon, and Judith Torney-Purta. Needless to say, any remaining errors are my sole responsibility.

This research would not have been possible without the cooperation of local education administrators, school principals, teachers, and students. My most important debt is to the adolescents who agreed to participate in the study and shared with me their opinions of politics. I am also thankful to Olga Glagoleva for introducing me to participants in the Tula Civic Education Project and Elizabeth Heide for putting me in touch with educators in Rostov-on-the-Don. The Department for Foreign Cooperation at the National University of Kyiv–Mohyla Academy provided skillful administrative support during my research in Ukraine. Special thanks also go to Larysa Iarovenko at the University of Toronto's Petro Jacyk Program for the Study of Ukraine for her superb administrative assistance.

Several people extended a warm welcome and overflowing hospitality during my fieldwork in the region. I am thankful to Nikolai Matveevich

Makarov for our long conversations and walks in Serebrianyi Bor to escape the bustling life of Moscow. Iryna Iosypivna Tatsyak-Bilyk embraced me like her own daughter; she introduced me to Lviv school teachers, exposed me to the city's rich cultural life, and even baked *perogi* for my train journey. Petro Vasylievich Iarovenko's sense of humor smoothed my moments of frustration with the red tape in Kyiv. Back in Canada, Oksana Zakydalsky helped me out in numerous ways, showing immeasurable generosity and kindness.

I also benefitted greatly from the many insightful comments and questions I received when presenting my work at the Stanford Center on Adolescence, February 2006; Stanford University's Center for European, Russian, and Eurasian Studies, March 2006; the Annual Meetings of the American Political Science Association in Philadelphia, September 2006 and Chicago, August 2007; the International Conference on Democratic Development and Civic Education in Ukraine, Yalta, Ukraine, September 2006; the Biennial Conference of the European Consortium for Political Research, Pisa, Italy, September 2007; and the First East Asian Conference for Slavic Eurasian Studies, Hokkaido University, Japan, February 2009.

A number of institutions provided a supportive environment during various stages of this research. The University of Toronto's Center for European, Russian, and Eurasian Studies served as a springboard for the development of this project and an exchange of ideas with fellow students and senior scholars. I thank William Damon for hosting me at Stanford Center on Adolescence and expanding my understanding of educational psychology during the data analysis stage of this research. As a postdoctoral scholar, I found an intellectually stimulating environment at Stanford University's Center on Democracy, Development, and the Rule of Law and made final revisions of the manuscript while interacting with a diverse body of scholars affiliated with the Center. At Fordham University, the Department of Political Science generously supported the completion of this research project.

For financial support, I am grateful to a number of institutions. At the University of Toronto, I received financial assistance from the Department of Political Science (C. B. Macpherson Dissertation Fellowship), Faculty of Arts and Science (Dmytro and Natalia Haluszka Scholarship in Ukrainian Studies), School of Graduate Studies (SGS Travel Grant and Doctoral Thesis Completion Grant), Center for European, Russian, and Eurasian Studies (H. Gordon Skilling Fellowship), and Petro Jacyk Program for the Study of Ukraine (Graduate Scholarship in Ukrainian Studies). I also gratefully acknowledge financial support by the Canadian Institute of Ukrainian Studies (Neporany Doctoral Fellowship), Ontario's Ministry of Training, Colleges, and Universities (Ontario Graduate Scholarship), and the Open Society Institute (Global Supplementary Grant).

Parts of Chapter 4 appeared in "Contextual Effects on Historical Memory: Soviet Nostalgia among Post-Soviet Adolescents," *Communist and Post-Communist Studies* 41 (2) (2008), 243–59. I am grateful to the publisher for granting permission to include the material here.

I thank Peter Sowden at Routledge and Richard Sakwa (BASEES series editor) for their enthusiasm for my book project. I am also grateful to an anonymous reviewer for thoughtful comments during the submission process.

Over the years, my family has been a steady source of support for me. I am deeply indebted to Akram, my husband and my best friend. His love, along with our countless conversations about politics and social science, lightened the writing process. I dedicate this book to my parents, who inspired me to explore the world and pursue my academic goals.

Note on transliteration

In this book, I follow the Library of Congress system of transliteration, with minor exceptions. I use conventional English-language spelling of commonly used Russian and Ukrainian proper names and omit soft (') and hard (") signs in the text. The Romanization Tables approved by the Library of Congress and the American Library Association are available at http://www.loc.gov/catdir/cpso/roman.html. Unless otherwise indicated, translations from Russian and Ukrainian are my own.

1 Introduction

The first generation of citizens without any firsthand experience of communism is now coming of age in the post-Soviet region. This generation was born at a turning point in East European history marked by the fall of the Berlin Wall, the disintegration of the Soviet Union, and the collapse of communism. As children, they witnessed how their families sought to make sense of dramatic political changes and eke out a living in the new socioeconomic environment. By adolescence, this generation began to observe the normalization of life and an improvement in living standards. The Communist Party was no longer in power to serve as an indisputable, monolithic source of political news and provide ideological training for young people. Instead, youth learned about national history and politics from their relatives socialized during the communist period, textbooks penned in the post-Soviet era, and TV programs interrupted by McDonald's ads and Hollywood trailers.

A parallel development in the post-Soviet region has been the rise of hybrid regimes falling somewhere between democracy and dictatorship (Diamond 2002; Levitsky and Way; McCann 2006; Ottaway 2003; Wilson 2005a). Democratic institutions are formally present in such regimes, and elections are regularly held to maintain a façade of electoral democracy. Yet the ruling elite systematically violate democratic procedures to the extent that the turnover of political power is hardly possible. In particular, incumbent governments control the mass media and mastermind vote fraud in an attempt to manipulate election results and extend their grip on power.

Russia under Vladimir Putin (2000–8) and Ukraine under Leonid Kuchma (1994–2004) are prime examples of political regimes in which weak democratic institutions coexist with autocratic practices of the ruling elite (D'Anieri 2007; Darden 2001; Fish 2005; Kuzio 2005a; McFaul, Petrov, and Riabov 2004; Sakwa 2009; White 2008a; White and Kryshtanovskaya 2003). From 1991 to 2003, Freedom House ranked Russia and Ukraine as "partly free," signifying deficiencies in the extent of civil liberties and political rights.[1] In particular, one of the central features of the democratic state – press freedom – has been regularly violated in the former Soviet republics. In Russia, the Kremlin took control of TV channels critical of the government and toughened restrictions on the media coverage of events in Chechnya (Lipman and McFaul 2001; Pietilainen

2 Introduction

2008; Simons and Strovsky 2006; White 2008b). In Ukraine, Kuchma's presidency was marred by the issuance of the so-called *temnyky*, government instructions on how to cover current events in the mass media, and the president's alleged involvement in the murder of the journalist Georgiy Gongadze (Dyczok 2003; Koshiw 2003). For a systematic assault on the mass media, the Committee to Protect Journalists placed Putin and Kuchma on the list of Ten Worst Enemies of the Press in 2001.[2] Apart from curtailing press freedom, the incumbent governments sought to introduce a wide array of formal and informal barriers to political participation and stifle civic activism.

Nonetheless, the extent to which non-democratic regimes have consolidated in Russia and Ukraine varies. Since 1991, Russian citizens have observed twice the transfer of power from the incumbent president to a handpicked successor. In 1999, Borys Yeltsin stepped down to pass the reins of power to Prime Minister Putin. More recently, Putin endorsed Dmitry Medvedev as the next Russian president. Ukrainians, on the other hand, have twice experienced the peaceful handover of power through competitive elections. In 1994, Leonid Kravchuk lost his bid for re-election to Kuchma, a former prime minister. In turn, Kuchma failed to place in the president's office his successor Viktor Yanukovych. The massive protests against fraudulent elections, which culminated in the Orange Revolution, made Viktor Yushchenko the country's third president. Based upon the "two-turnover test,"[3] one may conclude that the political trajectories of the two countries diverged.

In addition, Russia and Ukraine differ in terms of their official position on the legacy of the previous political regime. The Russian government placed great emphasis on the accomplishments of the communist state and perpetuated Soviet-era myths about the invincible political system. Specifically, the Kremlin covered up the dark side of the communist regime by stifling an open public discussion about the human costs of Stalinism and celebrating with fanfare Soviet victory in the Great Patriotic War of 1941–45.[4] In televised remarks, President Putin dismissed Stalinist crimes with the statement, "Other countries have done even more terrible things" (quoted from Kuzio 2007). Compared to his Russian counterpart, President Kuchma adopted a more critical view of the communist system and its leadership. In particular, the commemoration of the famine of 1932–33 (the Holodomor) became a focal point for denouncing human rights violations under communism. In his address to the nation in November 2002, for example, Kuchma condemned the communist ideology and Stalinist methods of social control.[5] In this political environment young Russians and young Ukrainians formed their worldviews.

How supportive is the first post-Soviet generation of the new political order? How much trust do young people place in incumbent authorities? Which images of the Soviet Union prevail in the minds of contemporary adolescents? How proud are high-school students to be citizens of the new states? It is important o address these questions in order to understand the extent to which new regimes can ride the wave of public support in the near future.

This book provides an in-depth analysis of adolescents' attitudes toward democracy, authorities, and the political community in Russia and Ukraine. On the basis of an original survey conducted in 2005, I demonstrate attitudinal differences within the post-Soviet generation. It is clear from the analysis that Russian adolescents tend to place more trust in the incumbent president and harbor more regrets about the disintegration of the Soviet Union than their peers in Ukraine. Furthermore, the political attitudes of Ukrainian adolescents from different borderland regions diverge. High-school students from the city of Lviv, located within a short drive from the Polish–Ukrainian border, tend to display more national pride and less Soviet nostalgia than their peers from the city of Donetsk, situated close to the Russian–Ukrainian border. It is striking that post-Soviet adolescents in the two neighboring states hold such divergent political attitudes.

Argument

In this book, I argue that state policies on patriotic education affect adolescents' political attitudes in Russia and Ukraine. More specifically, I posit that the content of patriotic education tends to generate more skepticism about Western-style democracy, more trust in the incumbent president and more Soviet nostalgia in the core of the Soviet Union (Russia) than in the periphery (Ukraine). It is further argued that lack of policy consensus about patriotic education in Ukraine leads to the reproduction of region-based political cleavages within the younger generation.

The broad aim of patriotic education is to cultivate love of one's country and the commitment to act upon it. The pursuit of this educational policy, however, can serve different political ends. On the one hand, patriotic education can be envisioned to strengthen the democratic polity by fostering a sense of national unity and rallying popular support for reforms (see Ben-Porath 2007). Dankwurt Rustow (1970) refers to national unity as a "background condition" for the transition to democracy. On the other hand, the notion of patriotism can be abused to consolidate a non-democratic regime. The autocratic ruler can invoke the idea of unconditional love of the motherland as a pretext for blocking an open public debate and obstructing collective action against the powerholders. Promoting a narrow, illiberal form of patriotism may cause the loss of the society's "moral sensitivity" to the wrongdoings of the ruling elite.[6]

World history abounds with examples of how non-democratic rulers exploited the idea of patriotic education to enlist the broad-based support of youth and solidify their power. In the aftermath of the 1989 Tiananmen Square protest, the Chinese Communist Party turned to patriotic education to bolster mass support for the non-democratic regime (Zhao 1998). Infused with patriotic fervor, Chinese school textbooks taught students about the humiliation at the hands of foreign powers and instilled pride in the country's

4 *Introduction*

recent economic accomplishments. Acting upon these beliefs, thousands of university students participated in anti-American demonstrations in reaction to US bombing of the Chinese Embassy in Belgrade in May 1999. More recently, President Hugo Chavez of Venezuela appealed to youth to back up his political vision. Amid growing tensions between the United States and Venezuela, approximately 1,400 young people from different parts of the country held the founding congress of United Socialist Party of Venezuela Youth in September 2008 (Pearson 2008). The main task of the newly formed party is to promote youthful commitment to the defense of the Bolivarian revolution and the socialist model of development. Similarly, the government of Belarus set up the youth organization Belarusian National Youth Union to mobilize youth support for the non-democratic regime.[7] In various forms, the for the hearts and minds of young people is still waged worldwide, reflecting the ubiquitous ambition of the ruling elite to co-opt youth.

Patriotic education (*patrioticheskoe vospitanie* in Russian and *patriotychne vykhovannia* in Ukrainian) has been a prominent component of the Soviet educational system. According to the Russian *Encyclopedia of Pedagogy*, such education denotes "directed creation of the conditions (material, spiritual, and organizational) that are necessary for the development of the individual" (quoted from Nikandrov 2008: 58). As the Soviet Union was engaged in the ideological battle against the West, patriotic education was designed to foster commitment to Marxist-Leninist ideology, respect for the military, and readiness to defend the country's interests.

The demise of the Soviet Union, however, cast doubts over the relevance of military-patriotic education in newly independent states. In particular, lionization of the army and the build-up of patriotic fervor to defend one's country against external enemies appeared to be out of step with the post-Cold War reality. Yet the incumbent governments in the core of the Soviet Union and its peripheries dealt with Soviet legacies of military-patriotic education in different ways. In Russia, President Putin was determined to build upon the strengths of Soviet-era patriotic education to bolster popular support for the political regime, whereas Kuchma's government opted to downplay patriotic education in public schools. More specifically, national programs on patriotic education differed along four dimensions: content, length, budget, and coordination.

The Russian federal government adopted the National Program on Patriotic Education in 2001 and extended it for another five-year period in 2005. The objective of the national program was to foster "high patriotic consciousness, loyalty to the Fatherland, and readiness to fulfill one's civic duty to defend interests of the country."[8] At the symbolic level, the program's renewal signaled the government's commitment to the inculcation of patriotism in Russia's citizens. Additionally, the federal government increased monetary support for the program from 178 million roubles (US$6 million) during the first phase of the program (2001–5) to 498 million roubles (US$18 million) during the second phase (2006–10). Furthermore, the federal government set up the National Patriotic Center to coordinate educational activities throughout the country. Over the course of Putin's presidency, the Kremlin has increasingly exploited the idea of patriotism to rally the population around the non-democratic ruler, legitimize the so-called "sovereign democracy,"[9] and implement a belligerent foreign policy.

By contrast, the Ukrainian government during Kuchma's term in office underestimated the importance of a unified program on patriotic education, allowing different notions of patriotism to develop in eastern and western parts of the country. The National Program on Patriotic Education, Healthy Lifestyle, Spiritual Development, and Moral Values adopted in September 1999 proclaimed that its objective was to foster the moral development of the population and inculcate a sense of patriotism in citizens.[10] But the government failed to specify a budget allocated to this program and assigned all the coordination efforts to the Vice Prime Minister Volodymyr Seminozhenko, who lasted in his job for only four months. Moreover, the Cabinet of Ministers annulled the national program in less than two years since its adoption and did not enact a new one.[11]

Lack of political consensus regarding patriotic education interfered with the adoption of a viable educational program in Ukraine's national parliament. In December 2003, the Ukrainian government headed by the Prime Minister Yanukovych introduced a bill outlining the national program on patriotic education for 2004–8. The proposed program was divided into two stages. During the first stage in 2004, parliamentarians in consultation with local governments and civic organizations were expected to revise and improve the legal basis for carrying out patriotic education. During the second stage in 2005–8, both government officials and civil society actors were supposed to facilitate the implementation of patriotic education in Ukraine. Yet the political opposition objected to the specifics of the bill. Andriy Shkil, a member of Tymoshenko bloc and a former leader of Ukrainian National Assembly–Ukrainian People's Self-Defense, made a motion to block the passage of the bill (see Shkil 2004). Despite the opposition's efforts, the national parliament passed the bill and forwarded it to a parliamentary committee for revisions before bringing it back to the parliamentary floor for a final vote (see Verkhovna Rada 2003). In the wake of the 2006 parliamentary election, however, the newly elected national parliament revoked the previous parliamentary decree and removed the bill on patriotic education from the parliamentary agenda (see Verkhovna Rada 2006). At the time of this writing, the content of patriotic education is still hotly contested in Ukraine, hampering the passage of a widely accepted national program on patriotic education.

These policy choices had far-reaching implications for the development of political ideas among post-Soviet adolescents. Since the Russian government has accorded considerable attention to patriotic education and has consolidated a lot of power in its hands, it has the leverage to bombard Russian youth with state-sanctioned messages about the country's political development and Soviet heritage. Most importantly, the Russian government appears to speak with one voice on this issue. As a result, Russian adolescents tend to obtain less systematic knowledge about human costs of political stability and economic prosperity during Soviet and post-Soviet Russian history. In contrast, lack of policy consensus in Ukraine leaves adolescents free to explore different interpretations of Soviet history and debate the significance of current events. Compared to their Russian peers, Ukrainian adolescents tend to become exposed to a wider range of opinions about current political processes and Soviet history.

Mechanism

The governments in the former Soviet republics can deploy various pedagogical tools to drum up support for the nation-state among young citizens. This study focuses on the content of history textbooks as an instrument of patriotic education. A major advantage of examining school textbooks is that they provide an official version of society's historical memory (Ciobanu 2008; Janmaat 2005; Kisanne 2005; Lisovskaya and Karpov 1999; Osborne 2003; Ram 2000). The state-run educational agencies in Russia and Ukraine are heavily involved in the design and implementation of history teaching, since the construction of state-sanctioned historical narratives has significant repercussions for electoral politics.[12] Specifically, the Ministries of Education regularly review available learning aids and compile a list of textbooks approved for school use. An additional advantage of focusing on school textbooks is their captive audience. Every high-school student in Russia and Ukraine is required to take courses in national history. Hence, the majority of young people are exposed to state-sanctioned historical narratives at school.

Sources of policy differences

This study singles out the social cleavage structure as a factor that contributes to cross-country differences in patriotic education. It is well established that ethnic diversity may explain policy choices of a government (Easterly and Levine 1997). Furthermore, splits within the core ethnic group, or titular nation, are likely to impose constraints on policy-making processes. If the titular nation is divided along cultural lines, then it becomes difficult to arrive at a consensus and adopt a viable educational policy.

In addition, the social cleavage structure may exert indirect effects on public policies by affecting the robustness of political competition. By robust political competition, I refer to the presence of opposition parties that offer "a clear, plausible, and critical governing alternative" to the incumbent government (Grzymala-Busse 2007: 1). Ethnic diversity may serve as a base of voter mobilization, giving rise to multiple identity-based political parties. Under such circumstances, political competition in culturally heterogeneous societies may be quite intense, which, in turn, puts additional pressure on politicians to accommodate policy preferences of various social groups. When politicians representing diverse social groups fail to agree upon the appropriate policy option, it is likely to produce a policy gridlock.

In turn, the robustness of political competition affects the time horizons of incumbents. Time horizons refer here to how long the incumbent president envisages staying in power. By long time horizon, I mean the temporal period that extends beyond the two-term constitutional limit on the president's tenure. If the incumbent president has a long time horizon, then he is likely to display commitment to patriotic education. If the incumbent president has a short time horizon, then he is likely to neglect policies regarding patriotic education. This line of reasoning can be applied to account for policy differences in the selected states.

Both post-Soviet republics have a core ethnic group of comparable size: ethnic Russians constitute 80 percent of Russia's population and 77 percent of Ukraine's population is comprised of ethnic Ukrainians.[13] Yet ethnic Ukrainians in contemporary Ukraine are sharply divided along linguistic and regional lines. According to the Ukrainian Census (2001), 15 percent of ethnic Ukrainians consider the Russian language as their mother tongue. This linguistic cleavage overlaps with the country's regional divisions. The Russian-speaking population is heavily concentrated in the southern and eastern parts of the country, while Ukrainian is more frequently spoken in western and central parts of the country. More broadly, Ukrainians disagree over what it means to be a citizen of Ukraine. The presence of the divided titular nation poses a challenge for the design of public policies on patriotic education.

Furthermore, the political salience of cultural cleavages has an indirect impact on educational policies by keeping in the political arena a diverse mix of political forces. In Ukraine, major political parties built a regional base of support. As evidenced by the results of the 2004 presidential election, Yushchenko and his "Our Ukraine" bloc was most popular in the western and central parts of the country, while Yanukovych, the leader of the Party of Regions, enjoyed popularity in eastern and southern parts of the country. Each of these political forces offering a different set of policy options was an important player to be reckoned with. For comparison, cultural diversity does not produce similar political repercussions in Russian society. Since ethnic minorities and, in particular, non-Slavic ethnic groups tend to be marginalized in domestic politics,[14] ethnic Russians are well placed to deliver political victory to the party of power regardless of the ethnic minorities' vote. As a result, Russia's parliament faces fewer hurdles to introduce policy changes in the educational sector.

Finally, policy choices regarding patriotic education are constrained by the time horizons of incumbent presidents. In the case of Russia, President Putin's close circle has established itself as a major political force and eliminated a credible threat to the domineering position of the Kremlin-backed party United Russia.[15] Having cleared the playing field, Russia's ruling elite pursued the long-term goal of maintaining the repressive regime and nurturing compliant citizens, or "subjects." In the case of Ukraine, President Kuchma exercised less absolute power, since political competition was quite robust.[16] Constrained by electoral uncertainty, Ukraine's ruling elite focused on the short-term goal of winning elections and overlooked the far-reaching consequences of patriotic education.

Why study adolescents?

This book seeks to broaden the scope of public opinion research in the post-Soviet region by shifting the focus of attention from voting-age citizens to adolescents. Over the past two decades, most academic effort has been expended on investigating public opinion of the adult population socialized during the communist period (Colton and McFaul 2003; Evans and Whitefield 1995; Finifter and Mickiewicz 1992; Gibson, Duch, and Tedin 1992; Haerpfer 2002; Mishler and Rose 1997, 2002, 2005; Reisinger *et al.* 1993; Rose, Mishler, and Haerpfer 1998; White and McAllister 2008). Much less is known about the political attitudes of the younger generation growing up in the post-Soviet period (Blum 2007; Diuk 2004; Fournier 2007; Mendelson and Gerber 2005, 2006, 2008; Nikolayenko 2008). The neglect of youth attitudes in post-communist literature is somewhat surprising, given the growing political significance of the younger generation. A spate of recent empirical work examined the role of youth movements during the so-called colored revolutions (Bunce and Wolchik 2006; Collin 2007; Forbrig and Demes 2007; Nikolayenko 2007). Political scientists traced how young people staged nonviolent resistance to autocratic incumbents, but the analysis of how youth acquired political attitudes conducive to participation in protest activities is largely missing in these empirical investigations.

In the 1990s, scholars began to analyze how young people in post-Soviet societies adjusted to dramatic societal change (Chuprov 1992; Lisovskii 1996; Roberts *et al.* 2000; Zubok 1998). Since Russia is regarded as an inheritor to the Soviet Union, the study of Russian youth has attracted most academic attention. Influenced by Margaret Mead's seminal study of adolescent behavior in a Polynesian society, the anthropologist Fran Markowitz (2000), for example, examined how Russian teenagers coped with the dramatic consequences of the transition from communism in the early 1990s. Through her extensive work, Hilary Pilkington (1994, 1996; Pilkington *et al.* 2002) made a significant contribution to the study of youth cultural practices in post-communist Russia. In particular, she traced how an interaction between global and local forces shaped the production of youth culture in Russia. While anthropologists and sociologists took keen interest in the study of post-communist youth, political scientists neglected the linkage between adolescence and politics.

To date, there is a dearth of large-N surveys of adolescents' political attitudes in the post-Soviet region. Among notable endeavors to assess civic skills and knowledge from the cross-national perspective is the Civic Education Study of the International Association for the Evaluation of Educational Achievement.[17] Within the framework of the Civic Education Study, four former Soviet republics – the Baltic states (Estonia, Latvia, and Lithuania) and Russia – participated in the 1999 survey of 14-year-old adolescents. Given my focus on non-democracies and the timing of the survey (coinciding with the last months of Yeltsin's presidency), I collected my own survey data on adolescents. By administering a survey in three Russian and three Ukrainian cities, I seek to provide a snapshot of adolescents' political attitudes in the region to stimulate further discussion of the topic.

Beyond the region-bound focus on post-Soviet adolescents, this inquiry calls for a closer integration of youth studies in the field of political science. The initial impetus for the empirical analysis of pre-adult political socialization – processes related to the acquisition of politically relevant attitudes and beliefs – came from the breakdown of the Weimar Republic and the rise of Nazism. In the aftermath of World War II, social scientists looked for a key ingredient to ensure the survival of democracy. Early political socialization research posited that the induction of children into politics could serve as a mechanism for the durability of the political regime (Easton and Dennis 1969; Greenstein 1965; Hyman 1959). As empirical evidence about lifelong fluctuations in political attitudes began to accumulate, this line of research fell out of fashion in the field of political science. More recently, however, transformative events in Eastern Europe and the disengagement of youth from politics in Western democracies has sparked renewed interest in political socialization (Hahn and Alvair-Martin 2008; Niemi and Hepburn 1995; Sapiro 2004).

Still, there remains a degree of skepticism about the utility of studying political attitudes of pre-adults. As Torney-Purta (2004: 471) put it, "most psychologists have to be convinced that anything happening *after age 12* makes a difference, whereas political scientists have to be convinced that anything happening *before age 18* makes a difference." Skeptics argue that political attitudes change over the life span so political scientists should focus their attention on the study of voting-age individuals whose political preferences have immediate, detectable effects on domestic politics. Proponents of life-learning theory, for example, contend that such proximate factors as satisfaction with incumbent job performance and the subjective well-being are much stronger predictors of political attitudes than pre-adult political socialization (see Mishler and Rose 2002). This study does not question the lifelong ability of individuals to learn and alter their political opinions. But this book is grounded in the belief that the political character of adolescence is a valid area of empirical research.

There are several reasons why the study of adolescents merits academic attention. First, adolescence is a critical period for the formation of political identity. By the time of adolescence, individuals develop cognitive skills necessary to understand abstract ideas and exercise critical thinking (Adelson and O'Neil 1966; Feldman and Elliot 1990; Keating 2004). Obviously, individuals modify their opinions over the life span in response to changes in their personal lives or shifts in the political environment. Still, it is reasonable to assume that the political outlook developed during adolescence provides a point of reference for grown-ups.

Second, a closer look at adolescents' political attitudes offers us a glimpse into the lives of ordinary citizens and popular perceptions of political processes through the prism of the young generation. Unlike early political socialization research, this study does not assume that adolescents are passive recipients of information. On the contrary, this book is based upon the assumption that high school students are capable of processing political news and making their own judgments about current events in the country.

Third, the analysis of political socialization processes in non-democracies has policymaking implications. As the ruling elite seek to build a sense of national unity and foster support for the political system in order to prolong their rule, educators wrestle with the challenge of teaching history and civics in a politically suffocating environment. Governments in mature democracies can assist educators in the region by facilitating a cross-national exchange of expertise and promoting the liberalization of citizenship education.

The concept of political support

In the chapters that follow, I distinguish between three objects of political support: the democratic regime, incumbent authorities, and the political community. This distinction draws upon David Easton's (1965) concept of political support. Easton (1975: 436) defines support as "an attitude by which a person orients himself to an object either favorably or unfavorably, positively or negatively" and identifies three objects of political support.[18] The above-mentioned political attitudes lie at the heart of three political processes characteristic of the post-Soviet period: regime consolidation, state-building, and nation-building.[19]

The first dimension of political support – an attitude toward democracy – refers here to the acceptance of the democratic political system as the preferred form of government. It is widely held that citizens' recognition of democracy as "the only game in town" is an important threshold in the transition from authoritarianism (Diamond 1994). Hence, youth preference of democracy as the best form of government is an important indicator of how popular the novel political concept has become in post-communist societies. In addition, this book recognizes that the concept of democracy is open to multiple interpretations.[20] The empirical inquiry gauges the wide array of meanings that high-school students attach to the word "democracy."

The second dimension of political support covers attitudes toward incumbent authorities. Given the importance of political trust for the effective functioning of state institutions (Putnam 1993), this study gauges the extent to which contemporary adolescents trust incumbent authorities. To probe the trustworthiness of various state actors, the analysis singles out occupants of political institutions (presidency, national parliament, and political parties) and occupants of order-related institutions (army, police, and courts).

Finally, the third dimension of political support is related to the notion of political community. By political community, I mean here the nation-state. Upon gaining independence, the former Soviet republics sought to reassert a national identity based upon the core ethnic group, or titular nation. Still, there was a concern that the abrupt demise of the Soviet Union would produce divided loyalties among citizens socialized during the Soviet period (Dowley and Silver 2005). Taking into account this argument, this book distinguishes between attachment to the "old" political community (the Soviet Union) and the "new" one (Russia or Ukraine, respectively).

Case selection

Since the end of the Cold War, the number of countries displaying a combination of democratic and authoritarian attributes has expanded. Freedom House indicates that the number of states "in which there is limited respect for political rights and civil liberties" has grown from 38 in 1972 to 55 in 2002 (Karatnycky 2003). Most of these countries are concentrated in Latin America and Eastern Europe. A principal advantage of selecting countries with similar political, socioeconomic, and cultural characteristics is that it minimizes the magnitude of extraneous variance.[21]

Russia and Ukraine are similar in several ways. From the political standpoint, the selected states meet the criteria for being classified as hybrid regimes. Formal democratic institutions are present in Russia and Ukraine, but the political leadership manipulates the rules of the game to the extent that turnover of power is hardly possible. Another reason why Russia and Ukraine are appropriate for comparison is their similar levels of socioeconomic development. Since 2000, the two former Soviet republics entered a streak of positive economic growth (EBRD 2007). In Russia, the economic growth rate increased from 5.1 percent in 2001 to 7.1 percent in 2004. In Ukraine, the economy grew at 9.2 percent in 2001 and 12.1 percent in 2004. Yet the poverty level remained quite high in the region. By 2003, 41 percent of Russians and 22 percent of Ukrainians still lived on less than US$4 a day, taking into account purchasing power parity (Asad *et al.* 2005). In addition, the Gini index measured on a scale from 0, no inequality, to 1, perfect inequality, indicates the post-Soviet states were crippled with similar levels of social inequality: 0.33 in Russia and 0.27 in Ukraine for the year 2003 (Mitra and Yemtsov 2006). Culturally, both states trace their origins to East Slavic civilization. Kievan Rus was a medieval state populated by several Slavic tribes and located on the territory of contemporary Ukraine and the European part of Russia.[22] In 988, Kievan Rus under the rule of Prince Vladimir adopted Christianity. In contemporary Russia and Ukraine, the population is predominantly Christian. Furthermore, cross-national communication is aided by the fact that both the Ukrainian and Russian languages stem from the Old Church Slavonic language and use the Cyrillic alphabet.

Despite these similarities, Russia and Ukraine represent some variation along the autocracy–democracy continuum. Without doubt, Russia under Putin has grown more authoritarian than Ukraine under Kuchma. The vulnerability of the hybrid regime under Kuchma's presidency was clearly seen during the 2004 presidential election. Thousands of people protested against the government's attempt to orchestrate large-scale electoral fraud and bring Yanukovych to power (Aslund and McFaul 2006; Kuzio 2009; Wilson 2005b). While Putin's approval rating stood at 85 percent shortly before Medvedev's inauguration,[23] Kuchma exited the political scene with a single-digit approval rating.[24] In the wake of the Orange Revolution, political differences between Russia and Ukraine are likely to persist.

At the sub-national level, this study is conducted in three Russian cities (Moscow, Rostov-on-the-Don, and Tula) and three Ukrainian cities (Donetsk, Kyiv, and Lviv). The survey is based on local samples from areas with contrasting political conditions, rather than a nationally representative sample. Moscow in Russia and Kyiv in Ukraine provide the stage for national politics and attract the lion's share of investment. In contrast, with the military-industrial complex turned to ashes, Tula and Donetsk host a large share of Communist Party supporters. Finally, Rostov-on-the-Don, famous for its Cossack heritage, and Lviv, heartland of Ukraine's nationhood, stand out as cities vocal in their support for the revival of national culture. The social context in each of the cities is briefly described in the following paragraphs.

Yuri Luzhkov, the city mayor from 1992 to 2010, presided over the transformation of Moscow into the center of Russia's crony capitalism. It is widely believed that the mayor's wife, Elena Batyrina, established a thriving construction company and became one of the world's richest women as a result of her husband's position. In fact, a report in *Forbes* magazine (quoted in Kalashnikov 2008) suggests that today's Moscow has more millionaires than New York City. In addition, the megapolis attracts the most educated segment of the Russian population. According to the 2002 census, almost one third of Muscovites – 2.6 million people – went through higher education.[25] The growing middle class turns out to support President Putin for bringing socioeconomic stability to the country and raising the profile of Russia in the international community. Protest rallies organized by the opposition usually draw small crowds in the capital city.

More discontent against the authorities might be brewing in the provinces. In Tula, a city located 124 miles south of Moscow, there is some lingering support for the Communist Party. As a former participant in the August 1991 coup, Vasily Starodubtsev has been the governor of the oblast for two terms, from 1997 to 2005. In the 2003 election to the Duma, Russia's lower house of parliament, 14 percent of voters in Tula oblast cast their ballot for the Communist Party. To a large extent, the communist vote can be attributed to citizens' economic grievances in response to the meltdown of the military-industrial complex. In 1712, Peter the Great commissioned the building of Russia's first armament factory in Tula, turning it into a large weapons-making center. In the 1990s, however, the highly educated personnel working for the military-industrial complex began to lose jobs and suffer economic hardships. Now the region experiences a slow economic recovery.

Dramatic economic restructuring occurred in another Russian city, Rostov-on-the-Don, the capital of the southern federal district of Russia. The Rostov-on-the-Don oblast borders on Ukraine's Donetsk region in the west, the Volga region in the east, and the Caucasus in the south. Nicknamed the Gate to the Caucasus, the city serves as a major transportation hub connecting the Caucasus with the European part of the country. In addition, the city is known for its revival of Cossack culture.[26] Since 1991, Vladimir Chub has governed the oblast. In 1996 and 2001, Chub beat his contenders in the election race. For his unwavering support of United Russia, the politician was nominated governor of the oblast for a third term, from 2005 to 2010.

Kyiv is the largest Ukrainian city, with the population of more than 2.7 million people. Historically, it is known as the political center of Kievan Rus and the cradle of Eastern Orthodox Christianity. Since Ukraine's independence, the city has attracted almost one third of foreign direct investment and has expanded along the banks of the Dnieper River. Over the past few years, Kyivites have often taken a critical stance toward the incumbent government. In December 2000–March 2001, Ukrainians protested to demand the resignation of President Kuchma and the investigation of Gongadze's murder. During the 2002 parliamentary election, the Kuchma-backed For United Ukraine bloc garnered only 4 percent of Kyiv votes.[27] In December 2004, 75 percent of Kyivites voted for Yushchenko, signaling their yearning for political change.

Located less than 45 miles from the Polish–Ukrainian border, Lviv is the cultural center of Halychyna, the territory once controlled by the Polish–Lithuanian Commonwealth and the Austro-Hungarian empire. In the aftermath of World War II, the Soviet Army occupied the territory and trampled the idea of Ukraine's independence. For years, Halychyna's inhabitants waged an unequal battle against the communists and meticulously preserved the national culture. For its fusion of the architectural and artistic traditions of Eastern Europe with those of Germany and Italy, a historic quarter of Lviv called the Old Town was placed on UNESCO's world heritage list. Lviv residents overwhelmingly support the country's integration into the European Union and advocate the revival of Ukrainian culture. In December 2004, 92 percent of the electorate in Lviv oblast voted for Yushchenko, whereas 96 percent of the electorate in Donestk oblast cast their ballot for Yanukovych.

Donetsk has established itself as the informal capital of Donbas, an abbreviation for the Donets Basin coal-mining region. In the nineteenth century, the Welsh businessman James Hugh laid the groundwork for the city by opening several coal-mines and a steel mill in the vicinity of the newly built railroad. Given its impressive record of steel production and its flagship role as an industrial region, the city was renamed Stalino in 1924 and took its present name in 1961, amidst the de-Stalinization campaign. As industrialization unfolded, people of different ethnic origin flocked to Donbas, making Russian the language of inter-ethnic communication.

The once-flourishing industrial region sank into poverty during the transition from communism. Hundreds of low-profit coal-mines and bankrupt industrial enterprises were shut down, fueling nostalgia for Soviet-era prosperity. In the 1990s, Donetsk emerged as a stronghold of Communist Party supporters, but the popularity of the party declined with the passage of time. In Donetsk oblast, voting for the Communist Party of Ukraine dropped from 36 percent in 1998 to 3 percent in 2006. At the same time, the Party of Regions received 74 percent of votes during the 2006 parliamentary election. Tapping into the idea of a region-based identity, the Party of Regions burst into the local political scene and catapulted Yanukovych into the limelight of national politics.

The cities of Lviv and Donetsk symbolize the east-west regional cleavage that ruptures the fabric of Ukrainian society. Ethnic and linguistic cleavages overlap in the selected cities. According to the 2001 census, ethnic Ukrainians comprise 94.8 percent of total population in Lviv oblast and 56.9 percent in Donetsk oblast.[28] In addition, 58.7 percent of ethnic Ukrainians residing in Donetsk oblast consider Russian, rather than Ukrainian, their mother tongue. These differences spill out into the political sphere. Since Ukraine's independence, region of residence has been a strong predictor of the vote choice (Barrington and Herron 2004; Birch 2000a; Khmelko 2006; Kubicek 2000). From the political standpoint, the capital city of Kyiv represents the middle ground between the two polarized regions.

Methods of investigation

This study uses a combination of qualitative and quantitative research methods, reflecting "an awareness of the limitations of any single method and the advantages of using other methods to compensate for those limitations" (Levy 2007: 200). I designed and administered a large-N survey in the six selected cities to sketch a broad pattern of adolescents' attitudes. I refer to the resultant dataset as the 2005 Survey of Adolescents in Russia and Ukraine. In addition, I conducted semi-structured interviews with high-school students. The added value of this strategy is that it provides a leverage to gain a wider range of insights into the meaning of political support in post-communist societies.

Nine hundred and twenty-five adolescents in Russia and 889 adolescents in Ukraine filled out a pen-and-pencil questionnaire. Approximately 300 respondents were recruited in each city. Within each city, three school districts have been identified for participation to ensure a representation of various social groups. The first school district, with an upper-class bias, is located downtown. Another school district is situated in the bedroom community populated mainly by middle-class families. The third school district is located in the working-class neighborhood. Within each school district, schools have been randomly selected. Throughout the book, I mostly use the adjectives Russian and Ukrainian to describe the surveyed respondents, not the whole adolescent population in each country.

The demographic characteristics of survey respondents nonetheless closely correspond to the characteristics of the country's population. Males make up 49.5 percent of those surveyed and females 50.5 percent. Similarly, according to the 2002 Russian census, men make up 50.8 percent in the Russian population aged between 15 and 19. The ethnic composition of the sample also adequately represents the population at large. In the survey, the measurement of the sample's ethnic composition is tailored to the national context. In Russia, students were prompted to identify their membership in an ethnic group. Given the frequency of mixed marriages, however, the Ukraine students were asked to report their parents' ethnicity (separately for mother and father). Eighty-nine percent of Russia's respondents identified themselves as ethnic Russians, compared to 80 percent in the general population. Given that the survey sites were concentrated in the European part of the Russian Federation and excluded regions with a dense concentration of non-Slavic ethnic minorities, the 9 percent over-representation of ethnic Russians is rather modest. Representatives of various ethnic groups, including Armenians (2.9 percent), Tatars (1.1 percent), and Ukrainians (2.1 percent), participated in the survey, capturing in part the ethnic diversity of Russian regions. In Ukraine, the participation rate of ethnic Ukrainians and ethnic Russians serves as an indicator of the sample's correspondence to the general population. Based upon the adolescents' recall of father's ethnicity, 75 percent of respondents were ethnic Ukrainians, compared to 77 percent in the total population. Moreover, the 18 percent of ethnic Russians in the sample is a close match to the 17 percent of ethnic Russians in the country's total population. Notwithstanding some limitations, any political attitude patterns shared by these respondents are likely to be at least somewhat characteristic of Russian and Ukrainian adolescents at large.

By the same token, a total of 40 students from Russia and 36 from Ukraine participated in semi-structured interviews. The interviewees were recruited from the pool of students who filled out the written questionnaires. All the interviews were conducted in Russian or Ukrainian on the school premises. To reduce anxiety about the confidentiality of these conversations, the interviews were not tape-recorded. Rather than presenting students with a limited choice of responses, I asked them open-ended questions and encouraged them to freely express their ideas. To elicit as much detail from the interviewees as possible, the discussions were geared toward the adolescents' assessment of incumbent authorities, the Soviet Union, and their home country.

Roadmap

The book is divided into two parts. The first part (Chapters 2–4) examines how adolescents understand the concept of democracy, view incumbent authorities, and imagine the Soviet Union. The second part (Chapters 5–6) examines sources of political attitudes, with the focus on history teaching. In Chapter 2, the analysis finds that post-Soviet adolescents tend to associate democracy with the rule by people (*vlast' naroda*) and civil liberties. In addition, high-school students from Kyiv and Lviv link the notion of democracy with national independence and the Orange Revolution. Chapter 3 is concerned with adolescents' attitudes toward political actors (president, parliamentarians, and political parties) and order-related institutions (police, courts, and the army). As corruption thrives in the former Soviet republics, the police emerge as the least credible order-related institution. Even less popular among young citizens are political parties and parliamentarians. Chapter 4 unveils the extent of Soviet nostalgia and national pride in the core of the former Soviet empire (Russia) and its periphery (Ukraine). The marriage of Russian and Soviet identities has been so intensely propagated in Putin's Russia that even a new generation of citizens finds it difficult to divorce identification with Russia from the alleged greatness of the Soviet Union. Chapter 5 discusses several agents of political socialization – parents, teachers, and the mass media – that supply adolescents with political news. The findings indicate that post-Soviet adolescents frequently discuss politics with their parents and obtain political news more frequently from online publications than from offline newspapers. Next, Chapter 6 investigates the content of history textbooks that provide high-school students with knowledge of controversial events in Soviet history. The book concludes by drawing out the implications of this research.

2 Attitudes toward democracy

Since the end of the Cold War, democracy has become a catch-all word in the post-Soviet region. Communism has discredited itself as a political ideology, while a viable alternative to democracy has not emerged (Fukuyama 1992). Given these normative constraints, the ruling elite in closed political systems has fallen into the habit of paying lip service to the dominant transnational political discourse. In the former Soviet republics, incumbent presidents frequently embellish their speeches with references to democracy, while the coercive apparatus cracks down on the opposition. Revealing this elite thinking, President Alyaksandr Lukashenka of Belarus, for example, articulated a colorful definition of democracy during his meeting with the workers of Minsk car factory. "We don't need democracy with hullabaloo," Lukashenka said in 1998, two years after massive protests in the street against the expansion of presidential powers. "We do need the type of democracy where people work and get paid, even if not much but enough to buy bread, milk, sour cream, cottage cheese, and sometimes a piece of meat in order to feed their children" (Radio Free Europe/Radio Liberty 2006). Likewise, incumbent presidents in Central Asia tend to put the emphasis on the growth of economic prosperity in the post-Soviet period. In the 2005 Annual Address, for example, President Nursultan Nazarbayev of Kazakhstan proudly stated: "Over these ten years, we have been moving forward, towards democratization taking into consideration the specific features of our country and following the principle of 'first economy, then politics.' Gradualism has not let us down."[1] A popular elite strategy in repressive regimes is to eschew the application of democratic ideas and principles by advocating a local version of democracy and praising the virtues of gradual reforms and social stability.

In the aftermath of Ukraine's Orange Revolution backed by international donor organizations and Western governments, the term "sovereign democracy" has seeped into Russia's political discourse (see Orlov 2008). The coinage of the term is attributed to Vladislav Surkov, the Kremlin's chief ideologist. In defending his country against Western criticism on the eve of G8 Summit in St. Petersburg, Surkov postulated that Russia would adopt its own version of democracy, on its own terms. According to the Kremlin's spokesperson, the notion of "sovereign democracy" was developed to capture the peculiarities of Russian culture and take into account the state of the country's economic development. Yet most analysts of local politics concur that the slick phrase was meant to reassert Russia's sovereignty and send a signal to the West not to meddle in Russia's domestic affairs (Lipman 2006a; Ryzhkov 2005).

In contrast, the concept of democracy with an adjective was absent from the official political discourse in Ukraine. Instead, Kuchma's team of spin doctors promoted the idea of stability. Since the Soviet times, people were led to believe that any hardship could be tolerated "as long as there is no war" (*lish' by ne bylo voiny*). Tapping into this idea, the incumbent president extolled the value of stability and positioned himself as the guarantor of peace.[2] On the eve of the first round of the 2004 presidential election, Kuchma (2004) remarked, "Stability is like air. If we have it, we don't notice it. If we run short of it or, God forbid, it stops flowing altogether, then we become aware of its real, vital value to human life." Several weeks later, citizens en masse shook the status quo by protesting against electoral fraud and speeding up Kuchma's exit from power.

There is a large body of empirical evidence indicating that the political environment in Putin's Russia and Kuchma's Ukraine was hostile to the spread of democratic ideas and practices, albeit to varying degrees. The consolidation of Russia's sovereign democracy entailed attacks on investigative journalists, harassment of nongovernmental organizations concerned with human rights issues, and tightening control over the educational system (for an overview, see Petrov 2005). Along similar lines, Kuchma sought to safeguard the status quo by obstructing the development of independent media and interfering with the election campaigns of opposition parties. But Kuchma's grip on power was less firm than that of the leadership in Russia, making the regime more vulnerable to the breakdown.

In this political context, post-communist youth observed the wide gap between the official rhetoric and the political reality. This chapter examines how adolescents made sense of what democracy is all about. The empirical analysis begins by gauging the extent to which pre-adults claim support for democracy. Next, the chapter discusses how the young generation understands the concept of democracy.

Adolescents' support for democracy

Scholars have long argued that broad-based public support for democratic ideas and principles underpins the durability of democracies (Almond and Verba 1963; Eckstein 1998; Norris 1999). In his seminal work, Easton (1965) developed the concept of diffuse support to explain why the regime is able to withstand political and economic turbulence. According to this perspective, it is the appreciation of democracy as a value in itself that carries the political regime through periods of social turmoil. A wide dispersion of pro-democratic attitudes is of even greater importance in countries that fall somewhere between democracy and dictatorship. The in-built tension between the official rhetoric touting the virtues of democracy and governmental actions undercutting the viability of democratic institutions injects a modicum of uncertainty into the political environment. Specifically, the potential emergence of a genuine pro-democratic majority spells grave danger for the powerholders by swaying the direction of the country's political development in favor of democracy. Though the ruling elite routinely violate electoral procedures and marginalize the opposition, there is a limit to the magnitude of electoral fraud permissible in hybrid regimes. That is why the incumbent government needs a reservoir of public support or, at minimum, resigned acceptance of the status quo.

It is reasonable to assume that individuals during adolescence form opinions about democracy. Though teenagers cannot directly participate in politics by exercising the right to vote or joining political parties, they develop cognitive skills necessary to grasp abstract ideas and pass judgments about political phenomena. Nor is the younger generation completely shielded from the official political discourse. High-school students learn about democracy from conversations with their parents, civics courses at school, and the mass media. It is unclear, however, to what extent post-communist youth in hybrid regimes embraces democracy as the political value.

In this study, adolescents were prompted to report their level of agreement with the following statement, "Democracy is the best form of government for my home country." The findings presented in Table 2.1 reveal that approximately two-thirds of those surveyed endorse the democratic political

Table 2.1 Adolescents' support for democracy: a cross-city comparison

Level of Support	Russia			Ukraine		
	Moscow	Rostov	Tula	Kyiv	Lviv	Donetsk
High	58.1	68.7	68.1	60.1	74.7	55.9
Low	23.9	18.1	19.4	14.5	5.1	15.5
Don't know	18.1	13.2	12.5	25.4	20.2	28.6
Total	100% (310)	100% (310)	100% (304)	100% (283)	100% (292)	100% (304)
Cramer's V	0.074**	—	—	0.130***	—	—

Source: Survey of Adolescents in Russia and Ukraine, 2005.

Notes
The question wording was: "To what extent do you agree with the following statement: Democracy is the best form of government for my home country." The variable is a four-point scale ranging from 1, strongly disagree, to 4, strongly agree. In the table, the response categories for "strongly agree" and "agree" and "strongly disagree" and "disagree" are collapsed to summarize the level of support for democracy. In addition, the table reports the percentage of "don't know" responses. N = 1,803. The correlation coefficient Cramer's V measures the strength of the relationship between the two variables. It ranges from 0, no relationship, to 1, perfect relationship.
***p <.001, **p<.01, *p <.05.

system. There are, however, detectable cross-city differences. Within Russia, Moscow adolescents tend to be less supportive of democracy than their peers in the provinces. To some degree, this empirical observation challenges the traditional image of the capital city as the home base of liberal-minded indivisuals. One possibility why Moscow adolescents are less enthusiastic about democracy is that they tend to hold fewer grievances against the incumbent government and more optimism about their abilities to make a living within the parameters of the current political regime. Another explanation for a higher level of democratic support in Rostov-on-the-Don and Tula might be that the cycle of competitive gubernatorial elections has fostered "democratic tendencies" in Russian provinces (Moses 2002). Until 2004, governors in each Russian oblast were elected by popular vote, creating limited opportunities for political competition at the local level. As a result, adolescents in Rostov-on-the-Don and Tula might have observed how the idea of democracy plays out in their hometowns. Furthermore, the cross-national diffusion of ideas and the heavy traffic of people across the Russian–Ukrainian border might have contributed to the spread of democratic ideas in the borderland region of Rostov.

The broad-based dispersion of democratic support among Ukrainian adolescents is compounded by the fact that the local social context has a significant impact on the political attitudes of young citizens. Apparently, the younger generation contributes to the reproduction of the east–west regional cleavage in Ukrainian society. On the one hand, Lviv, located close to the Polish–Ukrainian border, stands out as a beacon of democratic support. On the other hand, Donetsk, tucked away on the Russian–Ukrainian border, emerges as a drag on Ukraine's break with the communist regime. Respondents from the capital city of Kyiv occupy the middle ground: they score lower than their peers in Lviv, but higher than their counterparts in Donetsk. In general, the east–west regional cleavage does not bode well for Ukraine's capacity to rally behind a common political ideal.

Furthermore, there are empirical grounds to argue that the level of democratic support has declined among Russian adolescents during the post-Soviet period. In spring 1996, a team of Russian scholars at the Center for the Sociology of Education, Russian Academy of Sciences conducted a survey of 1,604 Moscow adolescents aged 14–16. When confronted with the choice of the preferable political regime for Russia, 71.5 percent of Moscow high-school students selected democracy (Sobkin 1997). For comparison, only 58 percent of the surveyed Moscow adolescents endorsed democratic support in spring 2005. Apparently, the luster of liberal democracy has tarnished among Russian youth.

Given the passage of time since the collapse of communism, the proportion of adolescents who express ambivalence about the democratic political system is remarkably high in 2005. Almost a quarter of the Ukrainian adolescents surveyed still appear to be uncertain about the virtues of democracy. In particular, 28 percent of Donetsk respondents hesitate to approve of the political regime that allowed the political loss of Yanukovych as a result of the nullification of the initial election results and the re-run of the second round of the 2004 presidential election. In contrast, the re-election of Putin for a second term in office was a virtual certainty, and Russian adolescents observed "boring" national elections. In March 2004, Putin held a 56 percent lead over the second-place presidential contender, the leader of the Communist Party of the Russian Federation. This air of political stability smoothes away some doubts about the virtues of democracy: only 14 percent of Russian adolescents are ambivalent about the suitability of democracy for their homeland.

Who is hesitant to endorse or reject democracy as the best form of government? To answer this question, I turn to the results of binary logistic regression analysis presented in Table 2.2. The findings provide the empirical basis for sketching a socio-demographic profile of adolescents who "don't know" whether democracy is a good fit for their home country. The dependent

Table 2.2 Support for democracy: profiling don't knows

	Russia			Ukraine		
	B	Robust S.E.	Exp. (B)	B	Robust S.E.	Exp. (B)
Gender (male = 1)	−0.455	0.311	0.634	−0.174	0.216	0.840
Ethnicity: Russian	0.340	0.452	1.404	0.196	0.276	1.216
Father's education: higher	0.305	0.360	1.357	−0.177	0.230	0.838
Mother's education: higher	−0.107	0.371	0.899	0.019	0.230	1.020
International travel (yes = 1)	−0.617*	0.319	0.540	−0.043	0.218	0.958
Grade 10	−0.228	0.342	0.796	−0.516**	0.218	0.597
Local context						
Rostov-on-the-Don[a]	−0.561**	0.282	0.571	—	—	—
Tula[a]	−0.927***	0.302	0.396	—	—	—
Donetsk[b]	—	—	—	0.305	0.246	1.356
Lviv[b]	—	—	—	−0.106	0.240	0.900
Constant	−1.288	0.533	—	−0.891	0.252	—
Chi-square	15.100*	—	—	14.750*	—	—
−2LL	−334.416	—	—	−365.561	—	—
Pseudo R-square	0.032	—	—	0.020	—	—

Source: Survey of Adolescents in Russia and Ukraine, 2005.

Notes
Cells contain coefficients from binary logistic regression, robust standard errors, and odds ratio. The dependent variable is coded 1 if "don't know" and 0 if otherwise. The question wording was: "To what extent do you agree with the following statement: Democracy is the best form of government for my home country."
N = 1,803.
***p <.01, **p<.05, *p <.10.
a Moscow is the reference category for the other two Russian cities.
b Kyiv is the reference category for the other two Ukrainian cities.

variable is coded 1 if respondents chose "don't know" and 0 if otherwise. The model includes such indicators of socioeconomic status as parental level of educational attainment and international travel.

The results provide partial support for the argument that schools play a positive role in solidifying students' attitudes toward democracy. In the Ukrainian model, the regression coefficient for the tenth grade is negative and statistically significant, implying that enrollment in the tenth grade decreases the odds of being unsure about the suitability of the political regime for the home country. All Ukrainian students take a mandatory civics course in the ninth grade, and exposure to the course material is likely to strengthen students' knowledge about various political systems and solidify their opinions about democracy. Yet the relationship between enrollment in the tenth grade and a "don't know" response is statistically insignificant in Russia. Instead, the results suggest that international travel breeds ambivalence toward the democratic ideal among Russian adolescents. The regression coefficient for international travel is negative and statistically significant, signifying that those students who have traveled abroad are more categorical in their opinions about the suitability of democracy than those who have never left the country. As the number of Russian students with international experience grows, school trips to London or a romantic rendezvous in Paris might undermine the credibility of the official political discourse regarding the attractiveness of sovereign democracy.

In addition, the regression results confirm some cross-city differences in attitudes toward democracy. In the Russian model, the regression coefficients for Rostov-on-the-Don and Tula are negative and statistically significant, indicating that the proportion of Russian adolescents ambivalent about democracy is higher in Moscow than in the other two cities. In the case of Ukraine, the share of "don't know" responses is higher in Donetsk and lower in Lviv, compared to the capital city of Kyiv.

Since Russian adolescents tend to be less supportive of democracy than Ukrainian ones, it is hardly surprising that the same trend is observed within the adult population. As shown in Table 2.3, the level of democratic support has been significantly higher in Ukraine since the mid-1990s. Furthermore, the attitudinal gap between Russia and Ukraine has widened over the past decade. In 1995, according to the data from the World Values Survey, 45 percent of Russia's respondents, compared to 55 percent of Ukrainian ones, reported support for democracy. In 1999, the level of democratic support remained almost unchanged in Russia (46 percent), while it increased by more than 8 percent in Ukraine. Moreover, the results from the 2006 Life in Transition Survey reveal that Russia's voting-age population is almost equally split into three parts: the slim plurality of the surveyed (36.5 percent) prefer democracy over other political alternatives, 31.7 percent of Russians are willing to endorse an authoritarian government "under some circumstances," whereas the remainder (31.8 percent) claim that the regime type does not make any difference for people like them. In contrast, the majority of Ukrainians (56 percent) endorse the democratic political system, while

Table 2.3 Adults' support for democracy, 1995–2006

	1995[a]		1999[a]		2006[b]	
Level of support	Russia	Ukraine	Russia	Ukraine	Russia	Ukraine
High	45.0	55.1	46.0	63.6	36.5	56.0
Low	33.0	13.7	28.6	11.5	31.7	22.6
Don't know (Doesn't matter)	22.0	31.2	25.4	24.9	31.8	21.3
Total	100% (2,040)	100% (2,811)	100% (2,500)	100% (1,195)	100% (1,000)	100% (998)
Cramer's V	0.233***	—	0.202***	—	0.196***	—

Sources
a World Values Survey (WVS). The survey was administered in Russia and Ukraine in 1995 and 1999. N = 8,546. For more information, visit the website http://www.worldvaluessurvey.org.
b The Life in Transition Survey was administered by the European Bank for Reconstruction and Development in collaboration with the World Bank in 2006. N = 1,998.

Notes
The question in the WVS was formulated as follows: "I'm going to describe various types of political systems and ask what you think about each as a way of governing this country. For each one, would you say it is a very good, fairly good, fairly bad, or very bad way of governing this country? ... having a democratic political system." The response categories in the table are relabeled to indicate the level of support for democracy. For example, a "high" level of support for democracy in the table corresponds to a combination of "very good" and "good" response categories in the survey. The Life in Transition Survey prompted respondents to choose which of the following statements they agreed with most: (1) democracy is preferable to any other form of political system; (2) under some circumstances an authoritarian government may be preferable to a democratic one; (3) for people like me, it does not matter whether a government is democratic or authoritarian. The percentage of those who preferred democracy is reported in the table.
***p <.001, **p<.01, *p <.05.

one fifth of those surveyed share skepticism about the impact of the political regime on their lives. More specifically, Ukraine's respondents attach greater importance to the presence of an independent press and strong political opposition.[3] These attitudinal differences account, in part, for the divergent political paths that Russia and Ukraine have taken.

Are adolescents content with the way democracy works in their home country? To explore this issue, the survey prompts high-school students to grade the level of democratic development in Russia and Ukraine, respectively. As seen in Table 2.4, approximately one fifth of Russian and Ukrainian adolescents have difficulty answering this question. Another one fifth of adolescents reports dissatisfaction with the way democracy functions in the country. The results also reveal some cross-country and within-country variations. Compared to Russian adolescents, Ukrainian ones tend to assign a higher score to the level of democracy in the country. Within Ukraine, according to the survey results, Donetsk adolescents rank the level of democracy Ukraine has achieved higher than Lviv adolescents. A possible

24 *Attitudes toward democracy*

Table 2.4 Adolescents' evaluation of democracy

	Russia			Ukraine		
	Moscow	Rostov	Tula	Kyiv	Lviv	Donetsk
Excellent	2.3	6.5	1.6	9.9	2.4	17.3
Good	17.4	15.2	13.5	35.2	19.0	34.2
Satisfactory	38.4	38.8	40.8	20.8	22.8	23.7
Unsatisfactory	17.4	21.7	30.6	17.3	30.0	4.8
Don't know	24.6	17.8	13.5	16.9	25.9	20.0
Total	100% (305)	100% (309)	100% (304)	100% (284)	100% (290)	100% (295)

Source: Survey of Adolescents in Russia and Ukraine, 2005.

Note
The question wording was: "How would you grade the level of democratic development in your home country?" The variable is a four-point scale ranging from 1, unsatisfactory, to 4, excellent. In addition, the table reports the percentage of "don't know" responses.

explanation for this empirical observation is that Lviv adolescents set a much higher bar for the application of democratic ideas and principles in the country.

Overall, the findings suggest that the prospects for democratic development in the selected states are rather mixed. Optimists might draw our attention to the high percentage of adolescents endorsing democracy as the "best form of government." But a more sober finding is that almost one third of young citizens fail to develop positive attitudes toward the democratic political system a few years before reaching the voting age. In addition, there is a palpable danger that the presence of youthful indifference toward the regime type in their home country may boost support for an authoritarian ruler in exchange for socioeconomic stability. At this point, these interpretations have to be regarded as conditional. Taking the side of the optimists or aligning with more cautious observers of regional politics depends on a clearer understanding of what respondents mean by democracy. For this reason, this chapter proceeds with the discussion of how adolescents understand the concept of democracy.

Contested meanings of democracy

The academic literature yields a variety of definitions of democracy (Bollen and Jackman 1989; Collier and Levitsky 1997; Collier and Adcock 1999). According to the minimalist perspective (Schumpeter 1942), democracy is associated with open political competition. Przeworski (1991: 3), for example, argues that "democracy is a system in which parties lose elections." Other scholars have developed a much broader definition of democracy. Dahl (1971), for example, insists upon citizen participation as a critical dimension of the democratic system. We can infer from this line of research that ordinary citizens interpret the concept of democracy in different ways.

Given the novelty and the contestation of regime norms, post-communist citizens, in particular, attach a wide array of meanings to the word "democracy." Freedom is widely considered as a fundamental value that binds individuals in open societies (Rose 1995). In 1990, more than half of citizens in Czechoslovakia, Lithuania, Poland, and Romania associated democracy with freedom (Simon 1998). In addition, the impoverished population conflated the economic prosperity of Western societies with democracy. Meanwhile, democracy can disrupt the lives of ordinary citizens because it grants individuals the freedom to protest and it slows down policymaking processes. In particular, students of Russian politics tend to scrutinize the ranking of public preferences when it comes to choosing between social order and liberal democracy (Bahry, Boaz, and Gordon 1997; Miller, Hesli, and Reisinger 1997; Sakwa 1995). Through a series of in-depth interviews in six Russian cities and a variety of small towns, Carnaghan (2008) uncovers how daily existence generates multiple interpretations of order and affects the appeal of democracy. Likewise, pre-adults are likely to display a diversity of opinions about the meaning of democracy. A close inspection of various conceptions of democracy among adolescents is important, since it provides insights into their reasoning behind support for the political regime.

This empirical investigation is driven, in part, by the following question: *Does a particular understanding of democracy lead to higher support for the political regime?* The choice of rights and freedoms, on the one hand, and good governance, on the other, deserves particular scrutiny because it represents a major dilemma in countries undergoing a variety of political and socioeconomic transformations simultaneously. The findings from large-N surveys show that mass support for democracy depends, to a large extent, on the performance of political and economic institutions in post-communist societies (Mishler and Rose 2005; Tucker 2005; Whitefield and Evans 1999). Some qualitative evidence also suggests that institutional performance plays a decisive role in shaping mass attitudes toward democracy. Using in-depth interviews with respondents, Carnaghan (2001), for example, finds that Russian adults tend to value material rewards more highly than democratic processes. Does the same finding apply to adolescents? Or is this new generation more inclined to cherish individual rights and freedoms? The study seeks to shed some light on this issue.

The results presented in Table 2.5 confirm our expectation about variations in adolescents' conceptualization of democracy. The survey prompted adolescents to list phrases or words associated with the word "democracy." Based upon a qualitative analysis of students' responses to the open-ended question, the study identifies six themes capturing the essence of democracy.[4]

When it comes to defining democracy, a large proportion of Russian adolescents bring up the phrase "people's rule" (*vlast' naroda*). As many as one third of Tula respondents come up with this response. At first glance,

26 *Attitudes toward democracy*

Table 2.5 Adolescents' conceptions of democracy

Conception	Russia			Ukraine		
	Moscow	Rostov	Tula	Kyiv	Lviv	Donetsk
Rule by the people	20.3	29.7	35.5	12.5	13.3	7.8
Freedoms/rights	17.4	30.3	38.5	26.6	29.4	27.4
Good governance	4.8	4.2	5.9	4.5	10.6	2.3
Bad governance	0.6	1.3	2.0	2.8	1.0	2.9
Independence	—	0.6	—	5.2	10.6	2.0
Orange Revolution	—	—	—	2.1	2.7	3.6
Don't know/non-response	56.9	33.9	18.1	46.4	32.4	54.1
Total	100% (311)	100% (310)	100% (304)	100% (289)	100% (293)	100% (307)
Cramer's V	0.242***	—	—	0.190***	—	—

Source: Survey of Adolescents in Russia and Ukraine, 2005.

Notes
The open-ended question was: "Please list words or phrases with which you associate the word democracy." Percentages are reported in the table.
N = 1,814.
***p <.001, **p<.01, *p <.05.

it seems like a standard, textbook definition of the political regime based upon the literal translation of the word "democracy" from Greek. There is, however, another layer of meaning to this phrase in the post-communist region. The slogan "Power to the People!" is very familiar to Soviet citizens. Upon overthrowing the Russian tsar, the Communist Party of the Soviet Union proclaimed that all the power in the state would belong to the people. In reality, the ruling party usurped state power and brutally suppressed any dissenting voices. Thus, given the communist legacy, the reference to *vlast' naroda* might be a poor indicator of what democracy means to adolescents in the selected cities.

It is clear from the analysis that the percentage of adolescents to fall back on the textbook definition is much lower in Ukraine. One reason why relatively few Ukrainian respondents regurgitated the textbook definition of democracy is that they could draw upon their personal experience. Having lived through a period of massive mobilization against flagrant electoral fraud in 2004, Ukrainian adolescents are likely to have developed a more personalized understanding of democracy at work. In contrast, contemporary Russian adolescents tend to become exposed to democracy only in the abstract.

Nonetheless, it is possible that the phrase "people's rule," reminiscent of the communist past, carries a new meaning for young citizens. Some critical remarks by adolescents dissatisfied with the political situation in the country suggest such an interpretation. For a number of respondents, one of the major sources of frustration with the status quo turns out to be the perceived concentration of power in the hands of a few people:

> Democracy means the rule by the people. But Russia is no democracy, although it is described this way. It is an oligarchy.
> (14 year old, Moscow, Russia)

> Democracy, if translated literally, means the rule [*vlast'*] by the people. But people in our country have no power [*vlast'*].
> (14 year old, Tula, Russia)

> Democracy is when decisions are made not by a single person, but by the people as a whole (nation).
> (13 year old, Kyiv, Ukraine)

Almost one third of respondents in Russian and Ukrainian cities, with the exception of Moscow, connect democracy to the provision of individual liberties. Arguably, this conception of the political regime is crucial for genuine democracy to take root in the post-communist states because it suggests some understanding of democratic processes. Freedom of expression was a popular point of reference. A few respondents expressed awareness of the dangers associated with articulating an opinion in a politically hostile environment:

> When people can say whatever is on their mind, and nobody will stop them from doing it, and nobody will do anything to them afterwards.
> (16 year old, Tula, Russia)

> Owing to democracy, one can express one's point of view without the fear that one will be killed.
> (14 year old, Kyiv, Ukraine)

The references to physical harassment and death in the aftermath of a controversial public statement might reflect students' awareness of recent assassinations of local independent journalists. Evidence of attempts on reporters' lives abounds in the post-communist region (Committee to Protect Journalists 2004). Kuchmagate – the tape scandal in the wake of Gongadze's death – made headlines in the year 2000. Like many other high-profile crimes, this murder remained unsolved, reinforcing popular beliefs in the failure of the ruling elite to protect the human rights of ordinary citizens.

Adolescents also criticized the failure of the existing political system to guarantee the right to choose the president and parliamentarians through free and fair elections. Among some Russian respondents, views of the corruptive power of money fueled skepticism about the possibility of ordinary citizens to run for parliament and be elected:

When people can choose whatever they consider necessary and useful; when they have the right to vote. But everything is bought up now. There is corruption everywhere. Nobody can be completely trusted.

(15 year old, Rostov-on-the-Don, Russia)

Many adolescents regarded the supremacy of statutory law (*verkhovenstvo zakona*) and equality before the law as defining features of the democratic political system. The respondents pointed to the glaring gap between existing laws and their uneven enforcement:

Democracy implies just laws for all the layers of the population.

(15 year old, Tula, Russia)

The citizen feels good in the state. His rights and freedoms are protected by law.

(15 year old, Donetsk, Ukraine)

It is worth noting that the proportion of respondents who make a link between good governance and democracy is quite low. The adolescents stressed the need for the government to be responsive to citizen needs and accountable for the implementation of public policies. Indeed, a number of Ukrainian respondents, in particular those originating from Lviv, associated democracy with honesty and truth. The public demand for transparency and accountability was expressed clearly and loudly during the Orange Revolution:

Democracy implies the development of the country, i.e. when our high-ranking officials stop taking bribes [*khabari*].

(15 year old, Lviv, Ukraine)

When the authorities [*vlada*] do everything in their power for the betterment of the country, rather than [putting money into] their pockets.

(15 year old, Lviv, Ukraine)

The government pays attention to people's opinions.

(14 year old, Moscow, Russia)

By observing the negative consequences of politicians' self-serving behavior, some adolescents began to associate democracy with moral degradation and self-aggrandizement:

Democracy is the so-called "freedom" of the individual so that he can humiliate the president and other people; so that he can do whatever he wishes, discarding any moral principles, violating the laws, living in fear that others will do to him what he has done to them.

(14 year old, Tula, Russia)

> Democracy is the means for politicians to make money.
> (14 year old, Rostov-on-the-Don, Russia)

> Democrats are swindlers.
> (15 year old, Kyiv, Ukraine)

> Democracy involves old views and stupid ideas. To bring order in the country, eliminate crime, unemployment, and poverty, one needs absolute monarchy.
> (15 year old, Donetsk, Ukraine)

In their musings upon the concept of democracy, Ukrainian respondents raised the issue of nation-building. The collapse of communism opened up an opportunity for establishing an independent Ukrainian state. In December 1991, Ukrainians were free to vote in the national referendum and express support for Ukraine's sovereignty without the fear of political repressions. By conflating democratization and nation-building processes, 10 percent of Lviv adolescents identified democracy with the word "independence" (*nezalezhnist'*). In contrast, less than 1 percent of Russian adolescents reported a link between democracy and national independence. This is not surprising, because the majority of Russians still bemoan the dissolution of the Soviet Union.

Another more recent event, the Orange Revolution, framed the mass understanding of democracy in Ukraine. Citizens in western and central parts of the country overwhelmingly endorsed and actively participated in protests on Maidan, Kyiv's main square, to defend their votes for Yushchenko. In contrast, the electorate densely concentrated in eastern and southern parts of the country voted for Yanukovych and questioned the grassroots nature of the protests on Maidan. The analysis of responses from the three Ukrainian cities vividly illustrates the repercussions of this political rift within the younger generation. When prompted to comment on the meaning of democracy, a Lviv adolescent recited lines from the unofficial anthem of the Orange Revolution, entitled *Together We Are Many, We Won't Be Defeated*. Another respondent from Kyiv wrote "Yushchenko" next to the drawing of the horseshoe (a campaign symbol of the Our Ukraine bloc during the 2004 election), suggesting the endorsement of the political leader. A teenager from Donetsk, by contrast, poured onto the page his vision of the incumbent government through the vulgar Russian-language rhyme "Yushchenko is an impotent, Yanukovich is the president." To some extent, such contempt for the incumbent president may be a reflection of systematic anti-Yushchenko media campaigns in eastern parts of the country.

More than one third of respondents declined to provide a substantive answer to the open-ended question. One possibility is that respondents were reluctant to reveal their understanding of the political regime. But the adolescents seemed to be quite comfortable, even forthright, when answering the bulk of the other survey questions on politics. An alternative explanation for a high percentage of non-responses is that these respondents either hold no opinion about democracy or feel ambivalent about the essence of the democratic political system. Given the political turmoil surrounding the Orange Revolution, Ukrainian adolescents are less settled in their understanding of democracy than their counterparts in Putin's Russia. A 14-year-old from Kyiv, for example, candidly admitted, "My understanding of democracy is muddy [*smutno*] at this moment."

The proportion of don't know/non-responses is too high to be ignored. Using binary logistic regression analysis, I seek to sketch a profile of these respondents. As shown in Table 2.6, students with only a vague understanding of democracy tend to come from families with less-educated parents. Moreover, students in lower grades are less likely to articulate a conception of democracy than tenth-graders. These findings suggest that education empowers young people with the basic knowledge of political concepts.

Table 2.6 Conceptions of democracy: profiling don't knows

	Russia			Ukraine		
	B	Robust S.E.	Exp. (B)	B	Robust S.E.	Exp. (B)
Gender (male = 1)	0.065	0.236	1.067	0.522***	0.188	1.686
Ethnicity: Russian	0.121	0.317	1.129	−0.028	0.245	0.972
Father's education: higher	0.047	0.258	1.048	−0.185	0.202	0.831
Mother's education: higher	−0.211	0.259	0.810	−0.437**	0.205	0.646
International travel (yes = 1)	0.220	0.240	1.246	0.364*	0.191	1.439
Grade 10	−0.160	0.245	0.852	−0.436**	0.189	0.647
Local context						
Rostov-on-the-Don	0.413***	−0.883	0.413	—	—	—
Tula	0.180***	−1.713	0.180	—	—	—
Donetsk[b]	—	—	—	0.465**	0.215	1.593
Lviv[b]	—	—	—	−0.334	0.206	0.716
Constant	0.015	0.377		−0.293	0.226	—
Chi-square	70.100***	—	—	41.680***	—	—
−2LL	−520.956	—	—	−449.867	—	—
Pseudo R-square	0.033	—	—	0.047	—	—

Source: Survey of Adolescents in Russia and Ukraine, 2005.
Notes
Cells contain coefficients from binary logistic regression, robust standard errors, and odds ratio. The dependent variable is coded 1 if non-response/don't know and 0 if otherwise. The open-ended question was: "Please list words or phrases with which you associate the word 'democracy'."
N = 1,814.
***p <.01, **p<.05, *p <.10.
a Moscow is the reference category for the other two Russian cities.
b Kyiv is the reference category for the other two Ukrainian cities.

Apparently, there are gender differences in the level of articulating one's conception of democracy. The conventional view holds that men tend to display more interest in politics and, by extension, more political knowledge, than women (Bennett and Bennett 1989; Delli Carpini and Keeter 1991). In a highly politicized social environment, however, everyone is likely to start following politics. In the aftermath of the 2004 presidential election, Ukrainian adolescents regardless of gender took a keen interest in politics: more than half of male and female students reported a "high" or "very high" level of interest in politics.[5] In addition, the empirical results presented in Table 2.6 indicate that male students were less likely to provide a definition of democracy. It is possible that a higher refusal rate among male students reflects gender differences in learning habits and academic achievement.[6] Anecdotal evidence from Russia and Ukraine suggests that female students tend to do homework more diligently and attend classes more regularly than male students. In the survey, male respondents might have been less inclined to provide thoughtful answers to the open-ended question about their conception of democracy, since this task demands considerable attention and diligence.

Another important factor that influences the level of adolescents' understanding of the democratic political system is the local context. More Moscow youngsters chose the "don't know" option than those in the Russian provinces. Within the capital city, most "don't knows" came from students in the working-class neighborhood who daily observe the glitz of the megapolis and the poverty of their households.[7] In addition, those youngsters tend to grow up in unstable families stricken with alcoholism and drug abuse. For them, daily existence is often of greater concern than academic performance. As a result, Moscow adolescents from disadvantaged backgrounds appear to be quite ignorant of the political issues gripping the country. In contrast, Donetsk adolescents are quite knowledgeable about domestic politics. But they are ambivalent about the meaning of democracy. For months, local TV channels have reiterated Russia's version of events during the Orange Revolution. The massive propaganda machine informed Donetsk adolescents that protesters in Maidan were paid with US dollars to protest against the election of Yanukovych as the new president. Yanukovych's wife appeared on national TV herself, claiming that protesters had consumed large quantities of drugged oranges and had worn winter boots imported from the United States. This distorted media representation of democracy in action raised doubts in the minds of Donetsk teenagers about the true meaning of the open society.

The implications of different concepts of democracy are explored by linking them to the levels of democratic support among adolescents. As shown in Figure 2.1, the association of democracy with freedom generates, on average, the highest level of support for democracy (82.6 percent in Russia and 82 percent in Ukraine). Yet there are some detectable cross-country differences. The perceived link between good governance and democracy tends to draw more support for the political regime among Russian adolescents, whereas

32 *Attitudes toward democracy*

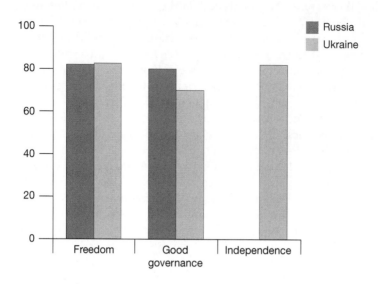

Figure 2.1 Adolescents' support for democracy by conceptions of democracy (percentages)

Source: Survey of Adolescents in Russia and Ukraine, 2005.

Note: The percentages refer to the proportion of respondents who reported support for democracy within the sample of respondents who associated democracy with a specific concept (freedom, good governance, or independence).

the connection between democracy and national independence supersedes concerns about good governance among Ukrainian adolescents. Further reinforcing the east–west regional cleavage, the conceptual connection of the Orange Revolution to democracy boosts democratic support in Lviv and weakens it in Donetsk.

Additional analysis reveals that adolescents' ambivalence about the appropriateness of democracy for their home country is related to their understanding of democracy. First, the difficulty of articulating a conception of democracy makes students reluctant to make judgments about the suitability of a political regime. This source of attitudinal ambivalence can be found in diverse political settings. When respondents are unfamiliar with the political concept, they might be less inclined to report an opinion about it. The second source of adolescents' ambivalence, however, is more characteristic of societies grappling with the negative consequences of the transition from communism. A large proportion of those adolescents who associate democracy with bad governance are indecisive about the fit of the democratic political system with the national context. Overall, these findings suggest that a more solid grasp of the political concept may boost adolescents' support for democracy.

Conclusion

A close look at adolescents' attitudes toward democracy produces mixed results. The empirical observation that almost two-thirds of teenagers in the selected Russian and Ukrainian cities consider democracy as the best form of government gives us some grounds for optimism. Lending credence to the idea of generational replacement, post-communist youth appears to be more supportive of democracy than older generations socialized during the Soviet period. It is alarming, however, that almost one third of adolescents either harbor negative views of democracy or express ambivalence about the democratic political regime. A major implication of these findings is that neither staunch supporters nor harsh opponents of democracy are likely to consolidate power in their hands. Indeed, this limbo might be an optimum condition for the survival of the hybrid regime.

Furthermore, it is clear from the analysis that longstanding regional cleavages affect pro-democracy attitudes of adolescents and reinforce the far-reaching impact of historical legacies. Strikingly, the attitudinal differences between Lviv respondents, on the one hand, and Donetsk ones, on the other, are larger than aggregate differences between respondents in Russia and Ukraine. The persistent east–west cleavage may further contribute to the durability of the hybrid regime in Ukraine by hampering movement along the democracy–autocracy continuum.

3 Trust in authorities

Each year thousands of young men in Russia and Ukraine are called up for compulsory military service. Approximately 400,000 young men between the ages of 18 and 27 are annually drafted in Russia (Lokshin and Yemtsov 2008). Likewise, almost 60,000 young men are drafted to serve in the ranks of Ukraine's military (*Elvisti* 2004; *ProUa* 2005). Yet, fulfilling the quotas for mandatory conscription has been a serious challenge for military recruiters. According to some estimates, only 10 percent of conscription-age men serve a two-year term in the military (Lokshin and Yemtsov 2008: 360).[1] In droves, young men dodge the draft by ignoring call-up notices and seeking various exemptions and deferments. Some submit fake medical reports, others try to get university admission or take up exempt jobs in rural areas. Few are willing to spend two years of their lives in the barracks because of the prevalence of abuse in the military and, in particular, hazing.[2]

The fate of 19-year-old Andrei Sychov has become a gruesome symbol of atrocious practices in the Russian military (Brigg 2006; Finn 2006; Murphy 2006; Myers 2006; Vyugin 2006). On New Year's Eve in December 2005, Sychov was dragged from bed at 3 a.m. and forced to squat for three and a half hours. With his hands tied behind his back, the draftee was severely beaten by senior servicemen and sustained serious injuries. Given the lack of medical attention, the young man developed a gangrenous infection and became bedridden. By the time he was hospitalized, his condition had seriously deteriorated. The doctors had to amputate his legs and his genitals, while the Ministry of Defense tried to hush up the case. Between the surgeries, one of the doctors divulged information about the draftee's condition to Sychov's mother. Allegedly, the Ministry of Defense tried to keep a lid on the scandal by offering her a bribe, but she declined the offer. The media attention to Sychov's beating has exposed a litany of problems that afflict the Russian army. Amid the torrent of negative news, young men facing the prospect of mandatory conscription tend to question the military's credentials to provide a secure environment for the professional training of new conscripts. The army is often one of the first points of youth interaction with government institutions. To some extent, it sets the negative tone for citizen–state relations in the future.

Conventional wisdom holds that adolescence is a period of rebellion against dominant social norms and authority figures (Deutsch and Jones 2008; Mees 1988; Sugimura *et al.* 2009). In their search for identity, high-school students tend to challenge parental and teachers' assertion of control over their lives and make choices unavailable to them during childhood. Alcohol consumption, drug use, and sexual behavior are among the knotty issues adolescents grapple with. At the same time, young citizens try to make sense of the world around them and evaluate the behavior of authority figures outside family and the classroom. While psychologists have devoted considerable attention to the social behavior of adolescents (Adams and Berzonsky 2003; Lerner and Steinberg 2009), seldom do sociologists and political scientists probe the attitudes of post-Soviet adolescents toward authority figures. In this chapter, I explore the attitudes of Russian and Ukrainian adolescents toward the president, parliamentarians, political parties, police, the army, and judges. By trust, I mean "a basic evaluative orientation toward the government" (Hetherington 1998: 791).

Trust in political and social institutions is in short supply in the former Soviet Union. Cross-national research has consistently shown that citizens in the post-communist states place less trust in government than citizens in mature democracies (Klingemann and Fuchs 1995; Norris 1999). Within the post-communist region, governments in EU member states tend to garner more public support than in the non-Baltic former Soviet republics (Haerpfer 2002; Mishler and Rose 1997; Rose, Mishler, and Haerpfer 1998). In line with the results from the surveys of the adult population, the IEA Civic Education Study finds that adolescents in post-communist Europe have less trust in political and public institutions than their peers in mature democracies (Torney-Purta, Barber, and Richardson 2004). Without doubt, post-communist citizenry has well-grounded reasons to be dissatisfied with incumbent authorities. There is no shortage of examples of forgotten electoral promises and abuses of power. Evidence is also pouring in that public servants ranging from top officials in government agencies to clerks in district courts and police officers in the street regularly engage in corruption and overlook the public interest in the selected states.

Yet trust in government is a necessary ingredient for the successful completion of political, economic, and cultural transformations in the post-Soviet region. From the political standpoint, positive orientation toward government cements the durability of the political regime (Almond and Verba 1963). From the economic perspective, trust in political and social institutions is positively correlated with the growth of a viable market economy (Knack and Keefer 1997). At the cultural level, institutional trust facilitates nation-building processes by fostering attachment toward the nation-state. As adolescents are on the cusp of becoming first-time voters and entering the labor force, they are likely to leave their imprint on the dynamics of various transformations in their home countries.

Who do adolescents trust?

The trustworthiness of various political actors ranks in the same order in both countries, but the magnitude of trust varies across the selected cities. As shown in Figure 3.1, the president is the most trustworthy political figure among the younger generation. President Putin wins the support of 74 percent of Russian adolescents. Compared to his Russian counterpart, President Yushchenko is less popular in his home country. Almost a year after the Orange Revolution, 45 percent of Ukrainian adolescents hold favorable views of the incumbent president. Notwithstanding widespread disillusionment with the job performance of the newly elected president, Yushchenko remained more trustworthy than parliamentarians.

The national parliament is ubiquitously known for being the least trusted institution (Hibbing and Patterson 1994; Hibbing and Theiss-Morse 1995). Consistent with this trend, deputies to the Duma, the lower chamber of Russia's national parliament, elicit trust only among 17 percent of Russian adolescents. Remarkably, Verkhovna Rada, Ukraine's national parliament, wins the trust of a quarter of Ukrainian adolescents at a time when parliamentarians are embroiled in rancorous political exchanges.[3]

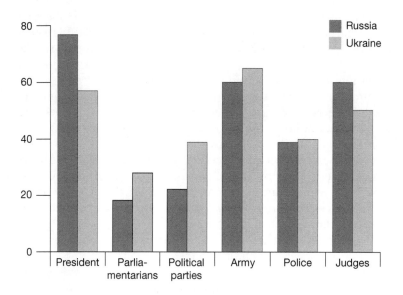

Figure 3.1 Adolescents' trust in authorities (percentages)

Source: Survey of Adolescents in Russia and Ukraine, 2005.

Note: The question wording was: "How much do you trust [doveriaete] the following: president, parliamentarians, political parties, army, police, and judges?" The variable is a four-point scale ranging from 1, not at all, to 4, very much. A combined percentage of "quite a lot" and "very much" is reported in the figure.

Moreover, political parties appear to be more trustworthy in Ukraine than in Russia. Thirty-eight percent of Ukrainian adolescents, compared to 22 percent of Russian ones, report trust in political parties. This finding suggests that the popularity of President Putin fails to trickle down to his party, United Russia. Furthermore, a two-party political system, with both parties continuing the course of Putin's reforms and maintaining the status quo, is unable to buttress support for the major political players.[4] The tranquility of Russia's political landscape fails to produce positive attitudes toward political parties. The Ukrainian political landscape, in contrast, is embellished with patches of blue (Party of Regions), red (the Tymoshenko bloc), and orange (the Our Ukraine bloc). In recent years, the rise of the Yushchenko-led 'Our Ukraine' bloc and the Tymoshenko bloc coincided with an increase of popular support for political parties. According to the 2005 survey of Ukraine's adult population, the level of trust in political parties jumped from 3.6 percent in 1999 to 8.5 percent in 2004. In addition, intense political competition might have contributed to the strength of citizens' attachment to a political party in Ukraine.

Among order-related institutions, the army turns out be the most trustworthy. In the survey, more than half of adolescents report trust in the army. If the survey question were more specific and gauged adolescents' attitudes toward mandatory conscription, then the results would be much less flattering for the image of the military. In contrast, the police is the single public institution that is equally distrusted by adolescents in Russia and Ukraine. Approximately two-thirds of teenagers report distrust in the law enforcement agency. A plausible explanation for this trend is the high extent of police involvement in semi-legal or illegal activities, often extracting money from ordinary citizens and forging ties with the criminal world (Hughes and Denisova 2001; Varese 2005). Finally, the analysis finds that adolescents' trust in judges is 10 percent higher in Russia than in Ukraine. More negative attitudes toward judges among Ukrainian adolescents can be attributed to the Supreme Court's ruling in December 2004.[5] As an extraordinary measure for resolving the political standoff, the Supreme Court ruled to annul election results claiming Yanukovych's victory and order the re-run of the second round of the 2004 presidential election. In the eyes of Yanukovych supporters, this controversial ruling might have tainted the reputation of the judiciary branch as an impartial mediator in legal disputes.

Not surprisingly, the east–west regional cleavage is a strong predictor of adolescents' attitudes toward the incumbent president and the national parliament in Ukraine. Lviv adolescents trust the incumbent president six times more than those in Donetsk (78 percent vs. 12 percent). Similarly, 60 percent of Lviv respondents and only 10 percent of their peers in Donetsk express trust in political parties that support Yushchenko.[6] And Donetsk respondents are least trustful of deputies to Verkhovna Rada. It is clear from these findings that local social context leaves a mark on adolescents' attitudes toward political players at the national level.

38 Trust in authorities

In sum, the results demonstrate that adolescents in post-communist societies exhibit a low level of trust in authorities. Politicians provoke a negative reaction among the respondents. Parliamentarians have yet to build a credible reputation among young voters in Russia and Ukraine. Among political actors, only the incumbent president wins a relatively high level of trust. As to order-related institutions, the army commands substantially higher levels of public support than the police.

These attitudes, however, might reflect the universal tendency of adolescents to defy authority. The life-cycle argument raises the question: how far does the adult population in Russia and Ukraine trust authorities? Data from the 2005 survey conducted by Democratic Initiatives, jointly with Kyiv International Institute of Sociology (Ukraine), and the Life in Transition Survey offer us an opportunity for a tentative cross-age comparison.[7] Contrary to the life-cycle argument, Russian and Ukrainian adolescents turn out to hold more positive attitudes toward authority than the adult population. As post-communist citizens advance into age, they tend to accumulate grievances against incumbent authorities and temper their expectations about the benevolence of the ruling elite.

A cross-age comparison suggests that trust in the incumbent president is almost 20 percent higher among adolescents in both countries. It is indisputable that President Putin is a popular political figure in Russia. Opinion polls

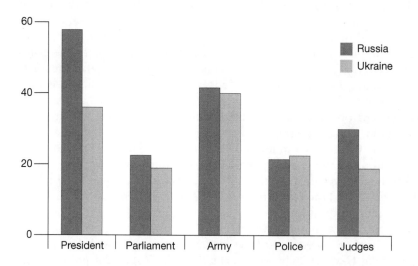

Figure 3.2 Trust in authorities among the adult population (percentages)

Sources: Democratic Initiatives/Kyiv International Institute of Sociology (Ukraine); Life in Transition Survey (Russia).

Note: The Ukrainian survey was administered on 18–23 September 2005. N=1,803. The Life in Transition Survey was administered in 2006. N = 1,998.

conducted by the Levada Center clearly demonstrate that the popularity of President Putin has been consistently high over his eight-year tenure.[8] During his first month in office in May 2000, Putin received the approval of 72 percent of Russian citizens. By the end of his presidency in February 2008, Putin's approval rating reached 85 percent.[9] In 2006, the results from the Life in Transition Survey indicated that 56 percent of Russia's adult population placed their trust in the incumbent president. In contrast, trust in President Yuschenko quickly dissipated upon his inauguration in January 2005, dropping to 33 percent in September 2005. Still, the adult population in both Russia and Ukraine takes a more critical stance toward the incumbent president than adolescents do.

Similarly, adolescents exhibit much higher levels of trust in order-related institutions. On average, the level of trust in the army and the police is 15 percent higher among adolescents. Only one fifth of adults in Russia and Ukraine report trust in policemen. Among reasons cited by Russia's citizens to account for distrust in the law enforcement agency, corruption ranks first.[10] Corruption has become ingrained in social practices to the extent that even young Russian recruits to the police academy claim that corruption is justifiable under certain circumstances (Beck and Lee 2002). As Walsh (2004) observes, "Mr. Putin is trying to build a police state without a functional police force." Likewise, attempts by Ukraine's former Minister of Interior Affairs Yuriy Lutsenko to introduce more transparency into the traffic police have fallen flat.[11] Furthermore, the results point to the failures of incumbent governments to promote rule of law. There is a 30 percent gap in the level of trust in judges between adolescents and adults, whereas the smallest attitudinal differences exist in public attitudes toward the national parliament. Youngsters and older citizens alike place little trust in politicians elected to the national parliament. These findings, however, need to be treated with caution, since the 2005 survey of adolescents is unrepresentative of the whole adolescent population in Russia and Ukraine.

Additional survey data support the argument that adolescents in post-communist Russia hold more positive attitudes toward authority than the adult population. Within the framework of the IEA Civic Education Study, a national representative sample of Russian adolescents was surveyed in 1999.[12] During the same year, Russia's voting-age population participated in the fourth wave of the World Values Survey, providing an opportunity for a cross-age comparison of political attitudes.[13] The results from the 1999 surveys indicate that the level of trust in the national parliament was 15 percent higher among Russian adolescents compared to Russian adults (35.6 percent vs. 19.9 percent). In a similar vein, 44.9 percent of Russian adolescents and 29.9 percent of Russian adults reported trust in the police, revealing a 15 percent difference in their attitudes toward the law enforcement agency. These attitudinal differences are consistent with what we observe in 2005.

Overall, the survey results reveal a low level of trust in political incumbents and public servants. The pervasive spread of corruption is a plausible explanation for distrust in authorities. According to the 2005 Corruption

Perceptions Index, ranking 159 countries from the most transparent to the most corrupt, Ukraine comes 113th and Russia lags behind at 128th, preceded by Colombia (56th), Saudi Arabia (75th), and China (78th).[14] Against this backdrop, it is not surprising that adolescents in Russia and Ukraine tend to distrust political incumbents. At this point, it is unclear how strong a link there is between political trust and interpersonal trust.

The link between interpersonal trust and political trust

The degree to which adolescents trust political institutions may have a profound effect on their social relations.[15] In societies riddled with corruption and political disaffection, individuals may lose trust in their fellow citizens. Alternatively, individuals may develop high levels of interpersonal trust as a coping strategy to overcome the failures of political institutions (Evans and Letki 2006). The results from the 2005 survey of adolescents provide support for the argument that the political environment in the former Soviet republics drives down the level of interpersonal trust. Twenty-two percent of Russian and 24 percent of Ukrainian adolescents believe that most people can be trusted.[16] From a cross-national perspective, the proportion of trusting adolescents is quite low in Russia and Ukraine. According to the results from the IEA Civic Education Study, for example, 64 percent of Hungarian adolescents and 53 percent of Polish adolescents place trust in fellow citizens.[17] At the sub-national level, respondents in the capital cities of Moscow and Kyiv express more caution in their social interactions than those in the provinces. For example, 31 percent of Tula respondents, compared to 23 percent of Moscow respondents, claim trust in their fellow citizens. In addition, Lviv adolescents have a significantly larger stock of social trust than those in Donetsk (27 percent vs. 19 percent).

Notably, the younger generation in Russia and Ukraine appears to be more wary of fellow citizens than older generations. According to the 2006 Life in Transition Survey, 36 percent of Russian and 41 percent of Ukrainian adults place trust in people. A plausible explanation for this trend is the imperative of the post-communist youth to survive in a socioeconomic environment marred by gross social inequality and cut-throat competition. Another possibility is that the reported higher levels of trust among adults socialized during the Soviet period reflect the tendency to disguise their true feelings. In the Soviet Union, citizens were used to professing collectivist ideas in public and practicing caution in private contacts with people (Kertman 2006).

Additional survey data from Ukraine show that the level of interpersonal trust increased by 19 percent after the Orange Revolution, going from 30 percent in 1999 to 49 percent in March 2005, but then it dwindled again.[18] Mass mobilization against electoral fraud and the subsequent victory of opposition forces have temporarily boosted a sense of solidarity among citizens in western and central parts of Ukraine, but lack of reforms in the post-2004 election period dampened citizens' trust in politicians and citizens.

Based upon data from the 2005 Survey of Adolescents in Russia and Ukraine, the statistical analysis finds a positive correlation between interpersonal trust and political trust. The more adolescents trust parliamentarians, the more they trust fellow citizens. Similarly, trust in army, police, and judges is positively related to interpersonal trust. Among Russian adolescents, however, favorable attitudes toward the incumbent president have a negligible effect on trust in people. These findings raise a broader question about sources of trust in incumbents and order-related institutions, and it is this question that the next section explores.

Political and order-related institutions through adolescents' eyes

Post-Soviet adolescents have opinions about politicians and government agencies, and they are not shy about vocalizing these opinions. The results of semi-structured interviews provide valuable insights into how adolescents perceive incumbent authorities. In expressing their attitudes toward the incumbent president, respondents mentioned his personality traits, his performance on the job, and broad social problems raging in the post-communist states. As far as the army, police, and courts are concerned, students dwelled upon the failures of these institutions to do their job and deliver public goods.

In my conversations with Russian adolescents, they expressed overwhelming support for President Putin. The post-Soviet generation found his lifestyle habits and his communication skills appealing. Unlike Yeltsin, Putin abstains from alcohol and stays in good shape. Sobriety, apparently, is an attractive quality, especially among female voters, in a country where more than seven million men are alcoholics:[19]

> Putin comes from the people [*chelovek iz naroda*], and he has his own principles.
> (Sveta, 15 years old, Moscow, Russia)

> I respect Putin. I also go in for sports, and I like judo.
> (Kirill, 14 years old, Tula, Russia)

> There is now a popular song, claiming that every woman dreams of a husband who would be like Putin – he won't beat her up, he won't abuse alcohol.
> (Liuda, 16 years old, Moscow, Russia)

> I like the way he talks – briefly and right to the point.
> (Liuda, 14 years old, Rostov-on-the-Don, Russia)

Furthermore, the Russian students inferred from Putin's frequent appearances on TV that he was working hard to improve the quality of life in the country and boost Russia's standing in the international community:

I see Putin very frequently in the news. He travels from one place to another. I believe that he does a lot of good for the country.

(Yana, 15 years old, Moscow, Russia)

I feel respect for Putin. He has enhanced the country's image in the world. Our economy is doing better. The president is carrying out the struggle for normal life in the country.

(Zhenia, 13 years old, Tula, Russia)

Even when Russian adolescents were not lavishing praise upon the president, they still refrained from sharp criticism of his policies. Some admitted that they had not felt a positive change associated with Putin's presidency, but they were reluctant to generalize from this experience to the whole country:

Personally, I don't feel substantial changes in my life after Putin has come to power. But I think that he is well suited for the job.

(Ania, 15 years old, Tula, Russia)

Moreover, a few Russian respondents shared a popular belief that the head of the state is unaware of any wrongdoings in the provinces. Back in Tsarist Russia, there existed a belief in the good tsar and his evil entourage. Similarly, a number of Soviet citizens genuinely believed that Stalin was unaware of their many sufferings under communism. In a similar vein, some students shifted the blame for state failures to deliver public goods to the executors of presidential decrees:

Putin is guiding the country in the right direction. But he has to rely upon people to follow his orders, and they don't do a good job.

(Roman, 15 years old, Tula, Russia)

Donetsk respondents, by contrast, branded President Yushchenko as the main culprit responsible for the dismal socioeconomic situation in the region. In particular, they castigated his neglect of the coal-mining industry, his re-privatization plans,[20] and his cozy relations with the United States:

Yushchenko is unworthy to be the President of Ukraine. Ukraine could fall apart because of him. Everything falls apart right now. Almost half of the coal-mines in the region are closed. He sold Krivorozhstal' [Ukraine's largest steel mill]. Donetsk is left with nothing. Approximately 35–40 percent of Donetsk's population currently resides in Moscow. There are more jobs there. It is difficult to make a living here. Only the elderly stay in the city.

(Kolia, 16 years old, Donetsk, Ukraine)

The president wants to see Ukraine in the European Union too soon. It is unrealistic. We are a poor country. Look at Poland. The president of

Poland set a personal goal to improve the well-being of ordinary people. Polish coal-miners earn much more than Ukrainian ones. When coal-miners in Poland go underground, they are not so scared that they will never see sunlight again. And many Ukrainian coal-miners die each year. If we aspire to become a part of the European Union, we shouldn't try to imitate the United States. We would do better to learn from Poland.
(Sasha, 15 years old, Donetsk, Ukraine)

Yushchenko has made a deal with Bush. Yushchenko put our country on sale. The United States conspired with Yushchenko to help him [get elected], but the USA doesn't care about us. They only care about Russia. Americans want to turn Ukraine into a big colony. They want to have a big military base here. And Ukrainians will end up working for the American army.
(Aniuta, 15 years old, Donetsk, Ukraine)

Moreover, Donetsk respondents questioned Yushchenko's stainless reputation and scorned his condescending attitude toward inhabitants of eastern Ukraine. These responses mirrored the key messages of the anti-Yushchenko campaign during the 2004 presidential election. Specifically, pro-Yanukovych PR specialists made insinuations about Yushchenko's biased treatment of Ukrainians in different parts of the country:[21]

Yushchenko has a negative attitude towards people in eastern Ukraine. The government has sold Krivorozhstal'. Now they want to sell Nikopol plant [a ferroalloy-producing plant owned by Viktor Pinchuk]. There were criminal charges both against Yushchenko and against Yanukovich. Yanukovich was exonerated from all criminal charges. He spent only 15 days in prison. And who knows how long Yushchenko had been imprisoned?
(Bohdan, 14 years old, Donetsk, Ukraine)

I distrust the president. His actions suggest that he wants to do a lot of good things for western Ukraine and worsen the life of people in eastern Ukraine. I've heard that people in western Ukraine are becoming disappointed with his policies too. He didn't do what he has promised them.
(Liuda, 14 years old, Donetsk, Ukraine)

Having alienated almost half of the Ukrainian population from the outset of his presidency, President Yuschenko also lost public trust in central and western parts of the country. Reflecting this trend, adolescents from Kyiv and Lviv expressed disenchantment with the national leader:

In the past, I had more trust in Yushchenko. He talked a lot about people when he was on Maidan [Kyiv's Independence Square, the main site of the Orange Revolution]. But I am not sure now how much I can trust him. I heard that his son has an expensive car, and he fired Tymoshenko [former prime minister and leader of the political bloc that supported Yushchenko during the Orange Revolution].

(Stas, 15 years old, Kyiv, Ukraine)

People's spirits have sunk in recent months. My mother used to be so committed to Yushchenko, but this feeling is now gone. People wanted to believe in something, they were looking for an ideal. I wouldn't have voted for Yanukovich. But Yushchenko is no good either.

(Nastia, 15 years old, Kyiv, Ukraine)

Speaking more broadly about elected politicians, adolescents in Russia and Ukraine shared a concern about the pervasive role of money during the election period. Students noted that ordinary citizens stood a slim chance of making a political career because of limited access to financial resources:

Now money decides everything. In the past, seasoned [*proverennye*] people were elected to parliament [those who passed a background check]. Now a person with a sack of money can get wherever he wants in politics. A person who has no idea about politics can become a deputy. It all depends upon the amount of money he puts into his election campaign.

(Zhenia, 13 years old, Tula, Russia)

Good politicians don't have enough money to succeed. They won't make it to the top.

(Denis, 15 years old, Tula, Russia)

By the same token, the adolescents pointed out that elected politicians abused their positions. Most respondents were convinced that members of the national parliament ruthlessly pursued their self-interest and looked upon a seat in the parliament as a golden opportunity for self-aggrandizement:

I heard on TV that Russia is ranked third by the number of millionaires. Japan is after us. At the same time, a lot of people are starving or have huge debts. It shows how much our politicians embezzle. They can't be trusted.

(Ania, 16 years old, Tula, Russia)

Duma deputies have only one thing on their mind – how to make quick money. There is always a shortage of money in the government because they embezzle state funds.

(Sasha, 16 years old, Moscow, Russia)

The would-be voters doubted the intentions of elected politicians to keep campaign promises and bring about tangible changes in the lives of their electorate:

I distrust politicians because they are hypocrites. They do everything to please the public when they need it. I watched a news report about a visit of some politicians to the local orphanage. I don't believe that they really care about those kids. They would do anything to boost their popularity.

(Liuda, 16 years old, Moscow, Russia)

I don't trust politicians. One day they say one thing, another day – the complete opposite. During the election period, politicians give out cars, money, and various gifts. Once they are elected, they don't do anything for people.

(Stas, 15 years old, Kyiv, Ukraine)

The respondents also expressed disapproval of the politicians' social behavior. Some adolescents claimed that it was inappropriate for deputies to interrupt a parliamentary session and get into a fist fight with their political opponents while the whole country was watching it on TV. These findings are consistent with other research documenting the link between televised incivility of political disputes and trust in government (Mutz and Reeves 2005):

Our current deputies are unworthy to sit in Verkhovna Rada. I watched on TV how they were fighting with their fists. They also curse on air. And these people govern the country.

(Kolia, 16 years old, Donetsk, Ukraine)

In part, these popular perceptions of elected politicians foment negative attitudes toward democracy. In this regard, it is instructive to scrutinize comments made by 15-year-old Aniuta from Tula. The Russian adolescent liked the poetry of Vladimir Maiakovsky, famous for his daring language and powerful rhythms. As an ardent critic of bourgeois democracy, Maiakovsky enriched the literature of the nascent communist state by producing numerous poems and campaign slogans. His play *Misteria Buff*, written in 1918 to celebrate the first anniversary of the October Revolution, struck a chord with 15-year-old Aniuta in contemporary Russia:

Deputies look upon the Duma as a trough [*kormushka*]. They don't care about the common people. My favorite poet is Maiakovsky. He wrote, "One gets a donut, another one gets a hole from the donut; that's what the democratic republic is all about" [*Komu-to bublik, a komu-to dyrka ot bublika. Vot takaia demokraticheskaia respublika*].

(Ania, 15 years old, Tula, Russia)

Turning their attention to order-related institutions, adolescents cited the appalling conditions of military service as a primary reason for distrust in the army. Since mandatory conscription was a major concern for male respondents, they frequently referred to the service in the army as "two years of my life wasted" or "serfdom." In addition, adolescents voiced discontent with indiscriminate recruitment of conscripts:[22]

> I have a negative view of the army. They don't care about young people. Once they attempted to recruit as a conscript a fellow with symptoms of heart defect.
>
> (Nastia, 14 years old, Moscow, Russia)

> The meaning of the word "fighter" [*bojets*] is lost. Now soldiers can be forced to paint grass with the green paint. In the past, a young man wouldn't be conscripted if he had flat feet. Now even a person with one leg or cancer can be drafted.
>
> (Roman, 15 years old, Tula, Russia)

Respondents also criticized the meager financing of the army and worried about adverse consequences of negligent state policies, including the pile-up of outdated military equipment and the provision of inadequate professional training.[23] More alarmingly, adolescents noted a link between military service and the deterioration of young men's health:

> Our army is incapable of defending the country. There are only three rusty ships in Sevastopol [one of the main seaports on the Black Sea].
>
> (Stas, 15 years old, Kyiv, Ukraine)

> Our army is cash-strapped. Generals own huge dachas, while soldiers go barefoot. Young men die of pneumonia in the army.
>
> (Kirill, 14 years old, Tula, Russia)

> I come from a dynasty of military men. Both my father and my brother served in the army. Earlier, there was also *dedovschina* [harassment of junior conscripts by senior ones], but on a smaller scale. Now the situation has worsened. Once electricity was turned off in a military hospital for 40 minutes, and a patient on the life-support machine died.
>
> (Lesha, 14 years old, Moscow, Russia)

Then there were complaints about endemic corruption in the army. Respondents pinpointed how the high-ranking military sell off military equipment and use soldiers as free labor to perform tasks unrelated to military service:

> Deep inside, every soldier wants to defend his home country. But the high-ranking generals are all bought up. They manage the army very poorly. The fish rots from the head. If there are good top managers, everything will be good.
>
> (Julia, 15 years old, Kyiv, Ukraine)

Soldiers toil on the general's plot instead of receiving proper training.

(Denis, 15 years old, Tula, Russia)

It is noteworthy that four students enrolled in a cadet class at a Moscow secondary school set themselves apart from other respondents by holding distinct views on the army.[24] While acknowledging budgetary problems in the military, young cadets preached pride in the army. These adolescents came from families with a military background. Moreover, they took extra courses in physical education and military training to jumpstart a military career:

> The army deserves public trust. It has some financial difficulties, but it is not bad in itself. The army reform is under way to improve things. I decided to enter the cadet class because it is necessary to defend the homeland.
>
> (Stas, 16 years old, Moscow, Russia)

> It is a shame that few conscripts are willing to join the army voluntarily, and many are looking for a loophole. They are afraid of *dedovschina*, they are scared of being sent to a hot spot. In my opinion, everybody must fulfill his duty and serve in the army. The young fellow becomes a real man after serving in the army ... I entered the cadet class because it is a lot of fun for me. I spend time at school until 5 or 6 p.m. Our major tells us stories about famous military men and teaches us the code of behavior. One becomes a real patriot here.
>
> (Alex, 16 years old, Moscow, Russia)

To young cadets, the military training was associated with positive experiences because it provided them with an opportunity to form a close-knit network of friends and stay out of trouble:

> I was born in the German Democratic Republic. My dad is in the military. He made me enroll in the cadet class so that I won't hang out in the street. And I like it here.
>
> (Artem, 15 years old, Moscow, Russia)

> I got tired of running in the streets without any particular aim. It is interesting to be a cadet. We go in for sports, we undergo military training. And there is good male company here. We take part in various extracurricular activities together.
>
> (Sasha, 16 years old, Moscow, Russia)

The police was another public institution negatively viewed by a large number of respondents:

> I distrust the militia. When an emergency happens and somebody needs help, one will not catch a sight of the militia for an hour or so. They will

come when there is no need for help anymore.

(Milana, 15 years old, Moscow, Russia)

Militiamen used to be more responsible. Now they get out of the water dry [get out of trouble without any consequences]. They even don't pick up drunkards off the street. In the past, they used to take them to the police station for a night.

(Katia, 15 years old, Donetsk, Ukraine)

The militia cannot be counted on. If a single militiaman is walking along the street now and sees a gang beating up somebody, he won't stop or call for help. He'll just pass by as if nothing had happened.

(Alex, 16 years old, Moscow, Russia)

The interviewees' narratives about the militiamen were filled with references to corruption. The traffic police was in particular criticized for harassing drivers with the sole purpose of extracting money:

All the traffic policemen are sold-out a**holes [*podkupnye kozly*]. They never give you a receipt when you pay them a fine. It is impossible to pass the driving test without giving them a bribe.

(Sasha, 16 years old, Moscow, Russia)

There are very few honest people left in the militia. Why would the traffic policemen fine anybody 80 rubles if he is offered a bribe of 500 rubles right in his pocket?

(Artem, 15 years old, Moscow, Russia)

Our traffic policemen drive foreign cars and say that they don't get wages for months on end. Everything is bought with money now. My friend was run over by a car. But the driver wasn't punished. He was released after three days in detention.

(Ania, 16 years old, Tula, Russia)

Furthermore, the respondents recounted rumors and personal stories about the alleged crimes of the militiamen:

I've heard that several militiamen approached young girls inside the metro station and asked them to show their personal identification documents. Then these militiamen found a pretext to drag the girls to the police station. The militiamen raped these girls, and they had nobody to turn to.

(Masha, 15 years old, Moscow, Russia)

I distrust militiamen. I watched news reports about turncoats in the militia [*oborotni v pogonakh*]. They have ties to the criminal world.

(Lesha, 16 years old, Tula, Russia)

> The militia can't be trusted. My friends told me a story about their own troubles with our militia. A Zhigul' [a make of car] was stolen in the city. And the militia knew only that the hijackers were wearing black jackets and black T-shirts. How many people wear black T-shirts in Kyiv? What kind of "special traits" are those? And my friends who happened to wear black T-shirts that day were arrested in the street in the broad daylight. They were just 15 or 16 years old. But the militiamen dragged them to the police station and beat them up. Then they let my friends go.
>
> (Ihor, 14 years old, Kyiv, Ukraine)

In Ukraine, some respondents sounded apologetic about the corrupt practices of militiamen. They shifted the blame onto a system that made it impossible to live on one's monthly wages as the only source of income. And some Kyiv respondents recalled a positive role of the militia during the Orange Revolution:

> I put some trust in the militia. The militiamen stood with the people during the Orange Revolution. They stood on Maidan. Well, they are corrupt, they take bribes, but they are human beings. They need to survive somehow.
>
> (Oleh, 14 years old, Kyiv, Ukraine)

The theme of corruption re-emerged in the adolescents' discussion of attitudes toward the justice system. The respondents claimed that judges were willing to sacrifice legal evidence and misinterpret existing laws for a kickback. In addition, some adolescents pointed out that judges were notorious for their sloppy examination of evidence during court hearings:

> Judges can always be bribed. A wealthy person can give the judge a bribe to have the case ruled in his favor, and the judge won't refuse the money. The judges don't care. Anyway, it is not their life that is being decided upon.
>
> (Julia, 14 years old, Kyiv, Ukraine)

> The judges are very rude. When my mother went to the court and asked them to clarify a few things regarding her citizenship application, they just shouted at her. They didn't want to explain the laws to her. You even have to pay a bribe to have your case opened.
>
> (Ilona, 14 years old, Donetsk, Ukraine)

> I've heard about a person who had been charged with a crime he hadn't committed. Somebody framed him, and the court didn't investigate the case well enough.
>
> (Larisa, 14 years old, Kyiv, Ukraine)

In addition, Ukrainian respondents rebuked the dependence of judges on politicians. As expected, distrust for judges among Donetsk respondents stemmed partly from the ruling by the Supreme Court in favor of President Yushchenko:

> Our judges depend on our politicians. Deputies have more power than judges. I trust only international courts.
> (Oleh, 14 years old, Kyiv, Ukraine)

> I don't trust the judges. When Yushchenko filed a complaint, the court reviewed the case. But when Yanukovich submitted a case about electoral fraud, they didn't even want to look at it.
> (Anton, 13 years old, Donetsk, Ukraine)

The analysis reveals some cross-national differences in adolescents' attitudes toward the incumbent president, but mostly highlights similarities in the negative assessment of politicians and public servants. Respondents in both Russia and Ukraine identify corruption as a major reason for distrust in authorities.

Conclusion

The survey results demonstrate that post-Soviet adolescents differentiate between different authority figures. The incumbent president is the most trustworthy political actor, whereas deputies in national parliaments and political parties generate less trust. Among order-related institutions, the army emerges as a much more trustworthy institution than the police. In addition, the data from semi-structured interviews reveal that corruption is the most prominent factor conducive to distrust in incumbent authorities. Across the region, young citizens vocalize discontent with the magnitude of self-aggrandizing elite behavior. The predominant mood is that politicians and public officials put selfish, profit-maximizing goals above concerns about the public good.

The results also illustrate that region of residence affects adolescents' attitudes toward political figures. Respondents from Russia's capital city of Moscow hold more positive views of the incumbent president than those from the provinces. The connection between region and trust in government is even more pronounced in Ukraine. As losers in the 2004 presidential election, adolescents from Donetsk are less inclined to trust the incumbent president than those from Lviv.

4 Building the new political community, remembering the old one

The search for national heroes is in full swing in post-communist Russia and Ukraine. Putting a local spin on the BBC's popular TV project *100 Greatest Britons*, Russia's TV channel Rossia (Russia) and Ukraine's TV channel Inter issued nationwide calls for nominating the greatest Russians and the greatest Ukrainians.[1] Approximately 2.8 million votes in Russia and 1.6 million votes in Ukraine were cast during the final round of voting.[2] A large proportion of participants in the interactive TV projects were technologically savvy youth who expressed their preferences by going online, sending SMS messages, and making phone calls. As a result of popular voting, members of the imperial family and such Soviet leaders as Lenin and Stalin made the shortlist in Russia, while writers and freedom fighters were top picks in Ukraine. According to the official results, Aleksandr Nevsky, grand prince of Novgorod who defended the land against the Swedish invasion and won the battle of 1240 at the confluence of the rivers Izhora and Neva (thus gaining the name of Nevsky), earned the honorary title of the Name of Russia. At the same time, Yaroslav the Wise, the grand prince known for uniting the principalities of Kyiv and Novgorod, drafting the first code of laws, and promoting the spread of Christianity, was officially declared the Greatest Ukrainian. Strikingly, medieval grand princes won the top spots in both countries.

Yet, characteristic of post-Soviet politics, these electoral outcomes were tainted with allegations of vote rigging. In Russia, controversy arose when Stalin surged to the top of the list and the TV project producers suppressed voting for the controversial political leader. Since the website initially lacked protection against illicit computer-generated votes, hackers were able to sway the voting results. In response, the TV project management annulled, at its discretion, more than 2 million votes cast for Stalin and announced Aleksandr Nevsky as the Name of Russia (*Vzgliad* 2008). Likewise, the final outcome of Ukraine's TV project surprised many observers. At the beginning of the final week of voting, Stepan Bandera, leader of the Organization of Ukrainian Nationalists, had a solid lead with more than 200,000 votes in his favor, while Yaroslav the Wise lagged behind, garnering only 60,000 votes throughout the whole month. On the last day of voting, however, 550,000 additional votes were cast for the medieval prince, sweeping Bandera off the first place. Rumors were circulating that the Party of Regions headed by Yanukovych opposed the nomination of Bandera as the greatest Ukrainian and masterminded the ballot stuffing (*Telekrytyka* 2008). These rigged elections of national heroes reflect the awkward attempts of the ruling elite to steer nation-building processes in a certain direction.

Attachment to the political community, conceived here as positive attitudes toward the nation-state, lies at the heart of nation-building processes. A healthy dose of national pride reinvigorates and sustains the political system by stimulating civic engagement and strengthening compliance with state laws (Bart-Tal and Staub 1997). A belief in national superiority, however, may destabilize the political order by justifying exclusionary citizenship laws and belligerent foreign policy (de Figueiredo and Elkins 2003; Feshbach 1994; Hjerm 1998).

In this chapter, I distinguish between the 'new' political community and the 'old' political community. Contemporary Russia and Ukraine are defined as "new," since these countries were put on the world map as independent nation-states only 20 years ago. The Soviet Union can be considered as the "old" political community in the sense that it precedes the formation of independent post-communist states.

National pride among adolescents

Adolescents in Russia and Ukraine have developed attachment to the independent nation-states. As shown in Figure 4.1, more than 80 percent of the respondents report positive attitudes toward their home country. This level of patriotism is remarkable, given the plethora of political and socioeconomic problems the post-communist societies have to grapple with. It is also noteworthy that cross-city differences are negligible in Russia: 89 percent of adolescents in Moscow, 87 percent in Rostov-on-the-Don, and 86 percent in Tula report a sense of pride in being a citizen of Russia. In contrast, the intensity of national pride varies across Ukrainian cities. Seventy-two percent of Lviv adolescents report "a great deal" of national pride, whereas only 29 percent of Donetsk adolescents display this level of attachment to the nation-state. Moreover, one fifth of Donetsk respondents do not feel proud to hold Ukrainian citizenship at all. These results support the argument that the political attitudes of adolescents reproduce conflicting ideas over national identity stemming from the east–west regional cleavage.

How patriotic are adolescents, compared to the older age groups? Survey data from the World Values Survey (WVS) and local opinion polls shed some light on this issue. The 2005 Survey of Adolescents in Russia and Ukraine and the WVS used the same survey item to measure the level of national pride, allowing for a cross-age comparison. But the WVS was administered in Ukraine and Russia during the 1990s, prior to significant political changes in the region associated with Putin's presidency in Russia and the Orange Revolution in Ukraine. Hence, the WVS data are supplemented with more recent public opinion data from the polls conducted by the Russian

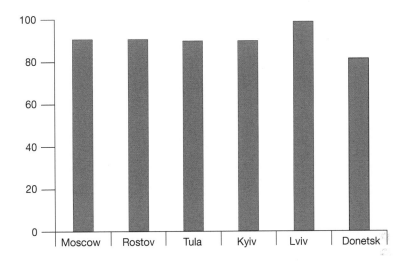

Figure 4.1 National pride among adolescents in Russia and Ukraine (percentages)

Source: Survey of Adolescents in Russia and Ukraine, 2005.

Note: The question was worded: "How proud are you to be a citizen of [country]?" The survey item was a four-point scale, ranging from 1, not at all, to 4, a great deal. N = 1,731.

public opinion firm Romir Monitoring in 2003 and Ukraine's Institute of Sociology at the National Academy of Sciences in 2005.

Table 4.1 records the level of national pride among the adult population in Russia and Ukraine. Throughout the post-Soviet period, more than half of the voting-age citizens of the former Soviet republics felt a sense of national pride. In the case of Ukraine, however, there was a spike in patriotism in the aftermath of the Orange Revolution. When the World Values Survey was conducted in 1999, voting-age Ukrainians lived in a country crippled with negative economic growth and governed by an unpopular government. In contrast, more than half of Ukrainians in 2005 were filled with pride at standing up to the corrupt authorities and defending their constitutional right to elect a political leader. Yet almost one third of Ukrainian adults in 2005 reported difficulty answering a question about their attitudes toward an independent Ukraine, whereas only 5 percent of the surveyed Ukrainian adolescents hesitated to articulate their attitudes toward the nation-state.

Overall, the survey results suggest that adolescents have a stronger attachment to the post-Soviet political community than adults. These findings, however, are open to multiple interpretations. One possibility is that the younger generation is less aware of the harsh political reality than the adult population and, thus, more idealistic about the home country. Another

54 Building the new political community

Table 4.1 National pride among adults in Russia and Ukraine

	1995[a]		1999[a]		2003[b]/2005[c]	
National pride	Russia	Ukraine	Russia	Ukraine	Russia	Ukraine
A great deal	30.4	25.0	31.6	23.8	11.2	22.3
Quite proud	40.9	42.4	38.8	37.1	34.7	56
Not much	21.4	20.3	21.3	25.9	37.8	14.1
Not at all	7.2	12.3	8.2	13.2	16.3	7.6
Total	100%	100%	100%	100%	100%	100%
	(1,961)	(2,545)	(2,394)	(1,125)	(1,470)	(1,233)
Cramer's V	0.097***	—	0.111***	—	—	—

Sources
a World Values Survey. The survey was conducted between November 1995 and January 1996 and April–June 1999. N = 8,546. The combined percentage of "don't know" and "missing data" is 6 percent. For more information, visit the website http://www.worldvaluessurvey.org.
b Romir Monitoring. 2003. Russkii kharakter (Russian character). Online report available in Russian at http://www.romir.ru/news/analitycs/russian_ch/ (accessed 4 June 2005). N = 1,500. Two percent of respondents chose the "difficult to answer" option.
c Panina (2005). The survey was conducted in March 2005. N = 1,800. Only two respondents declined to answer the question, but approximately one third of respondents (N = 565) chose the "don't know" option.

Note
The question wording in the World Values Survey and the 2005 survey of Ukraine's Institute of Sociology was: "How proud are you to be a citizen of [country]?" The survey item was a four-point scale, ranging from 1, not at all, to 4, a great deal. The 2003 opinion poll conducted by Romir Monitoring (Russia) prompted respondents to ascertain the overall level of patriotism by asking: "How developed, in your opinion, is the sense of patriotism among Russians?"

possibility is that older generations exhibit less allegiance to the post-communist state because they have lived most of their lives in another, more orderly political community and observe with dismay the social turmoil in the post-Soviet states. The findings raise another question: *what are the sources of a remarkably high level of national pride among Russian and Ukrainian adolescents?*

Sources of national pride

National pride is multidimensional (Evans and Kelley 2002; Smith and Jarkko 1998). Positive attitudes toward the nation-state may arise from a combination of political (political institutions, welfare system) and cultural (history, cultural practices) attributes of the political community. A close examination of student responses during semi-structured interviews reveals that there are at least six discernable sources of national pride: (1) history and culture, (2) people, (3) geography and natural resources, (4) achievements in science, (5) achievements in sport, and (6) the armed forces. The respondents in both Russia and Ukraine brought up the first three sources of patriotism. In addition, Russian adolescents mentioned achievements in science, sport, and the military.

National history has been a prominent source of national pride among the younger generation. Given the political and social turmoil of the post-communist period, adolescents looked back into the history of earlier centuries to build up a sense of patriotism. Nonetheless, the younger generation in each country differed in the selection of inspiring historic events.

The Russian adolescents admired the country's military accomplishments. 16-year-old Lesha from Tula, for instance, mentioned Suvorov's role in defending Russia from foreign invasion.[3] A number of Russian adolescents brought up Soviet victory in the Great Patriotic War of 1941–45 as a glorious event in the country's history. The younger generation appreciated the sacrifices their grandparents had made to defend the Soviet Union against Nazism. Sixteen-year-old Zhenia from Tula proudly concluded that many nations tried to conquer Russia, but failed. Along similar lines, Russian adults regard Soviet victory in the Great Patriotic War as the most important historic event that boosts their level of national pride (Public Opinion Foundation 2002).[4] The adolescents' focus on military accomplishments can be attributed, in part, to the emphasis of Russian history textbooks on the struggle against external enemies (see Berelowitch 2003).

Ukrainian history, by contrast, is the history of a colony striving for national independence. When prompted to comment on the country's accomplishments, 16-year-old Yura from Donetsk summarized: "At least, looking back upon Ukraine's heroic past, we should give it respect for its longstanding struggle for independence."

Rather than victories on the battlefield, folklore, songs, and national poems inspired Ukrainian adolescents to take pride in the motherland. In particular, Lviv adolescents praised the melodic qualities of the Ukrainian language. For example, Uliana from Lviv said, "I take pride in our beautiful language, our songs, and our poets: Taras Shevchenko, Ivan Franko, Lesia Ukrainka." Several respondents also recalled the magnificence of ancient edifices embellishing streets of Lviv and Kyiv, but they deplored the fact that many historical monuments had been on the verge of collapse. According to 15-year-old Kolia from Kyiv, "it is too bad that many people don't take proper care of our cultural treasures."

Another cited source of national pride was the people (*narod*). Russian respondents attributed to ethnic Russians such personal traits as hospitality, kindness, and open-heartedness (*dushevnost'*). And Ukrainian adolescents described ethnic Ukrainians as open, good-natured, and generous. The Orange Revolution has strengthened a positive image of Ukrainians among Lviv adolescents. The overwhelming majority of Lviv respondents participated in local rallies against electoral fraud. Some of the adolescents joined protesters in Kyiv's main square. That is why Yushchenko's victory in the 2004 presidential election had a personal meaning for them:

> I take pride in our unity and our courage to stand by our position. I mean the way we elected our president.
>
> (Andrij, 15 years old, Lviv, Ukraine)

> Our people have the guts to defend their point of view. But our government is worthless.
>
> (Olena, 14 years old, Lviv, Ukraine)

Meanwhile, Russian adolescents linked the country's military accomplishments with the personal traits of ethnic Russians, including stamina and spirituality:

> Russians have a strong character. They have become stronger as a result of living through wars and the [October] revolution.
>
> (Masha, 15 years old, Moscow, Russia)

> We have a strong character and a lot of stamina. We have endured more than any other nation.
>
> (Ania, 15 years old, Tula, Russia)

> People have tried to lift the country out of the ashes on many occasions. Russia survived because of the spiritual energy of its people.
>
> (Oleg, 15 years old, Tula, Russia)

In the course of semi-structured interviews, the juxtaposition of the titular nation with "the other" sometimes served as a means of illustrating the superiority of Russians or Ukrainians, respectively. The point of reference, however, differed across the countries. Russian adolescents emphasized the moral superiority of ethnic Russians over Americans. "I don't like America, in which everything is so artificial. People are more sincere and open-hearted here," said 15-year-old Sveta from Moscow. To some extent, such a response reflects the lingering effects of the Cold War in which the Soviet Union desperately tried to outdo the United States. In contrast, the responses of Ukrainian adolescents echoed the ongoing struggle over national unity. Stereotypes emanating from the east–west cleavage pit ethnic Ukrainians residing in different parts of the country against one another. Lviv adolescents tend to look upon visitors from Donetsk with suspicion. Similarly, Donetsk adolescents view inhabitants of western Ukraine as "the other":

> To me, Ukraine is the best country in the world. I like our people. They are very friendly [in this city]. They are different from those in Lviv [uttered in a condescending tone]. When several women from Donetsk went to Lviv as election observers, many local residents ran to the polling station to stare at "Donetsk bandits."
>
> (Natasha, 15 years old, Donetsk, Ukraine)

The country's natural beauty supplied another source of national pride. Russian respondents admired the immense scale of the country's territory spanning 11 time zones and hosting a diverse habitat. A 16-year-old student from Moscow, for example, spoke about Russia's taiga, a huge mass of land covered with coniferous forest. For Ukrainians, the black soil served as a source of national pride, since Ukraine's nickname as "the breadbasket of the Soviet Union" has been popularized in the country. In addition, the Russian–Ukrainian dispute over gas pipelines made Ukrainian adolescents more aware of the country's favorable geographical position. Sandwiched between Russia and the European Union, Ukraine is a transit point for Russia's gas flows to Western Europe.

The respondents rarely mentioned the other traditional sources of patriotism, including accomplishments in sport, science, and the armed forces. A few male students recalled that Russian sportsmen had won top prizes at world competitions. The militaristic theme re-emerged in student references to the country's scientific achievements. "The only thing that makes me proud is our weapons. Russia produces top-notch weapons," said 14-year-old Misha from Tula, a city historically known for its production of arms. Furthermore, some adolescents considered the massive emigration of Russian scientists as an indicator of Russia's accomplishments in the realm of science. Fourteen-year-old Liuda from Rostov-on-the-Don, for example, noted that "many Russian scientists are so good that they had found well-paid jobs in the United States." By comparison, Ukrainian adolescents did not make any references to the country's accomplishments in science or sports, implying that the range of reasons why young Ukrainians could feel proud of their home country was quite narrow.

Rather than boosting a sense of national pride among citizens, the performance of incumbent authorities often spawns negative attitudes toward the political community. The next section details why some adolescents hold their home country in low esteem.

Reasons for low national pride

Student responses during the semi-structured interviews reveal three interrelated reasons for a low level of national pride: (1) bad governance, (2) poverty, and (3) poor interpersonal relations. In addition, several Ukrainian adolescents, mainly from the Donetsk region, referred to the so-called "citizenship by accident." Upon the dissolution of the Soviet Union, thousands of ethnic Russians acquired Ukraine's citizenship just because they happened to live on the territory of the former Soviet republic at that time. Apparently, the children of such individuals developed weak emotional ties to Ukraine.

Russian and Ukrainian adolescents were unanimous in their belief that lack of government accountability and responsiveness weakened their attachment to the political community:

> We have a good country, rich in minerals and other natural resources. But our government is bad, it mismanages these resources. Teachers, for example, get low wages.
>
> (Stas, 16 years old, Moscow, Russia)

> I don't like to see how there is a growing division between those who try to build something and those who are just raking in money for themselves. The state doesn't treat the army well and does not provide a good-quality health care system. Civil servants are building dachas [country cottages] for themselves; yet, they don't have money for the needs of the ordinary population.
>
> (Artem, 15 years old, Moscow, Russia)

> The country is in the grip of a severe crisis. There is an economic crisis. There is a political crisis. The presidential election was held in three rounds. They say that Maidan was a manifestation of direct democracy. But it also shows that people have no certainty in the future. How many years has Ukraine been independent? How many reforms have we seen? It has been 14 years since independence, and the country isn't reformed yet.
>
> (Ihor, 15 years old, Kyiv, Ukraine)

Among other things, adolescents from Donetsk, located in a heavily industrialized and polluted region of Ukraine, articulated concern over the government's neglect of the environment:

> I don't like how our authorities treat people. For example, they brought some toxic elements from Romania and dumped them somewhere in Transcarpathia. Chernobyl was a huge disaster in the Soviet Union, and who has to deal with its consequences? The economically weak country.
>
> (Bohdan, 14 years old, Donetsk, Ukraine)

> If we compare our economy and ecology with the situation in other countries, it is easy to see why Ukraine doesn't deserve much respect. In other countries, people don't dump garbage on the street. When I walk in my neighborhood, I feel as if I live in some dumping area. There is garbage everywhere.
>
> (Ilona, 14 years old, Donetsk, Ukraine)

In addition, Donetsk adolescents blamed President Yushchenko personally for strengthening their alienation from the Ukrainian state:

> I was proud to be a citizen of Ukraine until Yushchenko became president. Under his presidency, the country's budget has shrunk, whereas his own pockets began to swell with money. There is no democracy in the country. And the judges are heavily influenced by politicians.
>
> (Rostik, 15 years old, Donetsk, Ukraine)

I don't like our political situation and the living conditions of our people. Ukraine will soon become an American colony. Why does the United States need Ukraine? The USA uses Ukraine just to get closer to Russia. That's all.
(Aniuta, 15 years old, Donetsk, Ukraine)

Some Russian adolescents saw the need for a higher level of state involvement in economic matters. Taking things back into the hands of the state seemed reasonable, given the murky business practices of Russian oligarchs:

Many branches of industry are now in private hands. But we need state enterprises. We can significantly increase the size of our budget by selling vodka and cigarettes alone.
(Liuda, 14 years old, Rostov-on-the-Don, Russia)

I disagree with the way our country is ruled now. Everything could have been done in a different way after World War II. Stalin has done something good for Russia, but the subsequent leaders only ruined everything.
(Ania, 14 years old, Tula, Russia)

Both Russian and Ukrainian adolescents worried over poverty and unemployment:

Our economy is doing quite badly. If the economic situation had improved, then Poles would have come to work in Ukraine. Now, it is the other way around.
(Volodymyr, 14 years old, Lviv, Ukraine)

There are a lot of unemployed. Russia is not that rich, it lags behind other countries.
(Milana, 15 years old, Moscow, Russia)

Complaints about the economic situation have been louder in Ukraine than in Russia. Though both countries struggled with the transition to a market economy, Russia has gained a competitive edge thanks to its rich oil deposits. Russia's economy was booming in 2005, whereas Ukraine's manufacturers and consumers awaited with trepidation another increase in energy prices. The superior performance of Russia's economy had become a reason for a low level of national pride among ethnic Russians in Ukraine. Many Donetsk adolescents visited Russia and saw with their own eyes how Ukraine lagged behind its northern neighbor:

My grandmother moved to Donbass [the Donetsk coal-mining region] and stayed here. But I have a lot of relatives back in Russia. It is better for Ukraine not to quarrel with Russia. Life in Russia is much better than in Ukraine. My aunt has recently visited the Ural region. There were computer clubs everywhere and plastic windows in new buildings. And here it is utter poverty. I am all for dual [Russian–Ukrainian] citizenship.

(Anton, 13 years old, Donetsk, Ukraine)

I am not very proud to be a citizen of Ukraine. All my relatives live in Russia. I am drawn to that country. From the economic standpoint, Russia is much better than Ukraine.

(Oleg, 14 years old, Kyiv, Ukraine)

And some Donetsk adolescents whose parents were ethnic Russians evidently felt trapped by changes in citizenship laws following the dissolution of the Soviet Union:

I can't say that I am proud to be a citizen of Ukraine. I am satisfied with my life here, but I won't call myself a patriot. My parents are ethnic Russians. My father served in the military, and I was born in Germany. Then my parents moved to Donetsk. The Soviet Union fell apart, and I received a Ukrainian passport.

(Lesha, 16 years old, Donetsk, Ukraine)

I am not very proud to be a citizen of Ukraine. Nobody asked me which citizenship I want to have. My parents happened to live here when the Soviet Union dissolved.

(Bohdan, 14 years old, Donetsk, Ukraine)

In addition to political and socioeconomic problems, some adolescents linked lack of national pride to the deterioration of interpersonal relations:

I am not very proud to live in Russia. People have become indifferent to each other. We have lost compassion for one another.

(Elena, 15 years old, Tula, Russia)

One thing I really dislike in our country is relations between people. Some people treat others very badly. They believe that they are superior to others in some ways.

(Julia, 14 years old, Kyiv, Ukraine)

The east–west regional cleavage added another layer of complexity to interpersonal relations in Ukraine. Social tolerance is in short supply in the postcommunist state. Some adolescents have experienced firsthand the hostility of the local population toward "the other":

I would have taken more pride in Ukraine if all people were treated as equals. All people are equal in the eyes of God. It would have been much better if people respected their culture and their language. I am

originally from western Ukraine. But many people around me don't know about it. And I often hear how others use derogatory words to describe those from western Ukraine. It makes me feel very bad inside.
(Katia, 15 years old, Donetsk, Ukraine)

I am not that proud to live in contemporary Ukraine. The eastern and western parts of the country are in a deep conflict with each other. In Lviv, somebody threw bottles at members of *Shakhter* [the Donetsk soccer team]. We have such a tense situation that we would rather set up a federal system.
(Anton, 13 years old, Donetsk, Ukraine)

In sum, the poor performance of incumbent authorities has dampened a sense of national pride among the younger generation. The students reported frustration with the way political leaders had addressed the political and socioeconomic tasks facing the country. Some Ukrainian adolescents also expressed discontent with the persistence of the east–west divide. As evidenced by student responses, the enduring regional cleavage has spilled over into intolerance toward inhabitants from different parts of the country.

While this generation of Russians and Ukrainians was born in the post-Soviet period, their attitudes toward the nation-state might be affected by what they have learned about the "old" political community. The next section examines adolescents' attitudes toward the Soviet Union.

Imagining the Soviet Union

For many Russian and Ukrainian adolescents, 7 November is an ordinary day on the calendar or just an extra day out of school.[5] Officially, it was a day off until 2002 in Ukraine and 2005 in Russia, while its political meaning has long been lost on post-communist youth. "It is just a pretext for people to get drunk and for me to get extra sleep," a Russian university student remarked in a street interview, held in the fall of 2006.[6] But it is better known among older generations as the date of the October Revolution, marking the fall of the Provisional Government and the victory of the Bolsheviks.[7] Back in the Soviet period, the overwhelming majority of citizens were induced to celebrate the dictatorship of the proletariat by participating in a mass demonstration. In the sea of red, high-school students adorned with red ribbons on their chests used to march in columns and carry red carnations, red balloons, and red banners with the picture of Vladimir Lenin. Now only a handful of staunch Communist Party supporters scattered across Russian and Ukrainian regions gather downtown to mark the superiority of Marxist-Leninist ideology. Meanwhile, 7 November has evolved into a commemorative event to pay tribute to victims of the communist regime. In Ukraine, numerous civic organizations and political parties organize public events to commemorate human suffering at the hands of the Communist Party, while public events denouncing the communist system are less popular in Russia. This day is emblematic of differences in citizens' interpretations of Soviet history. In this study, I scrutinize how adolescents socialized in the post-communist period perceive the Soviet Union and evaluate the dissolution of the USSR.

The official political discourse sets a framework for the adolescents' spatial imagination. The incumbent governments in the former Soviet republics espouse diametrically different interpretations of the communist period. Russia's political leadership tends to emphasize the accomplishments of the Soviet Union in the domestic and international arenas, whereas Ukraine's government has made modest attempts to expose the atrocities of the communist system. Furthermore, incumbent presidents differ in the way they perceive the demise of the Soviet Union.

President Putin has famously referred to the dissolution of the USSR as "a major geopolitical disaster of the century" (Putin 2005). Consistent with this historical perspective, Russia's dominant political discourse downplays the significance of nationalist mobilization in other former Soviet republics and shifts the blame for the disintegration of the communist state onto the West. Survey data reveal that ordinary citizens find this argument quite convincing. In 2006, for example, 18 percent of Russians identified a Western plot against the USSR as a major reason for the collapse of the communist state.[8] These anti-Western sentiments are fueled, in part, by public yearning for the restoration of the country's superpower status. In turn, Russian liberals and Western policymakers have long been wary of the so-called Weimar syndrome – the bottled-up sense of national humiliation that can catapult into power an autocratic ruler.[9] A popular belief is that Putin has brought Russia from its knees and strengthened the country's standing in the international arena.

The incumbent presidents of Ukraine, in contrast, professed a more sober assessment of the communist period and adopted a more positive perspective on the dissolution of the Soviet Union. In his inaugural presidential address, the first popularly elected president of Ukraine, Leonid Kravchuk, formally denounced Ukraine's participation in the 1924 act creating the Union of Soviet Socialist Republics. Ukraine's second president, Leonid Kuchma, presided over the official abolishment of November 7 as the national holiday. Furthermore, Yushchenko was an outspoken critic of the communist regime, irking the Russian government. Given these cross-country variations in the content of political discourse, the expectation is that adolescents in Ukraine are likely to view the dissolution of the Soviet Union in more positive terms than their peers in Russia.

Adolescents' attitudes toward the dissolution of the Soviet Union

The dissolution of the Soviet Union produces a mixture of different responses among post-Soviet adolescents. As shown in Table 4.2, 63 percent of Russian respondents disapprove of the Soviet disintegration, whereas only 38 of Ukrainians subscribe to this view. Moreover, it is striking to

Table 4.2 Adolescents' attitudes toward the dissolution of the Soviet Union

Appraisal	Country		Russian city			Ukrainian city		
	Russia	Ukraine	Moscow	Rostov	Tula	Kyiv	Lviv	Donetsk
Positive	37.4	62.3	40.1	38.9	33.1	64.4	91.8	31.4
Negative	62.6	37.7	59.9	61.1	66.9	35.6	8.2	68.6
Total	100%	100%	100%	100%	100%	100%	100%	100%
	(891)	(846)	(292)	(303)	(296)	(278)	(281)	(287)
Cramer's V	0.249***	—	0.063	—	—	0.512***	—	—

Source: Survey of Adolescents in Russia and Ukraine, 2005.

Note: The survey item was designed as a dichotomous choice between a positive appraisal of the Soviet Union's disintegration and a negative one. The question wording was: "Do you consider the dissolution of the Soviet Union as a positive or a negative thing in your country's history?" The combined percentage of "don't know" and "non-response" was 4.3 percent. N = 1,737.

observe how Ukrainian adolescents who have grown up in different parts of the country develop divergent perceptions of the Soviet Union. On the one hand, almost all Lviv adolescents – 92 percent – endorse the disintegration of the Soviet Union. On the other, only 31 percent of Donetsk respondents have abandoned nostalgia for the USSR. Kyiv respondents represent the country's average, stacked between the two extremes. In fact, Ukraine's within-country variations are greater than the cross-country variations (when Ukraine's responses are aggregated at the country level).

In contrast, the way Russian adolescents perceive the dissolution of the Soviet Union is quite evenly dispersed across the selected cities. Sixty percent of Moscow students, along with 61 percent of Rostov-on-the-Don students, report regrets about the dissolution of the Soviet Union. Nonetheless, respondents from Tula are 7 percent more likely than their peers from Moscow to emphasize the negative consequences of the Soviet demise. Tula's marginal lead in pro-Soviet attitudes might be attributable to the fact that regional politics are dominated by Communist Party supporters.

A close look at the adults' attitudes can help us understand the extent to which attitudes of post-Soviet adolescents reflect the political thinking of their parents and grandparents. Russian opinion polls regularly monitor the level of public attachment to the defunct Soviet state. The Moscow-based Public Opinion Foundation has gauged citizens' attitudes toward the Soviet Union six times since 1991.[10] The results indicate that more than half of Russians harbored regrets about the Soviet demise during Yeltsin's presidency (Public Opinion Foundation 2001; Vovk 2006). The level of nostalgia for the USSR was at its low point, 69 percent, in 1992, but then it peaked at 85 percent in January 1999. The 1998 economic crisis coupled with a streak of wild capitalism might have boosted the appeal of the Soviet system.[11] The perceived inability of President Yeltsin to put the country back on track and restore Russia's standing in the international community also contributed to the persistence of positive recollections about the USSR in the 1990s.[12] By 2006, the level of Soviet nostalgia dropped to 62 percent among Russian adults. In part, this trend can be attributed to the shrinking size of the Russian population socialized during the early Soviet period. The Russian mortality rate reached 15.2 per 1,000 people in 2006, compared to 8.1 in the United States.[13] Still, the 2005 Survey of Adolescents suggests that the level of Soviet nostalgia among Russian adolescents is on a par with the level of Soviet nostalgia among Russian adults.

Unlike attitudinal similarities between adolescents and adults in Russia, the attitudes of Ukrainian adolescents stand in sharp contrast to those of adults. According to the 2006 survey commissioned by the Kyiv-based Institute of Politics, 54 percent of voting-age Ukrainians considered the disintegration of the Soviet Union as a negative phenomenon.[14] Among Ukrainian adolescents, the level of Soviet nostalgia was much lower. Based upon these findings, one may tentatively conclude that the attitudinal differences between Russian and Ukrainian adults are much smaller than the attitudinal differences between Russia and Ukrainian adolescents.

The image of the Soviet Union in adolescents' eyes

The re-examination of Soviet politics, along with the life of ordinary citizens in the Soviet Union, has become a topic of electrifying debate in the post-communist period. On the one hand, Communist Party hardliners doggedly promote a positive image of the Soviet Union, brushing aside any criticism of socialism and calling for the resurrection of the Soviet state. During the 1996 presidential election campaign, for example, Gennady Ziuganov, leader of the Communist Party of the Russian Federation, promised that there would be "a gradual democratic voluntary restoration of democratic links" between the former Soviet republics (CNN Online 1996). On the other hand, liberals and civic activists have focused on exposing the ills of the Soviet system to warn against the abuse of power in the post-communist period. For example, the Moscow-based non-governmental organization Memorial annually publishes a *Book of Remembrance* (*Kniga pamiati*), containing a list of Soviet citizens repressed during the 1930s.[15] The younger generation has grown up in the midst of this political debate. This section examines how post-Soviet adolescents imagine the negative and positive attributes of the Soviet Union.

Table 4.3 summarizes key themes identified during semi-structured interviews with Russian and Ukrainian adolescents. A number of high-school students concur that the dissolution of the Soviet Union brought about an increase in civil liberties and political rights, along with greater access to consumer goods. Some adolescents, however, emphasize the deterioration of intra-regional ties, economic decline, and a crime spike in the aftermath of the Soviet demise. Furthermore, Russian adolescents bemoan the weakened position of Russia in the international community and the "unfair" treatment

Table 4.3 Adolescents' reasoning in evaluating the dissolution of the USSR

	Country	
Theme	Russia	Ukraine
Positive appraisal of the Soviet Union's dissolution		
National independence		+
Revival of national culture		+
Civil liberties and political rights	+	+
Access to a variety of consumer goods	+	+
Negative appraisal of the Soviet Union's dissolution		
Loss of influence in the world (superpower status)	+	+
Deterioration of intra-regional cooperation (Slavic unity)	+	+
Economic decline and loss of social security	+	+
Increase in crime	+	+
Worsening of community relations	+	+
"Unfair" treatment of ethnic Russians abroad	+	

Source: Survey of Adolescents in Russia and Ukraine, 2005.
Note: N = 40 (Russia); N = 36 (Ukraine).

of ethnic Russians in the former Soviet republics, whereas Ukrainian adolescents from Lviv and Kyiv hail the collapse of the USSR as an event conducive to the revival of Ukrainian culture and national independence. In the following paragraphs, adolescents' images of the Soviet Union are discussed in greater detail.

Communism: a dark page in modern history

Data from semi-structured interviews with adolescents suggest that there are four factors conducive to the positive appraisal of the Soviet demise: (1) national independence, (2) revival of national culture, (3) civil liberties and political rights, and (4) access to a variety of goods. Though Russian and Ukrainian adolescents endorsed improvements in political and economic freedoms, the spatial imagination of high-school students diverged.

Adolescents' attitudes toward to the Soviet Union hinge, in part, on how they imagine the boundaries of contemporary post-Soviet states. During semi-structured interviews, Russian students made it clear that they did not envision the disintegration of the Soviet Union as an opportunity for the restoration of the country's independence or the revival of national culture. On the contrary, like most Russian adults, the younger generation perceived the dissolution of the Soviet Union as a humiliating loss of the territory Russia was entitled to control. Not surprisingly, most Ukrainian adolescents subscribed to a different view of the Soviet demise. National independence was a key reason why most Ukrainian adolescents endorsed the dissolution of the communist state. As 15-year-old Volodymyr from Lviv put it, "Now we have our country to ourselves. We have an independent state." Another 15-year-old respondent, Stas from Kyiv, similarly took pride in the fact that "Ukraine can now evolve as an independent state, without the interference of other countries." Awareness of the domineering role of Moscow in Soviet times has influenced the attitudes of most respondents in Kyiv and Lviv. Yet only a handful of Donetsk adolescents referred to national independence as an actual gain. In addition, few respondents from the predominantly Russian-speaking Donetsk appreciated the significance of rolling down Russification policies.

The issue of cultural revival was central to Lviv adolescents growing up in the heartland of Ukraine's nationalism. According to 14-year-old Zhenia, "We have the freedom of choice now. We can speak Ukrainian, rather than Russian." For decades, inhabitants of western Ukraine resisted Soviet attempts to de-Ukrainize the local population. Language retention was a marker of national identity, and Lviv residents continued to speak Ukrainian at home and in public. In the post-Soviet period, the constitution granted young Ukrainians the freedom to attend public schools with Ukrainian as the language of instruction.

Beyond language practices, respondents in both Russia and Ukraine acknowledged that the collapse of communism has led to the removal of some restrictions on civil rights and liberties. "A person could be locked up in prison for a simple joke. It is good that this system is gone," 15-year-old Liuda from Tula said. The newly found freedom of religion was also identified as a favorable consequence of the Soviet collapse. In the words of 14-year-old Ilona from Donetsk, "There was no freedom of religion in the USSR. Now anybody can attend church. I am a Jehovah's Witness so it is important for me." While adolescents expressed appreciation of the freedom of movement, they were quick to point out the rising costs of international travel. As 16-year-old Sasha from Moscow noted, "It is good that we can now go on vacation abroad. But it costs US$350 to visit my uncle in Alma-Ata [a large city in Kazakhstan]." More broadly, young citizens recognized that the collapse of communism opened up opportunities for personal development:

> There was no room for individuality, only the grey mass.
> (Denis, 15 years old, Tula, Russia)

> The ideas of equality and socialism were used to brush everybody with the same comb. People were denied opportunities to develop their creativity and potential.
> (Lesha, 16 years old, Tula, Russia)

On a more materialistic level, the adolescents seemed to savor the greater availability and variety of consumer goods. The younger generation denounced the Soviet-era deficit of goods and relished the supply side of the open economy. A 16-year-old girl from Moscow put it this way:

> When the Soviet Union existed, one had a hard time finding such basic things as soap or laundry detergent in the store. I've got used to eating fresh fruit and yogurt for breakfast; these products were terribly scarce in the past.
> (Nastia, 16 years old, Moscow, Russia)

Favorable assessments of the market economy were, nonetheless, intermingled with criticism of the ruling elite. According to Nastia from Kyiv:

> Our politicians managed the transition very badly. Take the transition from a planned to a market economy, for example. When they [politicians] made Ukraine independent, there was just a struggle for high-ranking positions. The constitution was only adopted five years after independence. It is a shame. The politicians organized everything very poorly.
> (Nastia, 16 years old, Kyiv, Ukraine)

The dramatic consequences of incompetent political leadership tilt the attitudes of some adolescents in favor of the Soviet Union.

Sources of nostalgia for the Soviet Union

The analysis suggests that adolescents regret the dissolution of the Soviet Union for a combination of six reasons: (1) loss of influence in the world, (2) deterioration of regional cooperation, (3) economic decline and social insecurity, (4) increase in crime, (5) worsening of community relations, and (6) "unfair" treatment of ethnic Russians abroad. The first two factors evoking the notions of superpower status and Slavic unity merit special attention, because such pro-Soviet sentiments generate mass support for Russia's belligerent foreign policy in the region.

The description of the Soviet Union as a superpower endowed with military and economic might was a commonly held view among Russian adolescents. With a hint of pride, Russian students pointed to the fact that the USSR used to enjoy worldwide recognition as a state to be reckoned with. Consistent with the predominant view of Soviet historiography, 15-year-old Sasha from Tula praised Stalin's contribution to the industrialization of the Soviet Union. "Stalin had taken Russia in with a ploughshare and left it with nuclear weapons," was a political message propagated during Soviet times. To reinforce her point, another respondent from Tula recited a line from a poem by Vladimir Maiakovsky, a famous Soviet poet:

> The Soviet Union was a superpower, everybody respected it. It is no accident that Maiakovsky wrote about the Soviet passport in the following

lines: "Look at it, envy it – I am a citizen of the Soviet Union." Reagan labeled the USSR the evil empire, and others are still trying to break us. Many former Soviet republics became NATO members, they grow united against us.

(Ania, 15 years old, Tula, Russia)

But Russian adolescents grudgingly acknowledged that the country's current standing in the international community pales in comparison to the enormous authority exercised by the Soviet state. The respondents placed the blame for Russia's damaged reputation at the door of external forces:

I wish Russia got more respect worldwide. Upon the dissolution of the Soviet Union, Russia is blamed for everything. Who is responsible for Soviet debts? Russia. Who is to blame for war in Afghanistan? Russia. It is not fair.

(Lesha, 16 years old, Tula, Russia)

When prompted to comment on the dissolution of the Soviet Union, most Donetsk respondents echoed the views of their peers in Russia. It appears to be a vestige of socialization in a community densely populated with ethnic Russians and Russian-speaking ethnic Ukrainians. According to a 16-year-old from Donetsk:

We used to be an undefeatable, united state. Everybody was scared of the USSR. We even horrified the United States. The USA was scared of our missile defense system.

(Kolia, 16 years old, Donetsk, Ukraine)

Both Russian adolescents and their Donetsk counterparts seemed to relish the idea of Slavic unity. Artem, a 15-year-old respondent from Moscow, argued that a united Slavic fist (*edinyi slavianskii kulak*) posed an insurmountable threat to external enemies during the Cold War era. In his words, nobody would dare to launch an attack on Soviet territory at that time. Yet the geopolitical situation has drastically changed. Instead of the perceived friendship between the Soviet republics, a flurry of political and economic confrontations has become characteristic of Russian–Ukrainian relations. The Orange Revolution increased the rift between the two countries. Crucially, though, Russian participants in the survey placed the blame for Ukraine's leaning toward the West on US efforts to undermine Russia's geopolitical weight in the region, rather than on the independent choice of Ukraine's citizens.

A number of Russian adolescents still sincerely believe that the former Soviet republics lost a valuable asset – Russia's protection – after gaining independence. They seem to be ignorant of nationalist mobilization across the former Soviet republics prior to the collapse of the communist state:

> When Kievan Rus was formed, Russia, Ukraine, and Belarus were all together. Now Russia has lost some parts of its territory, and a great loss for the other countries is the loss of the protection Russia used to provide for them.
>
> (Roman, 15 years old, Tula, Russia)

Another source of Russians' frustration with the international community has been the perceived unfair treatment of ethnic Russians abroad. A 16-year-old respondent from Tula, for example, regarded the removal of monuments to Soviet soldiers in Latvia as a personal insult.[16] Russian public schools devote considerable attention to teaching World War II events, but an in-depth analysis of the Molotov–Ribbentrop pact and its implications for the region seems to be lacking. Instead, history textbooks glorify the victory of the Russian people over the Nazis and elevate the role of Stalin in solidifying the power of the Soviet state. Given this lopsided coverage of Soviet history, it is not surprising that the interviewed high school students seemed unfamiliar with the fact that the Red Army occupied Latvia in June 1940 and incorporated it in the former Soviet Union by force. If Russian students knew about these well-recorded historical facts, they might have shown greater understanding of the foreign government's decision to dismantle monuments to Soviet soldiers.

When it comes to domestic issues, adolescents lamented the level of poverty in the country. Given the high unemployment rate in the post-Soviet period, the respondents found the communist-era idea of lifelong job security appealing:[17]

> The dissolution of the Soviet Union had bad consequences for people. There used to be a lot of jobs. People could afford a lot of things. There was enough money to live on. It is not the same now.
>
> (Andriy, 15 years old, Lviv, Ukraine)

> In the Soviet Union, there were plenty of job opportunities. If you did well in school, you could find a job. There was some hope for the future.
>
> (Bohdan, 14 years old, Donetsk, Ukraine)

> The family budget of most families worsened after the Soviet Union fell apart.
>
> (Aniuta, 15 years old, Donetsk, Ukraine)

Another attractive feature of the Soviet system was the low crime rate. A 15-year-old respondent from Moscow argued that it was right to impose some restrictions on people because it ensured control over everything. Indeed, criminal activities underwent a hike in the 1990s (Shelley 2000; Solomon and Foglesong 2000). The impoverished population turned to petty crime and violence. Moreover, the absence of a transparent legal environment led to the expansion of opaque business practices and mafia-like organizations. This insecure social environment engendered adolescents' concern about the high crime rate:

> There wasn't so much crime in the past. One could walk quite safely at night. Now one trembles with fear when walking in a dark alley late in the evening.
>
> (Sveta, 15 years old, Moscow, Russia)

> People used to fear the letter of the law.
>
> (Oleg, 14 years old, Kyiv, Ukraine)

By the same token, concern over declining moral standards occupied a prominent place in the students' reasoning about the negative effects of the Soviet demise. For example, 16-year-old Olga from Moscow stated that there existed strict discipline and respect for the elderly in the Soviet Union. Now youth display less deference towards the older generation and selfishly look out for their own needs. Reflecting socialist ideology, several respondents viewed a high level of individualism as a sign of social degradation. In general, the idea of collective good resonated with the younger generation:

> We used to be very friendly, and we used to treat each other well. Now everybody stands up for himself. People care only about what is good for them. Just look at our politicians. They have no scruples.
>
> (Larisa, 14 years old, Kyiv, Ukraine)

In sum, the semi-structured interviews revealed adolescents' reasoning behind both positive and negative evaluations of the Soviet system. To some, positive features of the communist regime, including job security and international prestige, outweighed the disadvantages of living in a closed society. But others attached greater importance to the exercise of political freedoms and the revival of national culture.

Past and present intertwined: Soviet nostalgia and national pride

One might expect the feelings of Soviet nostalgia and national pride to be closely linked in Russia and Ukraine. Indeed, the higher Soviet nostalgia, the lower national pride among Ukrainian adolescents. As shown in Figure 4.2, those Ukrainian adolescents who perceive the dissolution of the USSR as a negative phenomenon are 27 percent less likely to report feelings of national pride. This is consistent with the assumption that attachment to the old political community will decline and the level of national pride will increase with the passage of time. Yet the results from Russia reveal a substantially different attitudinal pattern: 87 percent of those who negatively evaluate the dissolution of the Soviet Union and 89 percent of those who look upon the Soviet demise in a positive light take pride in holding Russian citizenship.

Building the new political community 71

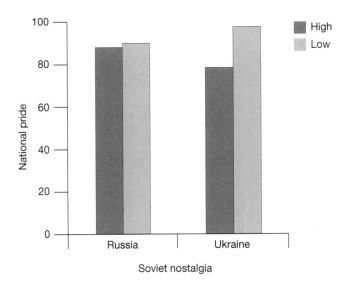

Figure 4.2 National pride by Soviet nostalgia (percentages)
Source: Survey of Adolescents in Russia and Ukraine, 2005.

This finding clearly shows how attachment to the old (Soviet) and new (post-Soviet) political communities seamlessly coexist in contemporary Russia. Russian and Soviet identities have been so closely intertwined that even a new generation of Russians finds it difficult to resist the perceived greatness of the Soviet Union.

Overall, the analysis presented in this chapter demonstrates how local social context sets the stage for the cultivation of national pride among the young generation. Soviet-era historical legacies appear to have left an indelible mark on the adolescents' imagining of political communities. Russian adolescents from Moscow, Rostov-on-the-Don, and Tula, along with their peers in Donetsk, tend to entertain favorable views of the Soviet Union, whereas Ukrainian adolescents from Kyiv and Lviv tend to denounce the communist past and embrace the idea of national independence.

Conclusion

The evidence presented in this chapter documents both cross-country and within-country variations in adolescents' attitudes toward the political community. Russian adolescents are more likely to disapprove of the Soviet demise than their Ukrainian peers. Moreover, the analysis confirms the salience of the east–west regional cleavage in Ukraine. Lviv adolescents display not a shred of nostalgia for Soviet times, whereas the majority of

Donetsk adolescents disapprove of the Soviet demise. In addition, respondents from Lviv, populated with predominantly Ukrainian-speaking ethnic Ukrainians, tend to exhibit much more national pride than their peers from the Russian-speaking city of Donetsk. Based upon the available survey data from Ukraine, the analysis uncovers the development of conflicting political allegiances among members of the same ethnic group residing in different parts of the country.

5 Learning about politics

In December 2000, Ukrainian civic activists launched the website *Maidan* (named after Kyiv's main square) to provide media support for the "Ukraine without Kuchma" movement.[1] While hundreds of people demanded the resignation of the incumbent president and set up tents in the city's main square, the online community spread the news about protest events and exchanged ideas about resistance to incumbent authorities. Since major TV channels bent to political pressures and offered a biased coverage of the movement's activities, the website sought to present an alternative account of protest events. Having accumulated extensive experience in the rapid collection and dissemination of news, this online community played a vital role during the Orange Revolution (see Goldstein 2007). In the post-2004 period, *Maidan* continues to supply media consumers with alternative information and press for democratic reforms. In particular, the website is popular with young, technologically savvy Ukrainians.

In addition to the Internet, young people obtain political news from a wide array of sources. Some messengers might be more influential than the others. The jury is still out as to the relative importance of family, schools, and the media in shaping worldviews of young citizens (for a review, see Beck 1977; Sapiro 2004).

As a first step in understanding these linkages, this chapter explores several sources of political news among adolescents. This chapter begins by analyzing the link between child-parent political discussions and adolescents' attitudes toward democracy, incumbent authorities, and the political community. Next, the relationship between political attitudes and exposure to media news is examined. Finally, this chapter investigates the role of student–teacher political discussions in shaping the political attitudes of students.

Family

Family plays a vital role in the lives of adolescents. Parents can greatly contribute to positive youth development by providing a safe social environment. From parents, children pick up appropriate models of behavior. Furthermore, children first learn about politics from their parents. Yet the expansion of female participation in the labor market has transformed the institution of marriage. Contemporary women tend to enter marriage and have children at a later age than their parents and grandparents.

This global trend means that family structure in Russia and Ukraine is undergoing change. Over the past two decades, there has been a slight postponement of first marriage. In Russia, the mean age at first marriage was 24 for women and 26 for men in 2002, compared to 22 for women and 24 for men in 1989 (*Demoscope Weekly* 2006). Likewise, the mean age at first marriage increased from 25 in 1989 to 27 in 2005 for Ukrainian women and from 27 to 30 for Ukrainian men (*Demoscope Weekly* 2007). While individuals in the former Soviet republics marry quite young, the divorce rates are among the highest in Europe. In 2001, Russia had a divorce rate of 5.3 per 1,000 people and Ukraine a divorce rate of 3.7 per 1,000 people (UNECE 2005). Inevitably, the prevalence of divorce has detrimental effects on the well-being of children. According to some estimates, 27 percent of Ukrainian children grow up in single-parent families (*Demoscope Weekly* 2007). Another recent development in Russia and Ukraine is a spike in one-child households. There are more abortions than live births in these former Soviet republics (UNECE 2005). Notwithstanding these negative trends, family tends to provide a modicum of stability in adolescents' lives.

In the post-Soviet region, politics is a popular topic for family conversations at the dining table or in the living room. Interest in politics is quite high, since ordinary citizens often endure the profound and painful impact of public policies on their lives. In Ukraine, for example, 72 percent of all voting-age adults and, in particular, 59 percent of 18–25-year-olds reported interest in politics in February 2005 (Buerkle, Kammerud, and Sharma 2005: 23). The introduction of educational reforms, the growth of private healthcare services, the closure of coal-mines, or the timely provision of pensions hinge upon the choices of the ruling elite and spark heated discussions in the confines of private homes and apartments. Growing up in Russia and Ukraine, adolescents not only bear witness to family discussions about politics, but also engage in conversations about current events with their close relatives.

Figure 5.1 shows how frequently adolescents in three Russian and three Ukrainian cities discuss politics with their parents. The survey results indicate that almost half of Ukrainian teenagers daily hear about politics from their parents. The frequency of political discussions is 10 percent higher in Kyiv and Lviv than in Donetsk. Similarly, an IFES survey conducted in February 2005 among voting-age Ukrainians found that supporters of the incumbent president, heavily concentrated in western and central parts of the country, reported a higher level of interest in politics than Yanukovych's electorate in the eastern part of the country (Buerkle, Kammerud, and Sharma 2005: 23). In contrast, Russian adolescents are less politicized, with 31 percent of respondents from Rostov-on-the-Don, 27 percent from Moscow, and 20 percent from Tula having politics as a topic of daily conversations with parents. Overall, less than 15 percent of adolescents in Russia and Ukraine never discuss politics with their close relatives, testifying to the salience of politics in post-Soviet households.

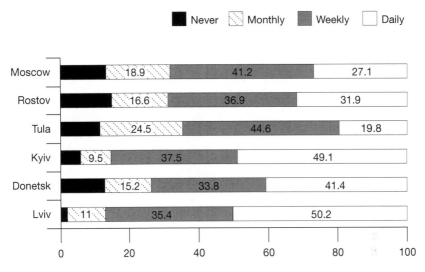

Figure 5.1 Political discussions with parents
Source: Survey of Adolescents in Russia and Ukraine, 2005.

Next, this study explores the link between political discussions with parents and political support. As shown in Figure 5.2, those adolescents who frequently converse with their parents about politics tend to report a higher level of support for democracy. But parents appear to have a negligible impact on the prevalence of national pride among the younger generation. In addition, the results suggest that parental reminiscences about the USSR tend to foster Soviet nostalgia among Russian adolescents, whereas conversations with parents in Ukraine tend to reinforce adolescents' approval of the Soviet demise. Strikingly, adolescents' trust in the incumbent president is positively correlated with discussions of current events with parents in Ukraine. This positive outlook might derive from the fact that some citizens, who protested against electoral fraud in 2004, pegged their hopes for better future on the new president.

Mass media

Since the collapse of communism, the media landscape in Russia and Ukraine has undergone tremendous transformation (Dyczok 2003; Mickiewicz 1999; Oates 2006; White 2008b). Following a short period of political liberalization in the early 1990s, the ruling elite attempted to reassert control over the flow of information. In Russia, the Kremlin took over the media empires built by Boris Berezovsky and Vladmir Gusinsky during the Yeltsin period. In Ukraine, the presidential administration introduced *temnyky*, clandestine guidelines for national TV channels and major newspapers on how to

76 Learning about politics

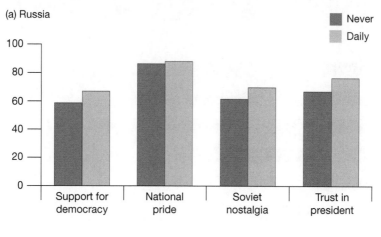

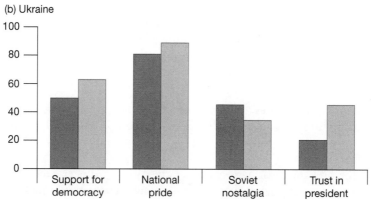

Figure 5.2. Political support and discussions with parents
Source: Survey of Adolescents in Russia and Ukraine, 2005.

cover current events (D'Anieri 2005: 236). Numerous reports indicate that the Russian government has effectively driven independent media out of the market and strengthened mechanisms of censorship and self-censorship among journalists.[2] While the Ukrainian media gained more independence in the aftermath of the Orange Revolution, the incumbent government continues to undermine the watchdog function of the press and treat journalists as instruments in the struggle for power. Before discussing patterns of adolescents' exposure to media news, this chapter examines the media environment in Russia and Ukraine.

Media development in Russia

The Russian media analyst Zassourski (2004) identified four stages in the media development of post-Soviet Russia. The first period spanning the early 1990s is the "golden age" of Russian media, since it heralded the breakdown of state censorship and the exponential growth of non-state media. During the second period (1992–96), however, most media outlets experienced a string of financial problems and fell under the influence of the so-called oligarchs. The period from 1998 to 2000 was marked by "an information arms race" in which powerful business groups carved up the media market. The election of Putin as the next president brought about another perestroika in the media sector.

A number of shake-ups occurred in the broadcasting sector during Putin's presidency (Lipman and McFaul 2001; Pietilainen 2008; Simons and Strovsky 2006; White 2008b). In 2000, the Kremlin regained control over the TV channel ORT by forcing the media baron Boris Berezovsky to sell his share in the company. ORT hit the rocks after it provided a critical coverage of the president's handling of the rescue operation to lift the *Kursk*, the sunken nuclear submarine, and its 118-member crew. That year, Berezovsky fled the country to shirk imprisonment on corruption charges. Another media tycoon, Vladmir Gusinsky, came under attack from the state apparatus for airing political satire on his TV channel NTV. Through a combination of legal and semi-legal means, the government made it clear that overt criticism of Putin is a taboo on national television.

Multiple restrictions on press freedom have left a mark on the content of media news. Based upon the content analysis of five Russian TV channels, the European Institute for the Media (2000) finds that Putin dominated the media coverage of the 2000 presidential election campaign and benefited from the unqualified support of state-controlled TV channels for the war in Chechnya. The results also indicate that the national TV channel ORT devoted most of its negative news coverage (82 percent) to Grigoriy Yavlinksy, another presidential contender and leader of the opposition party Yabloko, in the three weeks prior to the election. In addition, the media coverage of catastrophic events reveals the extent to which state-controlled media have bent to political pressures. In August 2000, NTV aired reports critical of the way the government organized a rescue operation to lift the sunken submarine. By the time of the siege of Beslan school in September 2004, the Kremlin had learned from its mistakes, restricted journalists' access to events and blanketed Russian TV viewers with misleading information (Lipman 2006b; OSCE 2004). Contemporary Russia lacks a national TV channel that has editorial independence and can act as a watchdog on the government.

Since it is precarious to air investigative reports and political talk shows, TV programming in Russia is dominated by entertainment programs and soap operas. By the same token, the Kremlin is intent on tapping into the potential of cinematography to build a sense of national identity. In his opening remarks at the 2008 conference of Russian film industry professionals, Putin brought up Lenin's famous saying, "Of all the arts, cinema is the most important art for us." With more than 100 films fully or partially funded by the government in 2007 alone, Russia has become Europe's second-largest film-maker after France (Coalson 2008). In particular, Russia's Ministry of Culture supports the production of Russian movies infused with patriotism. Like Soviet-era scripts, the portrayal of the Great Patriotic War is a stable feature of the Russian movie industry (Gillespie 2005), whereas artistic criticism of the current regime is banished from the public eye.

Furthermore, a pro-presidential media slant dominates the content of major newspapers. In recent years, the government has favored the acquisition of popular newspapers by businessmen close to the Kremlin. In 2006, Alisher Usmanov, a Russian steel magnate and general director of Gazprominvestholding, acquired *Kommersant*, Russia's leading independent newspaper, for $300 million (Kulakova and Cherkasova 2006). The newspaper *Novaia Gazeta*, previously 100 percent owned by the editorial staff, was forced to sell 39 percent of its shares to Aleksandr Lebedev, deputy of Moscow city council, and 10 percent to Mikhail Gorbachev, former president of the USSR (BBC 2006). In addition, local governments systematically distort media competition by extending rewards to loyal newspapers. According to some estimates, Russian regional authorities spent $0.5 billion subsidizing regional and local media in 2006 (IREX 2007: 170).

In this sea of state censorship and propaganda, the Internet is an island of political pluralism for principled journalists and information-hungry citizens (Semetko and Krasnoboka 2003). The use of the Internet is spreading across Russia. In 2002, one fifth of Russians knew how to use the Internet (Levada Center 2007: 191). By September 2007, one third of Russians reported familiarity with the World Wide Web. Nonetheless, only a small fraction of the Russian population has regular access to the Internet. In 2005, only 10 percent of Russians reported access to the Internet at home, with an additional 6 percent surfing the net at work. Most Internet users are young people. According to the Public Opinion Foundation, the proportion of Internet users among 15–17-year-old Russians jumped to 40 percent in 2005.[3]

Overall, the media environment in Russia creates numerous hurdles for the younger generation to obtain objective and reliable information on current events and Soviet history. National TV channels, along with major newspapers, provide a lopsided coverage of social reality, while the Internet remains inaccessible to a large segment of young Russians.

Media development in Ukraine

In the 1990s, Ukraine's pattern of media development resembled the media situation in Russia. The early 1990s were a honeymoon period marked by the relaxation of state control and the growth of independent media. In the mid 1990s, however, the consolidation of business interest groups has led to the division of the media market. Viktor Medvedchuk, head of the presidential administration, reportedly gained control over two TV channels with nationwide reach: Inter and Channel 1+1. In addition, Viktor Pinchuk, the president's son-in-law, acquired such TV channels as STB, ICTV, and Novyi Kanal (New Channel). By the time of Kuchma's re-election for the second term, it had become clear that the Ukrainian media had lost a large share of the press freedom it used to enjoy in the early 1990s (Nikolayenko 2004).

Kuchmagate sent shockwaves through Ukrainian society. Oleksandr Moroz, a member of the national parliament, released tapes implicating the incumbent president in the murder of the opposition journalist. The "Ukraine without Kuchma" movement organized protests demanding the president's resignation. Though Kuchma stayed in office until the end of his second term, pro-presidential TV channels failed to boost his approval rating. Furthermore, media strategies of the ruling elite, including news censorship and negative advertising, failed to prevent Yushchenko from coming to power (Dyczok 2005; Prytula 2006).

In 2005, the new government loosened control over the media, but stopped short of strengthening the fourth estate. On many occasions, media coverage of the abuse of power was met with neglect. Neither the police nor the courts looked into the publicized cases of corruption or provided a fair trial of public officials. Furthermore, Yushchenko himself vehemently objected to media scrutiny of his family's luxurious lifestyle. In particular, a political scandal erupted when the online publication *Ukrainska Pravda* (Ukrainian Truth) released a report about high-priced gadgets flaunted by 19-year-old Andriy Yushchenko (Amchuk 2005). The president's son drove a BMW M6, valued at more than $100,000, and used a Vertu cell phone with a platinum frame and a price tag of more than $6,500. Ukrainian journalists raised questions about how an undergraduate student whose father, the incumbent president, officially earned $510 in monthly wages could afford such expensive items. In response, President Yushchenko labeled an investigative reporter "a media killer" for the alleged attempt to smear his political career through a personal attack on his son. This highly publicized episode of the president's interaction with the independent media reveals, at minimum, a lack of elite understanding about the proper role of journalists in a democratic state.

Unlike the Russian TV audience, Ukrainian media consumers are exposed to a variety of political opinions. Most TV channels lavish criticism on the incumbent president. In contrast, Channel 5, owned by Petro Poroshenko, Yushchenko's close friend, directs its energy toward discrediting the incumbent prime minister, Julia Tymoshenko. Another TV channel – TRK Ukraina – is a mouthpiece of Rinat Akhmetov, Ukraine's wealthiest man, affiliated with the Party of Regions (*Newsru.Ua* 2008). A disturbing trend across the TV channels is the owner's impingement on editorial independence and the treatment of journalists as pawns in a power struggle.

The survey data suggest that Ukrainian media consumers tune into TV channels that conform to their political preferences. In November 2006,

20 percent of Yushchenko supporters and only 4 percent of Yanukovych supporters watched Channel 5 (IFES 2006: 10–11). Inter, on the contrary, was more popular with Yanukovych's electorate. Even clearer are the media habits of TV viewers if one scrutinizes media consumption patterns across regions. Channel 5 is the most popular source of political news in the western part of the country, whereas Inter, saturated with Russian-made movies and Russian-language entertainment programs, is the most watched TV channel in eastern and southern parts of the country.

Consistent with the global trend, newspaper readership is declining in Ukraine. In 2006, only 8 percent of Ukrainians identified the press as a major source of political news (IFES 2006: 10). The tabloid *Argumenty i Facty* (Arguments and Facts) has the largest circulation of 761,000 copies (IREX 2007: 174). Yet most newspapers tend to have less impressive sales. Media consumers tend to pick local newspapers to learn about happenings in their city or region.

Meanwhile, the growth of the Internet occurred at a slower pace in Ukraine than in Russia. In the course of the 2004 election campaign, the biased TV coverage of current events compelled a lot of voters to search for alternative information online. Within one month, the number of Internet users spiked from 1,593,305 during the first week of November to 2,016,100 during the last week of November (*Ukrainska Pravda* 2004). Yet 55 percent of all Internet users were based in the capital city of Kyiv. Overall, only 3 percent of Ukrainians in 2005 had access to the Internet at home, with an additional 8 percent using the net at work or Internet cafes (Panina 2005: 131).

This media environment provides a context in which Ukrainian adolescents gain exposure to news media. In the post-2004 period, TV channels and newspapers bombard media consumers with diverse political messages. Furthermore, the political significance of the Internet is growing, supplying young citizens with ample political information.

Adolescents' news media consumption

Figure 5.3 shows how frequently adolescents get informed about politics by watching national TV channels, reading newspapers or surfing the net. Clearly, television is a major source of political information among post-Soviet citizens. Approximately half of adolescents in the three Russian and three Ukrainian cities daily watch TV news. In contrast, only 10 percent of adolescents daily learn about current events from newspapers. In unison with the global trend, Internet usage supersedes newspaper readership among the younger generation. Almost 15 percent of adolescents turn to the Internet to keep track of public affairs. Notably, there are negligible differences in the use of the Internet across the cities. Fifteen percent of respondents from Moscow and 19 percent of respondents from Rostov-on-the-Don report daily exposure to political news via the Internet. Similarly, 14 percent of adolescents from Kyiv and 15 percent of adolescents from Donetsk daily get exposed to political information online.

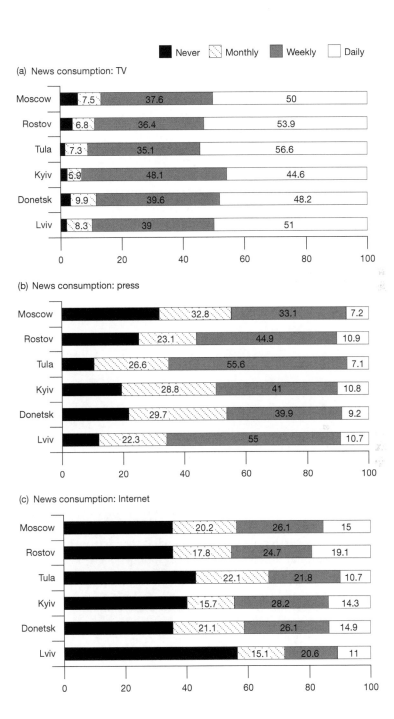

Figure 5.3 Patterns of media news consumption among adolescents (percentages)
Source: Survey of Adolescents in Russia and Ukraine, 2005.

Despite high levels of news consumption, Russian and Ukrainian adolescents might harbor skepticism about the credibility of domestic media outlets. As reported in the previous chapter, adolescents tend to believe that local politicians engage in profit-maximizing behavior and disregard the public interest. This negative view of the political elite might have spillover effects on the media's public image. In addition, contemporary adolescents might receive cues about distrust in media messages from parents socialized in the communist era. Having lived in the environment of intense state censorship, Soviet citizens learned how to question media messages and read between the lines.

In fact, the data obtained from semi-structured interviews with adolescents indicate that most high-school students perceive a bias in the media coverage of current events. Respondents from both Russia and Ukraine point out that the mass media tell "half-truths":

> I watch the news every other day, one needs to know what is happening in the country. But I like sports news more than politics. The media tell half-truths. They say that everything is great, but it is a lie.
>
> (Stas, 16 years old, Moscow)

> News is the window to the world. One can't trust the media, but it provides at least some information about the world. Any person can say one thing, but think in a completely different way. Nobody can be trusted.
>
> (Dima, 16 years old, Tula)

> I don't believe it when the mass media promises that everything will be just fine. It's hard to believe. A TV channel gets money from a politician, and then it talks only about this politician and keeps information about others off air. That's how it was during the presidential elections.
>
> (Iryna, 15 years old, Lviv, Ukraine)

Some adolescents, however, place more trust in what they see on TV than in what they read in national newspapers. These respondents espouse a belief that visual images are more difficult to manipulate:

> I don't trust the press. Who knows what stories they can make up? They write about something crazy every day. I trust TV reports more. TV journalists shoot everything on camera. I can see it.
>
> (Anzhelika, 14 years old, Kyiv, Ukraine)

In providing explanations for the media bias, Russian respondents bring up self-censorship and the unethical behavior of public relations firms, whereas Ukrainian respondents tend to emphasize the elite's manipulation of media coverage for political gain:

I only half-trust the media. Journalists are afraid to tell the whole truth because they can be killed like Listiev [a famous Russian journalist assassinated in 1995]. Everything was well thought out, and his case hasn't been solved yet.

(Artem, 15 years old, Moscow, Russia)

The mass media depend upon the information they receive from various PR firms. But these firms don't necessarily tell the truth. Each big company has a spokesperson working in the PR department. This person knows what he can tell and what he needs to hush up. That's why I don't trust the mass media.

(Zhenia, 15 years old, Tula, Russia)

I don't trust TV. Politicians may pay them for a report, and they will show it.

(Liuda, 14 years old, Donetsk, Ukraine)

Within Ukraine, the level of adolescents' trust in national TV channels varies across the cities. Lviv respondents tend to question the credibility of such Yanukovych-friendly TV channels as Inter and TRK Ukraina and place more trust in Channel 5, which is supportive of Yushchenko. Similarly, Donetsk respondents tend to express skepticism about the trustworthiness of national TV channels that diverge from their political sympathies:

To some extent, I trust Channel 5 and Novyi Kanal. They cover domestic politics better than others; they seem to tell more truth than others. I don't trust Inter at all. They even have all the programs in Russian.

(Volodymyr, 14 years old, Lviv, Ukraine)

I watch TV once a day: Channel 5 and a local TV channel. Some TV channels just work on their owner, for example, TRK Ukraina and ICTV. They don't tell the truth.

(Zhenia, 14 years old, Lviv, Ukraine)

I don't watch TV at all. We don't have a TV set in our apartment. In general, I don't trust mass media. Why do they impose the Ukrainian language? Even some DJs speak Ukrainian now.

(Ilona, 14 years old, Donetsk, Ukraine)

I don't believe the national TV channels. Yushchenko puts his people in top positions everywhere.

(Bohdan, 14 years old, Donetsk, Ukraine)

To navigate this pluralistic media environment, a few Ukrainian adolescents make a conscious effort to learn about politics from different media sources:

> I don't trust the mass media. I trust myself. I watch several TV channels to get different viewpoints.
>
> (Petro, 14 years old, Lviv, Ukraine)

> I don't watch TV frequently. It is necessary to watch several programs to understand what is going on. It is very easy to put a spin on events.
>
> (Nastia, 15 years old, Kyiv, Ukraine)

What is disturbing is that a few Russian adolescents justify the partial concealment of facts in the media coverage of current events:

> The mass media tell half-truths. On the one hand, it is bad because people need to know the whole truth. On the other hand, it is good because disorder can be averted in this way.
>
> (Yana, 15 years old, Moscow)

> TV journalists tell half-truths. If something terrible happens, they conceal some facts. For example, they reduce the number of dead in reports of a catastrophe. If the media told all the truth, there would be too much discontent among people. Sometimes it is better not to overwhelm people with too much information.
>
> (Misha, 14 years old, Moscow)

The prevalence of media skepticism among post-Soviet adolescents might weaken media effects on political attitudes. Figure 5.4 provides a visual representation of the relationship between media news consumption and political support. In particular, it contrasts exposure to mainstream media (television) and non-mainstream media (the Internet). Strikingly, exposure to TV news is positively associated with support for democracy in both Russia and Ukraine. There might be a self-selection process at play. Those high-school students who are positively oriented to democracy might be more inclined to watch TV news than those who care little about the provision of political freedoms and civil rights.[4] Likewise, adolescents distrustful of authorities are more likely to turn to the Internet for political news, since state-controlled broadcast media toe the official line and provide a biased coverage of current events. As shown in Figure 5.4, those adolescents who place less trust in the incumbent president tend to obtain more political news via the Internet.

Like parents, TV channels in Russia and Ukraine have divergent effects on adolescents' attitudes toward the disintegration of the Soviet Union. The more Russian adolescents watch national TV channels, the more they regret the demise of the Soviet Union. In contrast, heavy exposure to TV news is negatively correlated with feelings of Soviet nostalgia in Ukraine. This is consistent with a view that the mainstream Russian media propagate a positive image of the Soviet Union, while Ukrainian TV channels expose young citizens to a plurality of political views and challenge their thinking about Soviet history.

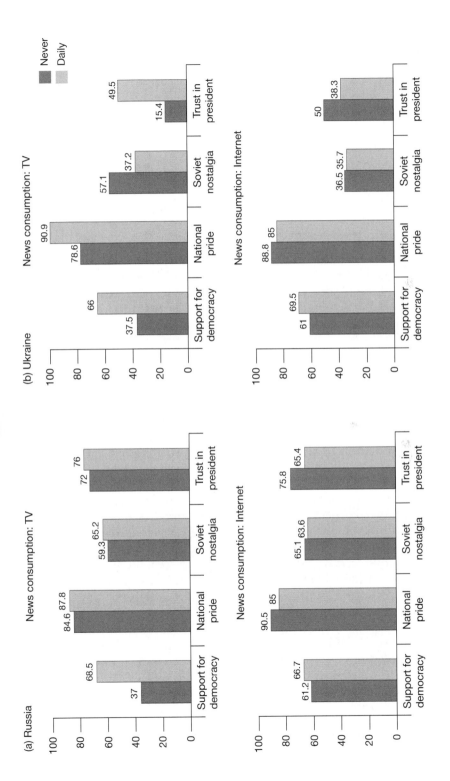

Figure 5.4 Political support and media news consumption (percentages)
Source: Survey of Adolescents in Russia and Ukraine, 2005.

Schools

Schools are charged with the responsibility to prepare a new cohort of citizens for entry to the labor market and integration into the political system (Bennett 1999; Nie, Junn, and Stehlik-Barry 1996; Niemi and Junn 1998; Torney-Purta 2002; Torney-Purta, Oppenheim, and Farnen 1975; Torney-Purta et al. 2001). As societies undergo dramatic transformations, the educational system also needs to adjust to changes in the political and socioeconomic environment. Institutional resistance to change, however, might hamper the success of educational reform. Before turning to the discussion of education in the post-Soviet period, this section sketches a profile of Soviet education.

The Soviet educational system

The objective of the Soviet educational system was twofold: (1) to train a labor force qualified for the advancement of industrialization and (2) inculcate Marxist-Leninist ideology in citizens. To a large extent, the Communist Party succeeded in accomplishing the first goal. The political leadership of the 1920s initiated a large-scale literacy program to transform the uneducated rural population into a competent workforce. Approximately 80 percent of the population was illiterate in 1917 (Jacoby 1974). By 1989, the national census registered near-total literacy: 94 percent of the employed urban population and 84 percent of the employed rural population in Russia had completed at least lower secondary schooling (Gerber 2000: 219). Furthermore, the massive migration of the labor force into urban areas led to a significant drop in the percentage of students in rural areas. Twenty-eight percent of all students in 1990, compared to 47 percent in 1960, were educated in rural areas (Dneprov, Lazarev, and Sobkin 1993). But the attempts by the Communist Party to mold the Soviet subject met with less spectacular success. The results from the Soviet Interview Project suggest that the experience of higher education fostered unfavorable attitudes toward the communist state (Bahry 1987). Despite the weight of evidence discrediting the Soviet project of engineering a new type of the citizen (*homo sovieticus*), the role of secondary schools in inculcating Marxist-Leninist ideas in children merits some attention. An examination of Soviet education will set the context for political socialization processes in the post-communist period.

The idea of absolute control lies at the heart of the communist state and clearly manifests itself in the management of the educational system. Saar (1997) identifies three key principles underpinning the Soviet educational system: (1) centralization, (2) standardization, and (3) imposition of utilitarian and egalitarian goals (Saar 1997). The Ministry of Education of the USSR controlled all aspects of the educational process, including the content of the curricula, the usage of textbooks, the language of instruction, the design of lesson plans, and the distribution of educational attainment and occupational choices across social groups. The teacher's task was to present learning material in an authoritative manner, and the student's responsibility was to memorize it without questioning. The teachers were stripped of any autonomy in designing curricula or using innovative teaching methods. Likewise, students were expected to subordinate their personal aspirations to the idea of collective public good by complying with state quotas for each occupation. The top-down approach to education discouraged creativity, initiative, and critical thinking. What the state required from its citizens was to endorse and follow the dogmas of Marxism-Leninism, as defined by the Communist Party.

Over the decades, the Communist Party maintained tight ideological control over teaching social studies. *A Short Course: History of the Communist Party of the Soviet Union (Bolsheviks)* (Kratkii kurs istorii Vsesoiuznoi Kommunisticheskoi Partii bol'shevikov) published in 1938 set the framework for formulating educational goals and writing school textbooks. For example, the 1968–69 syllabus in history (grade 9) explicitly allotted 20 out of 150 hours to the thorough study of works by Karl Marx, Friedrich Engels, and Vladimir Lenin (Dunstan 1978: 268). In conformity with Stalin's vision, history textbooks combined Marxist ideas with a narrative of Russian nationalism (Berelowitch 2003). Soviet-era historical writing elevated the role of ethnic Russians in world history and downgraded the cultural heritage of non-Russian ethnic groups.

In general, the Soviet cultural policy underwent substantial changes in the 1930s. With accession to power, the Bolsheviks supported a policy of cultural revival (*korenizatsiia*) aimed at reversing the effects of earlier discrimination toward ethnic minorities. Stalin, however, perceived the resurgence of indigenous cultures as a threat to the unity of the communist state. The security services launched massive purges of the local intelligentsia. Between 1930 and 1935, 15 conspiracies against the Soviet government were "discovered" in Ukraine alone (Kolasky 1968). Across the region, the state-sponsored imposition of Russian culture (Russification) intensified.

One of the mechanisms through which the Communist Party suppressed cultural diversity was its language policies in non-Russian Soviet republics (Bilinsky 1968). The Council of People's Commissars supported Russification by adopting a decree on the obligatory study of Russian in schools across the Soviet Union (1938). Stalin's successor as Soviet leader, Nikita Khruschev, applied a more subtle method of cultural assimilation by introducing the idea of voluntary choice. The new law (1959) delegated to parents the right to "choose" for their children a school with either Russian or another language of instruction. In fact, that law served as a tool for legitimizing the extensive usage of the Russian language in the multiethnic state (Silver 1974).

A new addition to the Soviet curriculum in the Brezhnev period was a course on principles of Soviet state and law (*osnovy sovetskogo gosudarstva i prava*). This course was designed to inform eighth-graders about the alleged advantages of the socialist legal system over the bourgeois one (Malinin and Pashkov 1978; Rzhevskii and Bondar 1982). Though students learned about the rights and obligations of Soviet citizens, it was ideologically unacceptable to challenge the superiority of the communist system or expose the shortcomings of a planned economy.

The emphasis on upbringing (*vospitanie*) was another mechanism for molding the younger generation. Soviet schools inculcated in children obedience, strict discipline, and respect for the elderly (Bronfenbrenner 1970). The Communist Party envisioned the child's identification with the collective as a powerful tool for inducing conformity to the rules. For example, in the wake of any misdoing, the student was "chastised more for letting the group down than for his individual errors" (Jacoby 1974: 21). Breaking away from the collective was a cardinal sin under the communist rule.

To draw students into the collective and utilize another venue for indoctrination, the Communist Party developed a hierarchy of youth organizations. All elementary school students were designated as "children of October" (*oktiabriata*) because the Bolsheviks had overthrown the provisional government in October 1917. These students were required to wear badges with the image of little Lenin until they were old enough to join the League of Young Pioneers. In addition to a new badge with another image of Lenin, red scarves adorned the drab school uniforms of middle-school students. Finally, high-school students joined Komsomol, the final school-based organization, designed to prepare young people for entering the ranks of the Communist Party. In this way, the political education of citizens was planned from early childhood to adulthood.

The political system, however, began to crumble in the 1980s. Though Mikhail Gorbachev envisioned *perestroika* (restructuring) and *glasnost* (openness) as means for salvaging the system, the new policies only accelerated the collapse of the communist state. The government adopted a series of laws in an effort to improve the quality of education (Kaufman 1994; Kerr 1990; Szekely 1986). But teachers' own initiatives to democratize the educational sector exasperated the ruling elite. Shortly after Vladimir Matveev, chief editor of *Uchitsel'skaia Gazeta* (Teachers' Gazette), exposed shortcomings in the system in his newspaper and formed an informal group of teacher-innovators, he lost his job (Kerr 1991). Apparently, the group's "Pedagogy of Cooperation," a teaching philosophy advocating a student-centered approach to education, went far beyond what the Ministry of Education was prepared to implement at that time.

In sum, the Soviet educational system was rigid. Conceptually, Marxist-Leninist ideology put a straightjacket on what could be taught at schools. From the management standpoint, the Moscow-based Ministry of Education controlled everything from the design of curricula and the selection of teaching methods to the constitution of youth organizations and the use of the Russian language in the classroom. Moreover, the state closely monitored and corrected, if necessary, the distribution of occupational choices among young people to satisfy the needs of a planned economy. That system suppressed critical thinking, individual initiative, and creativity. These personal traits, however, have become crucial to the start of a successful career in the post-Soviet period. The next sub-section highlights recent ideological changes at schools, with the emphasis on history teaching.

De-communization in the post-Soviet education system?

With the collapse of communism, the moribund educational system required drastic and immediate reforms. The Minister of Education of Russia, Edward Dneprov, was the driving force behind the Law on Education (1992) laying out the reform agenda:

- decentralization and regionalization – the devolution of responsibility for administration to regional (and republican) levels, municipal and district councils and the schools themselves;
- democratization – the introduction of greater public accountability; granting parents and the local community a greater say in the running of the schools;
- de-ideologization – removing the possibility of promoting one ideological viewpoint to the exclusion of others;
- differentiation/diversification – breaking the state's monopoly control of education;
- humanization – giving greater emphasis to the needs of the individual; improving teacher–pupil relations;
- humanitarization – giving greater emphasis to the humanities in the curriculum.

(Webber 2000: 33)

In the early 1990s, de-ideologization took the form of de-communization.[5] Since President Yeltsin sought to legitimize the revival of Russia as a powerful sovereign state, Russian historiographers assumed the task of establishing "continuity between the new democratic Russia and its pre-revolutionary predecessor" (Kaplan 2005: 254). Post-Soviet textbooks, for example, presented the aristocracy and the Russian Orthodox Church in a much more favorable light than Soviet historiography (Shevyrev 2005). Yet the revival of Soviet historical myths has been unfolding at a blinding speed in recent years.

A string of policies during Putin's presidency reveal the re-installment of ideological boundaries in the education sector and a move toward the consolidation of the so-called unified educational space (*edinoe obrazovatel'noe prostranstvo*). A draft of the Concept of History Education (2000) openly criticized diversity in the content of school textbooks on the grounds that it hampered the development of a unified approach to history teaching. In response, the Ministry of Education reduced the number of history textbooks and standardized, to a large extent, their content. Consistent with the Kremlin's rhetoric, the state-approved history textbooks reinforced three major themes: (1) the expansion of Russia in response to foreign invasions,

(2) glorification of the country's heroes and identification of its enemies, and (3) the unity and cohesiveness of Russian society (Berelowitch 2003).

Those textbooks that departed from the official political discourse were removed from public schools. Igor Dolutskii's textbook on twentieth-century national history (*Otechesvennaia istoriia, XX vek*), for example, came under heavy criticism from the educational authorities, since the textbook presented an overly critical summary of Russia's history. Dolutskii ended each chapter with a paragraph outlining different perspectives on a historical event. One chapter prompted students to discuss whether contemporary Russia was a democracy. Another chapter invited an assessment of Putin's leadership style.[6] The Ministry's response was that the textbook "elicits contempt for our past and the Russian people" (Bransten 2003; Lambroschini 2004). As in Soviet times, textbooks were supposed to narrate Soviet and Russian history without explicit questioning of the past or subtle criticism of the incumbent government.

Taking another cue from the Soviet educational system, the Russian government endorsed the formation of a nationwide youth organization *Nashi* (Ours) that would unite Russian youth supportive of incumbent authorities. This policy decision was, to a large extent, a reaction to the anti-regime mobilization of Georgian and Ukrainian youth during the so-called colored revolutions (Bush 2008; Corwin 2005; Myers 2007c). According to *Nashi*'s manifesto, the major objective of the youth movement was to "turn Russia into a global leader of the twenty-first century" by supporting Putin's "modernization policies" and building patriotic fervor among youth.[7] Among other things, *Nashi* activists focus on attacking the so-called enemies of the current regime, i.e. those who dare to publicly criticize authoritarian tendencies in contemporary Russia. The youth movement, for example, orchestrated a campaign against the British Ambassador to Russia, Tony Brenton, after he criticized the Kremlin at a summit organized by the opposition coalition The Other Russia (Blomfield 2006). In return for their work, a few prominent *Nashi* activists were rewarded with government jobs. For example, Vasily Yakemenko, *Nashi*'s leader from 2005 to 2007, took up the post of the head of State Committee on Youth. Like Soviet-era Komsomol, *Nashi* is supposed to become a springboard for making a career in Russian politics.

The pro-government youth movement has at its disposal considerable resources to train a new generation of Russians. *Nashi* annually holds a summer camp on the shores of Lake Seliger, located approximately 360 kilometers from Moscow, to provide ideological training for Russian youth. At the summer camp, young people recruited from various parts of the country learn about Russia's enemies, deconstruct US foreign policy, and rally behind the incumbent government. To spread these ideas among participants in the movement, *Nashi* increased the number of camp attendees from 3,000 in 2005 to 10,000 in 2007.[8] Although the exact number of *Nashi* activists is unknown, more than 50,000 young people have participated in the movement's major public events, showcasing the power of the regime to mobilize pro-government youth.

Overall, Putin's presidency marked the end of liberal reforms in the educational sector. In August 2001, the State Council (*Gosudarstvennyi Sovet*), an advisory body to the president of Russia, formulated a new policy document on the development of the educational system in the next 10 years (Dneprov 2002). This document symbolized a shift in the policymaking discourse from reforms to the modernization of education. More broadly, the Russian government brought back Soviet-era thinking about schools as tools of state indoctrination.

Like Russia, post-Soviet Ukraine embarked upon the project of de-communization in the early 1990s. The Ministry of Education and Science of Ukraine banished Marxist-Leninist ideology from schools and initiated the revision of national historical narratives. An additional challenge that Ukrainian educators faced was the expansion of Ukrainian-language schools in a country stricken with Russification.

The confrontation between the two schools of thought – Ukrainophile and East Slavic – set the stage for re-writing history in post-Soviet Ukraine (Janmaat 2006; Kennan Institute 2002; Kuzio 2005b; Marples 2007; Popson 2001; Stepanenko 1999; Wanner 1998). The first school focuses on the struggle of Ukrainians for independence and celebrates the distinctiveness of Ukrainian culture. The second school emphasizes ethno-cultural and political links between Russians and Ukrainians. Nonetheless, both of these schools depart from Soviet historiography's denial of Ukraine's aspirations for statehood. The country's history textbooks reflect the Ukrainophile approach to narrating the history of the Ukrainian people. Specifically, Kuzio (2002) identifies the revision of seven key phenomena in history textbooks:

1 Kyivan Rus' is either defined completely as a proto-Ukrainian state or as a state to which Ukrainians have the majority title;
2 the 1654 Treaty of Periaslav is no longer depicted as the "re-union" of two branches of one people. It is defined as a confederal alliance, not submission, and forced upon Ukraine by Poland's unwillingness to recognize Ruthenia (Ukraine/Belarus) as a third partner in the Polish–Lithuanian Commonwealth;
3 Tsarist rule is defined as something negative, leading to serfdom, a loss of elites and de-nationalization;
4 Austrian rule is seen in more favorable terms for having allowed nation-building to take place;
5 collapse of empires: the Ukrainian People's Republic (UNR), Directory and Hetmanate of 1917–21 are recognized as legitimate attempts at state-building;
6 Stalinism is perceived as a direct attack upon Ukrainian language, culture, elites; the 1933 artificial famine is viewed as "ethnocide" or the "terror/murder-famine";
7 World War II: the Ukrainian Insurgent Army (UPA) nationalist partisans are now largely depicted as having fought against the Nazis and Soviets.

Another controversy-ridden component of post-Soviet educational reform was the re-introduction of the Ukrainian language into classrooms (see Arel 1995). The 1996 Constitution of Ukraine granted Ukrainian the status of the sole state language, while Russian was designated as a national minority language. Given a heated debate over the place of the Russian language in Ukrainian society, the Ministry of Education and Science adopted a gradual approach to reversing the effects of Russification. Over the 1991–98 period, the proportion of students enrolled in Ukrainian-language schools increased from 48 percent to 63 percent (Janmaat 1999). Still, a majority of ethnic Ukrainians in the Donetsk region attended public schools with Russian as the language of instruction. To provide an incentive for learning Ukrainian, a new policy (1993) introduced a mandatory entrance examination in the Ukrainian language for admission to universities. By 2005, however, 74 percent of citizens still endorsed teaching Russian at public schools (Panina 2005). Throughout the post-Soviet period, the language issue has been so important that politicians took it up to boost electoral support by campaigning for either more comprehensive Ukrainization or continuing Russification.

Unlike the Kremlin, President Kuchma shied away from building a Komsomol-like youth organization to consolidate the political regime. Instead, various youth organizations unaffiliated with the government emerged across the country. Among potent youth organizations in western Ukraine, for example, was *Moloda Prosvita*, whose primary goal was to promote the development of Ukrainian culture. Though some political parties set up youth wings to rejuvenate the party ranks, these political entities appeared to be quite ineffective in recruiting and retaining youth. Only a small fraction of Ukrainian youth joined political parties. In 2002, the Union of Youth from the Regions of Ukraine (*Soiuz molodezhi regionov Ukrainy*, SMRU) was founded by the Party of Regions. According to the union's leader, Vitaly Khomutynnik, SMRU was the largest youth organization in Ukraine (Diagilev 2007). In many cases, however, SMRU emulated the Party of Regions' recruitment strategy and used administrative resources to expand its membership. For example, more than 1,800 high-school students received SMRU membership cards on the last day of classes in Donetsk, shortly before taking final exams at school (*Zhizn* 2004). Exposing the organization's lack of genuine popular appeal, the Union was hardly visible during the Orange Revolution.

In this context, school teachers are charged with the responsibility to present a revised version of national history to students. To some extent, teachers have the freedom to choose teaching methods and learning material. This freedom, however, is limited by a long list of guidelines supplied by the Ministry of Education.

Adolescents' conversations with the teacher

The teacher has a choice whether to make connections between the learning material and political reality.[9] A number of teachers in Russian and Ukrainian schools take the liberty to discuss current events with students. The results

Learning about politics 93

presented in Figure 5.5 suggest that Ukrainian teachers take advantage of this freedom more frequently than their Russian colleagues. In particular, one fifth of Lviv students reported that they daily spoke about politics with their teachers, implying the development of an open exchange of ideas in the school setting. In Donetsk, teachers drew their students into conversations about politics less frequently. Furthermore, a quarter of Russian high-school students never brought up politics during their interactions with teachers.

In part, the likelihood of an open political discussion in the school setting depends upon the presence of a trusting relationship between teachers and students. In the course of semi-structured interviews, some Lviv adolescents revealed that they had a common experience of protesting with teachers against electoral fraud in the fall of 2004.

> I traveled to Kyiv with my dad. We stayed at the October Palace. There were tons of people there. We also went to the rallies in downtown Lviv ... During the Orange Revolution, a lot of our teachers also went to Kyiv to support protesters. Two of our history teachers made a big poster dedicated to the Orange Revolution and hung it in the classroom. My picture is also here. I was wearing braided hair like Tymoshenko.
> (Olena, 14 years old, Lviv, Ukraine)

Yet the top-down approach is far more common in post-Soviet schools. Quite often, teachers expect to exercise unchecked authority over student experiences at school:

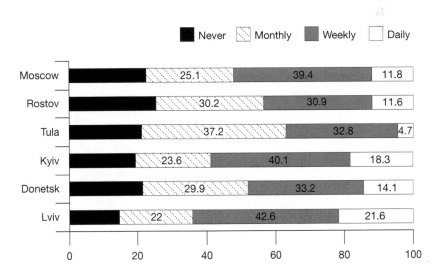

Figure 5.5 Political discussions with teachers (percentages)
Source: Survey of Adolescents in Russia and Ukraine, 2005.

94   Learning about politics

We have a school radio station. But teachers complained that young people had bad taste in music. And teachers insisted on having only classical music on Wednesdays.

(Uliana, 13 years old, Lviv, Ukraine)

There are very few things we can do on our own initiative at school, without the teachers' interference. Everything is closely supervised. For Teacher's Day, we made student newspapers. We were told to hang them in one place – on the first floor, with 5 centimeters between the adjacent newspapers. And the other walls remained bare.

(Nastia, 15 years old, Kyiv, Ukraine)

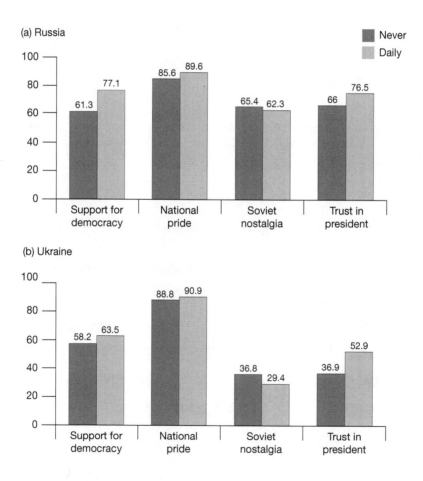

Figure 5.6 Political support and discussions with teachers (percentages)
Source: Survey of Adolescents in Russia and Ukraine, 2005.

The results further suggest that teachers in Russia and Ukraine tend to support the status quo. The more students speak about public affairs with teachers, the more young citizens support democracy, take pride in the home country, and place trust in the incumbent president. It is also noteworthy that Ukrainian students who frequently discuss politics with their teachers tend to endorse more strongly the dissolution of the Soviet Union, whereas this linkage is unobservable in Russia.

Conclusion

This analysis confirms that adolescents obtain political news from different sources. Like young people in mature democracies, Russian and Ukrainian youth tend to rely upon television as a major source of political information. Furthermore, the technologically savvy generation reads more online than offline publications. Since politics is a popular topic of family conversations, Russian and Ukrainian adolescents also absorb a lot of political information at home. Finally, schools hold the potential to supply students with a solid body of political knowledge and historical understanding. The next chapter provides an in-depth discussion of how school textbooks unravel national historical narratives.

6 Construction of Soviet history in school textbooks

> The state bears responsibility for the upbringing of youth. Thus, there must be responsibility for the quality of learning aids.
> Boris Gryzlov, Speaker of the Russian Duma, 21 June 2007

Teaching national history involves much more than the transfer of knowledge; it is a major vehicle for the reproduction of historical memory and the construction of national identity. In the post-Soviet period, Russian and Ukrainian historians embarked upon the revision of national history to buttress the legitimacy of new nation-states (Janmaat 2006; Kaplan 2005; Kuzio 2002; Lisovskaya and Karpov 1999; Marples 2007; Popson 2001; Shevyrev 2005; Wanner 1998). The hierarchical structure of the educational system in Russia and Ukraine facilitates students' exposure to the official version of national history. Each high-school student is required to take courses in national history. As a result, the entire population is exposed to official accounts of history through approved school textbooks. While conveying a particular version of the past, these textbooks provide adolescents with a lens through which they can interpret current events in the domestic and international arenas.

In general, history is one of the most popular school subjects among Russian and Ukrainian students. According to an opinion poll by Public Opinion Foundation in 2002, history is the third favorite subject among Russian high-school graduates, preceded only by math and literature (Petrova 2002).[1] Unlike most American high-school students,[2] post-communist youth rarely considers history as boring. Furthermore, the results from the 2005 Survey of Adolescents in Russia and Ukraine indicate that almost 90 percent of the surveyed students believe that the knowledge acquired in social studies courses (history and civics) will be of use to them in the future. Students' interest in history is likely to boost the power of the messages that history textbooks try to convey.

This chapter examines how major Russian and Ukrainian school textbooks cover twentieth-century history, encapsulating a series of highly contested historical phenomena. The analysis focuses on three key events in Soviet history: (1) the formation of the Soviet Union, (2) the dissolution of the Soviet Union, and (3) World War II. In addition, the chapter investigates how school textbooks cover the Holodomor (the famine of 1932–33), since it represents an episode of "forbidden history." While the Soviet leadership banned any discussion of the famine, Russian and Ukrainian historians have recently engaged in a heated public debate about the causes, scope, and consequences of the Holodomor.

For the purpose of textbook analysis, I select the Russian textbook titled *History of Fatherland XX Century* [Istoria Otechestva XX vek] by Nikita Zagladin *et al.* and the Ukrainian textbook titled *Modern History of Ukraine* [Noveishaia istoria Ukrainy 1914–2001] by Fedir Turchenko *et al.* The Russian textbook for the eleventh grade covers the period from the Russian–Japanese War of 1905 to the parliamentary election of 2003. The Ukrainian textbook consists of two volumes: the first volume covers the historical period from World War I to the eve of World War II (tenth grade), and the second volume deals with the history of Ukraine from World War II to 2001 (eleventh grade). The educational authorities in each country strongly endorse the use of these two textbooks. In 2002, Russia's Ministry of Education selected Zagladin's as the best history textbook on twentieth-century Russian history, giving it a significant boost in sales (Kirillova 2004). The fourth edition of the textbook was published in 2006. Likewise, most Ukrainian public schools use Turchenko's textbook to teach twentieth-century history. To accommodate the needs of Russian-language schools, 200,000 copies of the third edition were published in Russian in 2001.

The textbook analysis is divided into three steps. First, I scrutinize the content of textbook chapters to identify differences in the official discourse. Then I examine the content of visual aids that reinforce messages conveyed in the text. Finally, I compare the use of primary sources across textbooks.

Table 6.1 summarizes key findings of textbook analysis. The selected Russian and Ukrainian textbooks differ in the amount of space they devoted to the coverage of key events in Soviet history. Not surprisingly, the Ukrainian textbook discusses in greater detail events leading up to the dissolution of the Soviet Union and accords more attention to the nationalist mobilization during the late Soviet period. Furthermore, the Ukrainian textbook assigns two chapters (10 pages) to the Holodomor, while the Russian textbook buries references to the starvation of Soviet peasants in the chapter about the modernization of the economy and the defense system in the 1930s. As anticipated, both Russian and Ukrainian textbooks devote considerable attention to World War II, but the Ukrainian textbook breaks with the Soviet account of the war by illuminating the activities of the Organization of Ukrainian Nationalists (*Organizatsiya Ukrainskyh Nationalistiv*, OUN) and Ukrainian Insurgent Army (*Ukrainska Povstanska Armiya*, UPA). To provide a balanced account of Ukrainian resistance to the Nazis, Turchenko *et al.* discuss guerilla fighting by both Soviet partisans in eastern Ukraine and OUN–UPA members in western Ukraine. Another difference in the textbook coverage of historical events is related to the use of visual aids. The Russian textbook is replete with upbeat Soviet-era images, whereas the Ukrainian

Table 6.1 Textbook analysis: a summary

	No. of pages	No. of pictures	No. of documents
Theme 1 Formation of the Soviet Union			
Russia	12	3	0
Ukraine	10	1	4
Theme 2 Dissolution of the Soviet Union			
Russia	11	1	2
Ukraine	18	3	3
Theme 3 World War II			
Russia	65	25	8
Ukraine	69	17	24
Theme 4 Holodomor in Ukraine, 1932–33			
Russia	2 (10)	1 (7)	0
Ukraine	10	2	5

Sources: Turchenko et al. 2001; Zagladin et al. 2006.

textbook sparingly uses photographs to supplement the text. Furthermore, the Russian textbook rarely introduces students to primary sources, while the Ukrainian textbook stimulates students' thinking about historical events by placing excerpts from two or three original historical documents at the end of each chapter. The remainder of this chapter discusses these cross-textbook differences in greater depth.

Inclusion and omission in history textbooks

A critical task for historians is to decide what to include and what to omit in a summary of national history. In writing school textbooks, historians face an additional challenge. Since each course is allotted a limited amount of time, textbook writers need to exercise their judgment in identifying key points in national history and compressing volumes of historical documents and archival material into an easy-to-read format. This section examines how two teams of historians – Zagladin *et al.* and Turchenko *et al.* – approached the task of recounting Soviet history.

The formation of the Soviet Union

On 30 December 1922, the first Congress of Soviets (councils) composed of delegates from the Russian Federation, the Ukrainian Soviet Socialist Republic, the Belarussian Soviet Socialist Republic, and the Transcaucasus Federation ratified a treaty providing the legal basis for the establishment of the Soviet Union. In Soviet historiography, this event was celebrated as a voluntary union of different nationalities under the leadership of the Communist Party. Since 1991, however, the former Soviet republics, with the notable exception of Russia, have substantially revised official accounts of what had happened in the early 1920s and exposed the magnitude of popular opposition to integration into the USSR. Yet the Russian government continues to cling to the Soviet historical myth of Slavic unity within one state. Reflecting this trend, the selected textbooks cover the formation of the Soviet Union from different vantage points. The Russian textbook places emphasis on the legality of the union and its international recognition, whereas the Ukrainian textbook unveils the discriminatory policies of the central government toward the Ukrainian Soviet Socialist Republic (Ukrainian SSR) from the very inception of the Soviet state.

The coverage of this historical event in the Russian textbook reflects the persistence of Soviet historical myths in contemporary Russia. In the spirit of Soviet historiography, the USSR is described as a voluntary union of sovereign and equal republics. Like Soviet textbooks, the Russian one emphasizes the leadership role of ethnic Russians in building a multiethnic communist state. Russian students are taught that the Soviet Socialist Republics were formed "on the outskirts of the former Russian empire," implying the peripheral position of non-Russians in Soviet politics. Furthermore, Zagladin et al. (2006) justify the installment of the centralized state by emphasizing the benefits of center–periphery coordination in Soviet policymaking. Clearly, the textbook eschews the discussion of how non-Russians in the former Soviet republics opposed the concentration of all political and economic power in Moscow.

Instead, the Russian textbook devotes considerable attention to the Soviet struggle for international recognition and disparages subversive action by the Western powers. More specifically, Zagladin et al. (2006) suggest that a few Western European states were reluctant to recognize the legitimacy of the Soviet Union because of the righteous engagement of the communist state in an anti-colonial crusade. Another enemy of the Soviet Union identified in the textbook is the "white" émigré. The Russian historians describe how former aristocrats lived in dreadful conditions and took blue-collar jobs in the West, but never missed an opportunity to foment anti-Soviet sentiments in the host societies. In contrast, Lenin is praised for normalizing relations with bourgeois states without abandoning his commitment to the global spread of communism. The Russian textbook discusses at length the proceedings of international conferences that strengthened the position of the Soviet Union in the world.

The Ukrainian textbook offers a more gruesome account of the Soviet inception. A central message that the Ukrainian textbook delivers is that the Ukrainian SSR existed as a pseudo-state. Through various examples, Turchenko et al. (2001) meticulously trace Moscow-led processes of centralization at the expense of Ukraine's diminishing sovereignty. Another key message spelt out in the Ukrainian textbook is that the communist system was alien to Ukrainians. The textbook suggests that non-Ukrainians were responsible for imposing communist rule in Ukraine. According to some estimates, ethnic Ukrainians comprised less than one quarter of the membership of the Ukrainian Bolshevik Party (Turchenko et al. 2001: 238). Furthermore, the textbook points out that those members of the Ukrainian Bolshevik Party who criticized Russia's heavy-handed interference in Ukrainian affairs were swiftly removed from government positions. The discussion of the early Soviet period concludes by drawing an unflattering parallel between the Russian empire and the Soviet Union. The textbook cites an excerpt from an article by Mykhaylo Volobuev, an economist and a prominent member of the Ukrainian Bolshevik Party, who argued that Ukraine was an economically dependent colony of the Russian empire, and the Ukrainian SSR remained an economic colony of Russia within the revamped framework of the Soviet Union (Turchenko et al. 2001: 244). Overall, the Ukrainian textbook advances the idea that Ukraine's integration into the Soviet Union posed an obstacle to the country's political, economic, and cultural development for decades to come.

The dissolution of the Soviet Union

The Russian and Ukrainian textbooks offer divergent accounts of the Soviet demise. The Russian textbook shifts the blame for the disintegration of the Soviet Union on softliners within the Communist Party and scolds them for insufficient attention to "extremists" and inadequate reaction to nationalist mobilization in the former Soviet republics. In contrast, the Ukrainian textbook celebrates the struggle for Ukraine's independence and hails the Soviet breakdown as a renewed opportunity to build a sovereign state.

In their narrative of the Soviet demise, Zagladin et al. (2006) cannot ignore the rise of ethnic mobilization in the former Soviet republics, but they try to marginalize popular demands for liberation from the Soviet rule. The textbook treatment of Zheltoqsan, a popular uprising in Kazakhstan, is a vivid example of the gross misrepresentation of ethnic mobilization in the former Soviet republics. "Zheltoqsan" is a Kazakh word for December. In December 1986, thousands of young people protested against the replacement of Dinmukhammed Qunaev, leader of the Kazakh Soviet Socialist Republic, with Gennady Kolbin, an ethnic Russian without any personal or professional connection to the Central Asian republic (Pannier 2006). On the orders of the Soviet leadership, the Soviet military violently suppressed the protest. According to official Soviet statistics, 369 people were hospitalized with injuries, 600 protesters were arrested, and 99 of them were convicted (Helsinki Watch Committee 1990). The government's response was disproportionate to the citizens' action. A school teacher, for example, was sentenced to five years in a labor camp for just making leaflets. The Russian textbook summarizes this three-day protest event in one sentence and describes it as a "serious clash between Russian youth and youth of the titular nation" (Zagladin et al. 2006: 398). Furthermore, the Russian textbook refers to peaceful protests against the communist regime in Baku

(Azerbaijan, January 1990), Vilnius (Lithuania, January 1991), and Riga (Latvia, January 1991) as "violent clashes" between the Soviet military and supporters of independence.[3] In doing so, the Russian historians deflate the use of political violence by the Soviet leadership during the early 1990s.

Another recurrent theme in the Russian discussion of the Soviet demise is criticism of inadequate political measures to halt the mobilization of "marginal elements" in the former Soviet republics. The textbook repeatedly says that leaders of the Communist Party made a delayed response to "extremists" in the provinces. Furthermore, the textbook suggests that the Communist Party employed ineffective measures to deter further ethnic mobilization. Implicit in this text is the alleged absence of a "strong man" during a critical period in Soviet history. The Russian historians deplore a split within the Communist Party into hard-liners and soft-liners. Russian students are carefully brought to the belief that the presence of a more effective Soviet leadership could have kept the former Soviet republics together.

A major conclusion that the Russian textbook tries to draw is that the Soviet Union could have been preserved in a revamped form. To back up this claim, the textbook details how both the masses and the elite supported the idea of preserving the Soviet Union. The textbook cites the results of the referendum held in March 1991 to illustrate the extent of popular backing for the survival of the Soviet Union. Moreover, the textbook points out that Mikhail Gorbachev worked upon a new union treaty to set up a confederation of sovereign states. In an unprecedented move, the Soviet leader was prepared to make concessions and allow the Baltic states an exit from the Soviet Union. Russian students get the idea that the Communist Party showed some flexibility in the face of the looming political disaster.

In the Russian textbook, Ukraine is explicitly blamed for thwarting Gorbachev's plan to salvage the Soviet Union. The textbook indicates that Ukraine "harshly objected" to the new union treaty. According to Zagladin *et al.* (2006, italics added), "the process of *abrupt disintegration* of the USSR" began after Kravchuk announced Ukraine's exit from the 1922 treaty. Indeed, Ukraine's proclamation of independence delivered a devastating blow to the viability of the proposed Soviet confederation, since it shattered a Soviet myth of eternal brotherly love between Russia and Ukraine. Still, Ukraine was not alone in its lack of enthusiasm for the preservation of the Soviet Union. By December 1991, all the former Soviet republics proclaimed national independence, so piling up all the blame on the neighboring state reveals a bias in Russian foreign policy. In light of Gorbachev's political fiasco, the Russian textbook tries to end the chapter on an optimistic note by emphasizing the creation of the Commonwealth of Independent States as a continuation of close ties between the former Soviet republics.

The Ukrainian textbook provides another perspective on ethnic mobilization in the Soviet Union. In particular, the textbook supplies numerous examples of the growing popular demand for national independence. The Ukrainian historians report that Rukh, the Popular Movement of Ukraine, gained one third of seats in the Supreme Soviet of Ukrainian SSR during the first multiparty parliamentary election in March 1990. Another manifestation of popular demand for independence is the student hunger strike in October 1990. The textbook mentions that student protest in Kyiv's main square led to the resignation of Vitaly Masol, chairman of the Council of Ministers in Soviet Ukraine. In addition, the textbook debunks the myth that the drive for independence was limited to a handful of individuals from western Ukraine. To illustrate the growth of national unity, the textbook describes the formation of a human chain in 1990 between Lviv and Kyiv to mark the union of the Ukrainian National Republic and the Western Ukrainian National Republic in January 1919. Overall, Ukrainian students are brought to the belief that there were irreparable cracks in the edifice of the Soviet state. Unlike the Russian historians, Ukrainian ones conclude that the process of political liberalization and the popular drive for sovereignty were irreversible.

World War II

Without doubt, World War II is a monumental event in Soviet history. The international conflict had a devastating impact on the Soviet population. Estimates suggest that more than 27 million Soviet citizens perished during the war (Elman and Maksudov 1994). Almost every family in Russia and Ukraine has a relative who fought against the Nazis, so Victory Day (9 May) strikes a personal chord with millions of post-Soviet citizens. Likewise, West European states and their allies annually honor World War II veterans. Given the salience of World War II in world history, the Communist Party framed Soviet victory over Nazi Germany as an irrevocable testament to the moral superiority of the communist system. At the height of the Cold War, Soviet historiography extolled the self-sacrificing behavior of the Soviet people and the leadership role of the Communist Party during World War II, while Soviet politicians criticized the belated response of the West to the threat of Nazism. In the post-Soviet period, the commemoration of World War II remains an important venue for cultivating a sense of patriotism among citizens. Yet Russian and Ukrainian textbooks espouse different perspectives on World War II events. More specifically, historians in Russia and Ukraine disagree about the expansion of the Soviet Union through the Molotov–Ribbentrop Pact, the political acumen of Stalin, and the role of the Red Army and OUN–UPA in Soviet history.

An immediate cross-country difference in the coverage of World War II events is the demarcation of the war period. Part IV of the Russian textbook, comprising five chapters, is titled "The Great Patriotic War, 1941–1945." A broad overview of events preceding Germany's attack on Soviet soil is laid out in the last two chapters of Part III dealing with the Soviet Union in the 1920s to 1930s. In contrast, the Ukrainian textbook singles out the participation of Ukrainians in World War II, 1939–45. In fact, the Ukrainian historians suggest that "a majority of Soviet citizens" (not everybody!) perceived fighting against the Nazis as the Great Patriotic War (Turchenko *et al.* 2001: 13).

The Russian textbook divides the Great Patriotic War into three periods: (1) June 1941–November 1942, (2) November 1942–December 1943, and (3) December 1943–1945. The first period begins with Germany's attack on the Soviet Union on 22 June 1941 and deals with the military defeats of the Red Army. The battle of Stalingrad in November 1942 symbolizes a turning point in the Great Patriotic War, representing the first large-scale defeat of Nazi troops. The third period of the war covers the liberation of the Soviet Union from the Nazis. The last chapter concludes by pointing out the strengthened international standing of the Soviet Union in the aftermath of Soviet victory over Nazism.

Consistent with the country's master narrative, the Ukrainian textbook has a double burden of describing resistance to Nazism and communism. Accordingly, the Ukrainian textbook alternates between accounts of Nazi violence and narratives of Soviet occupation. The discussion of World War II begins with the forceful inclusion of western Ukraine into the USSR in 1939 and the violent imposition of Soviet rule. The next two chapters portray Germany's attack on the Soviet Union and the Nazi occupation of Ukraine. Subsequently, the Ukrainian historians elaborate upon the history of two resistance movements: Soviet partisans and OUN-UPA fighters. Upon pinpointing the defeat of Nazi Germany, the textbook shifts the focus of attention to the consolidation of the communist system on the territory of contemporary Ukraine. The Ukrainian textbook concludes by arguing that citizens' participation in World War II was a "milestone on the historical path of Ukrainians" toward national independence (Turchenko *et al.* 2001: 77).

Another point of difference between the two textbooks is the coverage of the Nazi–Soviet non-aggression pact, also known as the Molotov–Ribbentrop pact, signed on 23 August 1939. In Soviet historiography, any reference to the pact was banned, since the Communist Party framed the war as a battle of good (the USSR) against evil (Nazism). Public knowledge about secret negotiations between the two states would undermine the Soviet image as a champion of international peace. In the post-Soviet period, Russian textbooks began to divulge information about the pact and, in particular, the secret protocol spelling out the division of Eastern Europe between Nazi Germany and the Soviet Union. Yet Zagladin's textbook provides a rationale for striking a deal with the Nazis. Zagladin *et al.* (2006: 209) reassure high-school students that the Soviet Union had "no other choice," given the lukewarm reaction of France and the United Kingdom to the idea of signing a treaty on collective security with the USSR. In Stalin's defense, the textbook cites an excerpt from the memoirs of Winston Churchill, then British prime minister. Churchill wrote, "Even if its [Russia's] policy was cold-blooded, it was, to a large degree, realistic" (Zagladin *et al.* 2006: 209). Coming from another perspective, the Ukrainian textbook condemns the pact. Turchenko *et al.* (2006: 5) posit that the secret pact "exposed the imperial essence of both states and their leaders' cynical neglect of international principles accepted in the civilized world." Ukrainian students are brought to the conclusion that Stalin's deal with Hitler paved the way for the start of World War II, thus questioning the political acumen of the Soviet leader.

Furthermore, a glaring difference between the textbooks concerns the discussion of how Soviet rule was established on the newly occupied Soviet lands. The Russian textbook asserts that "Soviet diplomacy" coerced Estonia, Latvia, and Lithuania into signing treaties about cooperation with the USSR, which led to the establishment of Soviet military bases in the Baltic region (Zagladin et al. 2006: 212). By the same token, the Russian textbook is silent about the resistance of western Ukrainians to the imposition of Soviet rule. Yet the Russian historians claim that Finland put up the strongest resistance to the Red Army during the war period. Unlike the Baltic states and Ukraine, Finland has never been a part of the Soviet Union, so the account of Finnish opposition does not clash with the Soviet myth of voluntary entry into the USSR.

In contrast, before turning to the analysis of Germany's aggression toward the Ukrainian SSR, the Ukrainian textbook devotes considerable attention to the ruthless imposition of the communist system in Halychyna, Volyn, and Bukovina. The Ukrainian historians explain why the local population who initially greeted the Red Army with flowers quickly turned against it. High-school students learn that the NKVD, the Russian abbreviation for People's Commissariat for Internal Affairs, the KGB's predecessor, orchestrated massive purges of local intelligentsia, merchants, peasants, and priests. In the course of several months, thousands of people were put on freight cars and sent to labor camps in Siberia and the Far East. In addition, the Communist Party staged some show trials. For example, the textbook brings up a trial of 59 OUN members, held in Lviv in January 1941, which resulted in death sentences for 42 members, including 11 young women. The exposure of NKVD atrocities in the region helps students understand why OUN–UPA staged resistance to the communist regime.

Turchenko et al. (2001) try to strike a delicate political balance by covering two resistance movements on the territory of contemporary Ukraine. On the one hand, the textbook narrates how Soviet partisans undermined the power of the Nazis in the occupied territories. On the other, the textbook depicts how OUN–UPA combatants staged guerilla warfare against Bolshevism and, later, Nazism. In the past, Soviet historiography sketched a lopsided overview of guerilla warfare and branded OUN–UPA members as traitors. By confronting the controversial role of OUN–UPA during World War II, the Ukrainian textbook tries to emphasize the idea of a grassroots struggle for independence even under the worst possible conditions. The Ukrainian textbook indicates that Communist propaganda sabotaged OUN efforts to establish cooperation with Soviet partisans and fueled confrontation between the two resistance movements. What is largely missing in the Ukrainian textbook is an open discussion of Jewish–Ukrainian relations during World War II.

While emphasizing the fate of ethnic Russians and ethnic Ukrainians, both school textbooks devote little attention to the Holocaust. The Russian textbook writers obscure the magnitude of the genocide in the USSR (Lokshin 2008). The selected Russian textbook contains just one sentence, stating that the Holocaust took the lives of 7 million Jews (Zagladin *et al.* 2006: 261). But the textbook fails to specify the implications of the Holocaust for the large Jewish population in the Soviet Union. Some Russian eleventh graders might be left with the impression that the Holocaust occurred only in Europe. The Ukrainian textbook at least touches upon the national relevance of the Holocaust. The school textbook reports that large-scale massacres of Jews occurred in Ukrainian cities, specifying that 850,000 Jews were killed during the first three months of the Nazi occupation (Turchenko *et al.* 2001: 22). In particular, the Ukrainian textbook brings up the mass executions of Jews in Babiy Yar, a 1.5-mile-long and 164-foot-deep ravine in Kyiv (see Lower 2007). But the textbook fails to address the issue of anti-Semitism in Ukrainian society. More broadly, both Russian and Ukrainian textbooks fail to unravel the narratives of various ethnic minorities during World War II.

Turning to the Soviet leadership, Stalin's contribution to Soviet military victory is a point of contention in the selected textbooks. Soviet historiography praised Stalin as a skilled politician and a shrewd commander-in-chief. Given international criticism of Stalin's repressive policies, the Russian textbook admits the soiled reputation of Stalin, but still pays tribute to his leadership qualities. According to Zagladin *et al.* (2006: 259), the effective performance of the Soviet government during the World War II period derived "not only from well-thought-out state propaganda and ruthless repressions, but also citizens' trust in their leaders and, above all, Stalin." The Ukrainian textbook, on the contrary, gives Stalin little credit for Soviet victory in World War II. The Ukrainian historians criticize the Soviet leader for his reluctance to launch early preparations against the Nazi aggression and his failure to prevent excessive human casualties. Touching upon a taboo topic in Soviet historiography, the Ukrainian textbook reveals lack of adequate military training and dearth of weapons in the Red Army, causing a great numbers of deaths among young conscripts.

In the spirit of Soviet historiography, the Russian textbook emphasizes the importance of patriotism in ensuring Soviet victory. Zagladin *et al.* (2006: 227) point out that "an upsurge in patriotism swept the country" during the Great Patriotic War. The textbook is replete with examples of personal sacrifices on the battlefield and in the Soviet rear. Furthermore, the Russian textbook demonstrates how popular culture reflected the spirit of the day. The textbook quotes a few lines from the famous Soviet song "The Sacred War" by Vasiliy Lebedev-Kumach, "Rise up, the great country! Rise up to fight until death. With the fascist dark force. With the cursed horde."

Rather than dwelling upon Russian-dominated Soviet culture, the Ukrainian textbook illuminates the development of Ukrainian culture during the World War II period. Ukrainian students learn that the communist drive for mass mobilization triggered a temporary shift in Soviet cultural policy. The textbook indicates that the Communist Party allowed several

Ukrainian writers, previously arrested for popularizing Ukrainian culture, to put their artistic skills to use and foster love of the homeland among Soviet soldiers. For example, students are reminded that the Ukrainian poet Volodymyr Sosiura wrote the well-known poem "Love Ukraine" in 1944. Sosiura turned to his compatriots with the following words, "Love Ukraine with all of your heart and all of the deeds that you perform."

In sum, Russian and Ukrainian textbooks provide different interpretations of Soviet history during World War II. In keeping with Soviet historiography, the Russian textbook stresses unity and patriotism of Soviet people. The Ukrainian textbook, on the other hand, tries to place Ukrainian participation in World War II in a broader historical narrative of the struggle for national independence.

The Holodomor in Ukraine

As mentioned earlier, the Holodomor has become a contentious issue in Russian–Ukrainian relations. The Russian government denies Soviet targeting of ethnic Ukrainians during the massive famine in the 1930s, while the Ukrainian government regards the Holodomor as genocide against Ukrainians. The textbooks reflect divergent official positions on this issue.

The Russian textbook puts a positive spin on Stalin's economic policies and glosses over the human costs of collectivization. The chapter's title itself – "Modernization of the economy and the defense system in the 1930s. Cultural revolution" – introduces the topic in a rather positive way. The textbook describes in detail the accomplishments of Soviet industrialization, whereas references to the hardships of the rural population are hidden in the middle of the chapter. The authors briefly mention the law of five sheaves, setting out a legal basis for criminal charges against starving peasants who took just a few sheaves off the harvested fields. Furthermore, the textbook includes only one paragraph about the famine.

The Russian historians deny ethnic targeting during the famine of 1932–33. The textbook points out that the famine broke out in many parts of Ukraine, Kuban', and the Volga region, causing the deaths of somewhere between 3 million and 15 million people. Zagladin *et al.* (2006) acknowledge that the Soviet media were banned from covering the famine, but the textbook fails to discuss the role of the central government in masterminding the starvation of peasants in wheat-producing regions.

The Russian textbook further downplays the magnitude of the famine by swiftly turning to the discussion of "gradual stabilization" in rural areas. Russian students are brought to the belief that the harsh methods of collectivization were justified, since the living standards of Soviet citizens improved afterwards. In particular, the textbook highlights the positive effects of rapid industrialization on the lives of rural youth. Recalling Soviet-era propaganda, Zagladin *et al.* (2006: 173, italics added) claim that young people from rural areas "were *genuinely grateful* to the Soviet authorities [for the opportunity to move from villages into cities] and displayed *authentic enthusiasm*" about participation in state-initiated industrialization projects.

One might be led to believe that the Ukrainian textbook describes an entirely different country. The Ukrainian historians accord considerable attention to the analysis of the famine's causes and consequences. The textbook thoroughly documents the unbearable living conditions of Ukrainian peasants in 1932–33. In defiance of Soviet historiography, Ukrainian historians seek to expose the crass contradiction between Soviet propaganda and the socioeconomic situation in the villages. Turchenko *et al.* (2001: 297) point out that Stalin made assertions about substantial improvements in the well-being of Soviet peasants in January 1933, while thousands of people were dying of starvation in Ukrainian villages at that time.

Among other things, the Ukrainian textbook suggests that non-ethnic Ukrainians played an active role in decimating the Ukrainian peasantry. For example, Ukrainian students learn that Stalin appointed Pavel Postyshev, an ethnic Russian, to the post of Second Secretary of the Central Committee of the Communist Party of Ukraine and charged him with supervising the implementation of collectivization policies in the Ukrainian SSR. Turchenko *et al.* (2001: 296) report that Postyshev orchestrated purges of the Communist Party of Ukraine: more than 100,000 Ukrainian Bolsheviks were expelled from the party and either killed or sent in exile. These purges weakened local opposition to famine-inducing state policies.

One of the consequences of the Holodomor identified in the Ukrainian textbook is the influx of ethnic Russians into the Ukrainian SSR. Students learn that more than 117,000 ethnic Russians had moved to Dnipropetrovsk, Donetsk, Kharkiv, and Odesa oblasts by the end of 1933. The textbook suggests that newcomers settled in the regions decimated by the famine and compliantly carried out Soviet policies of collectivization.

Pictorial analysis

The analysis of visual aids reaffirms the presence of cross-country differences in teaching Soviet history. Table 6.2 presents a list of photographs that accompany the coverage of historical events in the selected textbooks. Clearly, the use of visual aids is more extensive in the Russian textbook than in the Ukrainian one. Beyond variations in sheer numbers, there are detectable differences in the content of messages that visual aids try to deliver. The substance of these differences is briefly discussed in the following paragraphs.

Consistent with the textual emphasis on the international recognition of the Soviet Union, visual images in the Russian textbook reinforce the perception of the country's high international standing. The first photograph pertinent to the formation of the Soviet Union portrays Lenin during the First Congress of the Comintern in 1919. Another photograph is a portrait of Georgiy Chicherin, Commissar for Foreign Relations in the USSR. The third image depicts Soviet diplomats at the international conference in Genoa.

Table 6.2 Pictorial analysis

Russia	Ukraine
Theme 1 Formation of the Soviet Union	
1 Lenin at the First Congress of the Comintern, 1919	1 Portrait of Oleksandr Shumskiy
2 History in faces: Georgiy Chicherin	
3 Diplomats at the conference in Genoa, 1922	
Theme 2 Dissolution of the Soviet Union	
1 Yeltsin, Kravchuk, and Shushkevich signing the Belovezhsk treaty	1 Human chain between Kyiv and Lviv, 21 January 1990
	2 "Better die than live in the USSR," October 1990
	3 Raising the blue and yellow flag above the parliament building
Theme 3 World War II	
1 Arrival of Soviet tank drivers in Spain	1 The map of divided Poland signed by Stalin and Ribbentrop
2 Top Soviet military personnel in Mongolia	2 Deputies to the National Assembly of Western Ukraine, 1939
3 Molotov signing the pact with Germany	3 Portrait of Mykhailo Kirponos
4 Clash during the Soviet–Finnish War	4 Ukraine during WWII
5 Ural machine-building factory	5 A Nazi public announcement
6 History in faces: Georgiy Zhukov	6 Partisans
7 T-34 tank	7 Portrait of Stepan Bandera
8 Yak-1 fighter aircraft	8 Portrait of Yaroslav Stetsko
9 The Nazi air strike on 22 June 1941	9 Greeting the liberators in Kharkiv
10 Face of the war (crying child)	10 Kyiv Offence Operation
11 Draftees, Moscow	11 On the liberated territory
12 Pilot at the helm	12 On the working front
13 The destroyed cathedral	13 The oath of OUN fighter
14 Helping the wounded	14 Portrait of V Kubiovych
15 Stalingrad, 1942	15 Portrait of Josip Slipyi
16 Teenage workers at a military plant	16 Berlin, spring 1945
17 Soviet tank drivers before the battle	17 The reconstruction of DniproHES
18 Radio news from the front	
19 The border signpost near the Soviet–Romanian border, March 1944	
20 Soviet soldiers fighting for Budapest	
21 Fireworks to celebrate the hoisting of the Soviet flag over the defeated Reichstag	
22 Zhukov signs an act marking the capitulation of Germany	
23 Victorious Soviet soldiers return home	
24 The eternal flame near the Kremlin wall	
25 A group portrait of Konev, Zhukov, et al.	
Theme 4 Holodomor in Ukraine, 1932–33	
1 Dinner in the field, 1934	1 The hard-earned bread, 1932
	2 The first tractor station in Ukraine, 1929

Sources: Turchenko et al. 2001; Zagladin et al. 2006.

The underlying message of these visual aids is that the USSR since its inception has won international recognition. Similarly, the depiction of the Soviet demise tries to emphasize the accomplishments of Russia's foreign policy by highlighting the formation of the Commonwealth of Independent States. The chapter on Soviet disintegration ends with the image of three former Soviet leaders – Borys Yeltsin, Leonid Kravchuk, and Stanislav Shushkevych – pledging their commitment to close cooperation between three Slavic states. In this way, the Russian historians attempt to shift the focus of attention from nationalist mobilization to Slavic unity during the early 1990s.

In contrast, the choice of visual images in the Ukrainian textbook reflects a focus on the internal dynamics of Ukrainian society in the 1920s and the 1990s. In the chapter on the formation of the USSR, the Ukrainian textbook underscores the opposition of Ukrainians to the concentration of power in Moscow by inserting a portrait of Oleksandr Shumskiy, Commissar for Education in the Ukrainian SSR. In a letter to Stalin, Shumskiy dared to criticize Soviet cadre policies – the appointment of non-Ukrainians to key government positions – and warn about the diminishing appeal of Bolshevism in the republic. In a similar vein, images of the early 1990s reflect the opposition of Ukrainians to the communist system. One of the photographs portrays a political event symbolizing Ukrainian unity: a human chain between Lviv and Kyiv formed on 21 January 1990 to mark the union of the Western Ukrainian National Republic and the Ukrainian National Republic in 1919. Another political symbol presented in the textbook is the blue-and-yellow flag, which was banned in the Soviet Union and raised above the parliamentary building on 4 September 1991. Yet the tent city with the poster "Better die than live in the Soviet Union" is the most telling image of Ukrainian opposition to communism. The picture portrays Ukrainian students who risked their lives by demanding political liberalization in Soviet Ukraine. Overall, the visual aids reinforce the idea that the communist system was alien to Ukrainian society.

Turning to the World War II period, the Russian depiction of the Great Patriotic War draws heavily upon Soviet imagery. Soviet textbooks were filled with images of Soviet soldiers who displayed extraordinary patriotism in defending the homeland and liberating Europe from the Nazis. Likewise, the imagery in the Russian textbook emphasizes the idea of patriotism. Strikingly, one of the photographs suggests that love of Stalin was a source of inspiration for Soviet soldiers. In keeping with Soviet historiography, Zagladin *et al.* (2006) include in the textbook a photograph of a Soviet pilot who kept a picture of Stalin in his cabin. Furthermore, a series of photographs reminds young readers that Soviet soldiers played a prominent part in the international arena and fought in Finland, Hungary, Mongolia, Romania, and Spain. Overall, most photographs from the selected textbook seem to recreate an atmosphere of unparalleled heroism and patriotism under Soviet leadership.

Compared to the Russian textbook, the Ukrainian one pays less tribute to Soviet soldiers and integrates images of OUN–UPA in the portrayal of

World War II. In defiance of Soviet historiography, the Ukrainian textbook contains portraits of such OUN leaders as Stepan Bandera and Yaroslav Stetsko.

The most startling cross-country difference emerges in the textbooks' treatment of the Holodomor. The Russian chapter on industrialization and modernization of the economy creates a string of positive images, portraying peasants reading their first book, a Bolshevik leader watching a new line of tractors at a factory, and Aleksey Stakhanov working in a coal-mine. The very page that contains references to the law of five sheaves has a bucolic image of relaxed peasants eating dinner on the meadow. Like Soviet historians, Zagladin *et al.* (2006) carefully select images to emphasize the positive effects of rapid industrialization and collectivization. The Ukrainian historians, however, expose the harsh reality of hard labor and starvation in the villages. The chapter on the Holodomor contains an image of an exhausted peasant toiling on the land.

In sum, the analysis of visual aids further confirms differences in the coverage of Soviet history. In the Russian textbook, visual images tend to highlight the international standing of the Soviet Union and mute shortcomings of the communist system. In contrast, the Ukrainian textbook weaves visual images into the narrative of the Ukrainian struggle for national independence and portrays the brutality of the communist regime. Analysis of primary documents will shed more light on cross-textbook differences.

Documentary analysis

The inclusion of primary documents in school textbooks is an important pedagogical tool for stimulating students' critical thinking. Students can develop their analytical skills by reflecting upon the content of historical documents and evaluating the significance of historical events. But Russian students appear to have less exposure to archival material than their Ukrainian peers. Table 6.3 displays a list of primary documents included in the selected textbooks. The cross-textbook comparison indicates that the Russian textbook includes fewer historical documents than the Ukrainian one. Contentwise, empirical analysis supports the argument that the Russian and Ukrainian textbooks construct different versions of Soviet history.

While Zagladin *et al.* (2006) avoid the use of original documents concerning the formation of the USSR, the Ukrainian textbook writers use historical documents as evidence of Ukrainian opposition to the communist state during its embryonic stage. The Ukrainian textbook, for example, includes a half-page excerpt from Volobuev's article published in the newspaper *Ukrainian Bolshevik* in 1928. The article supplies a list of measures proposed by Volobuev to halt the takeover of the Ukrainian economy by the Moscow-based central government. Subsequently, in the assignments section, students are prompted to explain why the Communist Party of the Soviet Union criticized Volobuev's perspective on Ukraine's economic development.

Similarly, the choice of historical documents regarding the dissolution of the Soviet Union reflects differences in the construction of national history. Both Russian and Ukrainian textbooks cite excerpts from the respective Declarations of National Sovereignty. Other historical documents included in the Ukrainian textbook also highlight the breakdown of the communist state. For example, Turchenko *et al.* (2001) present Rukh's statement calling upon citizens to put up resistance to the 1991 coup of communist hard-liners and wage a struggle for Ukraine's independence. The Russian textbook, in contrast, places more emphasis on the treaty proclaiming the formation of the Commonwealth of Independent States.

The coverage of World War II further reveals differences in the use of archival material. The Ukrainian textbook contains three times more historical documents on World War II than the Russian textbook. While Zagladin *et al.* (2006) select testimonies from top Soviet and Nazi military to emphasize the achievements of the Red Army, the Ukrainian historians provide a wider range of perspectives on the course of the war. In particular, the citation of some archival material reveals the ruthless implementation of the Soviet military draft. Assessing the impact of the Red Army on the demographic situation in Kharkiv, a Nazi officer reports that the Red Army drafted 15,000 men aged 15–40 and sent them to the frontline without any military training; 5,000 young women were taken to be trained as intelligence officers. Another document suggests the warm reception of the Nazis by Ukrainians and Belarussians in August 1941, a taboo topic in Soviet historiography.

Furthermore, a quarter of the documents in the Ukrainian textbook are devoted to the participation of OUN–UPA in World War II. Turchenko *et al.* seek to demonstrate that OUN–UPA members advocated Ukraine's independence and mobilized the local population to fight against communism. Ukrainian students have an opportunity to read a leaflet entitled "What UPA is fighting for." The inclusion of another historical document – an OUN memorandum to the Third Reich – points to the uneasy collaboration of OUN–UPA members with the Nazis against the common enemy, the communists. Yet the Ukrainian textbook dispels the notion of continuous partnership between OUN–UPA and the Nazis. Turchenko *et al.* (2001: 33) present an excerpt from an SD (Nazi security and intelligence) order of November 1941 to arrest and secretly execute OUN members for plotting the establishment of an independent Ukraine. Furthermore, the Ukrainian textbook prompts students to compare the texts of oaths of UPA fighters and Soviet partisans to identify similarities and differences among guerilla fighters. The Ukrainian textbook seeks to emphasize that both OUN–UPA fighters and Soviet partisans fought for Ukraine, but the reconciliation of veterans from the two resistance movements is unattainable in contemporary Ukraine.

Turning to the coverage of the Holodomor, the Ukrainian textbook incorporates several historical documents to back up the national historical narrative. Ukrainian students vicariously experience the horrors of the

Table 6.3 Documentary analysis

Russia	Ukraine
Theme 1 Formation of the Soviet Union	
N/A	1 Excerpt from the treaty between Russian Federation and Ukrainian SSR
	2 Speech by Mykola Skrypnyk
	3 Speech by K Rakovsky
	4 Article by Mykhailo Volobuev
Theme 2 Dissolution of the Soviet Union	
1 Declaration of sovereignty, 12 June 1990	1 Declaration of sovereignty, 16 July 1990
2 Statement of the heads of state of Russia, Belarus, and Ukraine, 8 December 1991	2 Secret telegram of the Secretariat of the Central Committee of the Communist Party of Ukraine, 19 August 1991
	3 Statement of the Popular Movement of Ukraine
Theme 3 World War II	
1 Winston Churchill's speech, 19 May 1939	1 Secret protocol, 23 August 1939
2 Secret protocol	2 Memoirs of G Kitaiskogo
3 Excerpt from Churchill's memoirs	3 Excerpt from the Barbarossa plan
4 Excerpt from Nazi report on the state of the Red Army, 15 January 1941	4 Directive, south-western front
5 Excerpt from memoirs of E Manstein, top Nazi official	5 Telegram about the defense of the right bank, Ukraine, 11 July 1941
6 Excerpt from memoirs of Georgiy Zhukov	6 Excerpt from memoirs of Nikita Khruschev
7 Excerpt from memoirs of K Rokosovsky, Soviet Marshal	7 Excerpt from SS report, 12 August 1941
8 Excerpt from memoirs of E Manstein, top Nazi official	8 Nazi Os plan
	9 Excerpt from the memorandum of OUN-B to the government of the Third Reich

Russia	Ukraine
Theme 3 World War II (continued)	10 Declaration restoring Ukrainian state, 30 June 1941
	11 SD order about the execution of OUN-B members, 25 November 1941
	12 Excerpt from memoirs of I Konev, Soviet Marshal
	13 Report of a Nazi officer, February 1943
	14 V Kondratiev's article on partisans
	15 Leaflet "What UPA is fighting for"
	16 Excerpt from memoirs of A Vasilevskii, Soviet marshal
	17 Material on the deportation of Crimean Tatars
	18 NKVD report on the organization and the results of anti-OUN work, 26 July 1945
	19 Report on flagrant legal violations by the special units, 15 February 1949
	20 Oath of the UPA fighter
	21 Oath of the Soviet partisan
	22 Nazi ruling on education in Zone B (Ukraine), 29 December 1941
	23 Stalin's speech about anti-Leninist errors and nationalist excesses in Oleksandr Dovzhenko's movie *Ukraine on Fire*
	31 January 1944
	24 Excerpt from Dovzhenko's diary
Theme 4 Holodomor in Ukraine, 1932–33	
N/A	1 Excerpts from memoirs of famine witnesses
	2 Statement of the secretary of Vinnitsa oblast Communist Party
	3 Ruling of the Central Committee, 8 November 1932
	4 Excerpt from an article by the Austrian scientist A Wonarburg
	5 Average agricultural output in 1895–1904 and 1933–38

Sources: Turchenko et al. 2001; Zagladin et al. 2006.

famine by reading memoirs of famine survivors. Based upon the recollections of Grigoriy Starostenko, a resident of the Donetsk region, students learn that little children in spring of 1933 ate weeds and lizards to survive. Furthermore, another famine survivor testifies to the incidence of cannibalism during that period. Onysia Nelipa from Cherkasy region recalls that "there was so much sorrow in 1933 that it can't all be written down on the ox skin" (Turchenko et al. 2001: 298). The Ukrainian textbook brings up some research findings testifying to the targeting of ethnic Ukrainians. The Ukrainian historians cite an excerpt from a manuscript by A. Wonarburg, an Austrian scientist, who finds that the famine occurred only in regions densely populated with ethnic Ukrainians, with the exception of Belarus. To contrast social reality with state propaganda, the Ukrainian textbook also includes a statement from I. Livenson, the head of the Communist Party of the Vinnitsa region. In March 1933, Livenson bluntly denied the starvation of peasants and asserted that only lazybones would experience food shortages in the absence of hard work. By the same token, Ukrainian students get to know about Molotov's order to halt the distribution of consumer goods in Ukrainian villages "until collective farms and individual peasants begin to honestly and diligently fulfill their duties before the working class and the Red Army regarding wheat production" (Turchenko et al. 2001: 299). These historical documents confirm the victimization of Ukraine during the Soviet period.

By the same token, the Ukrainian textbook uses historical documents to dispel the Soviet myth about effective agricultural policies under Stalin. In discussing the devastation of Ukrainian villages in the aftermath of the Holodomor, Turchenko et al. (2001) emphasize the ineffectiveness of forced collectivization. At the end of the chapter, high-school students are invited to compare agricultural output in 1895–1904 and 1933–38. It is obvious from the available statistics that output remained the same or even declined in the 1930s, documenting the futility of Soviet agricultural policies.

Conclusion

A comparative analysis of the Russian and the Ukrainian textbooks reveals cross-national differences in the construction of Soviet history and the production of historical memory. The content of the Russian textbook unveils a great deal of continuity with the Soviet official discourse. Like Soviet historians, Zagladin et al. (2006) emphasize the voluntary union of the former Soviet republics, the accidental nature of the Soviet collapse, and the greatness of Soviet leadership during the Great Patriotic War. The Russian textbook seeks to downplay the shortcomings of the communist system and emphasize the international recognition of the Soviet Union. In contrast, the Ukrainian historians significantly revise Soviet-era narratives of the communist period and produce an alternative version of Soviet history. Turchenko et al. (2001) expose the involuntary integration of Ukraine into the Soviet Union, the longstanding struggle for Ukraine's independence, and heroic resistance to both communism and Nazism during World War II. The Ukrainian textbook seeks to unravel the victimization of ethnic Ukrainians during the Soviet period and elucidate mass mobilization for national independence.

It is clear from this analysis that Russian and Ukrainian students acquire different understandings of Soviet history. Not surprisingly, Russian adolescents tend to take more pride in achievements of the Soviet Union, whereas Ukrainian adolescents tend to embrace with greater enthusiasm the demise of the communist state. These differences suggest that different political generations are coming of age in Russia and Ukraine.

7 Growing up, but growing apart

The emergence of the first generation without any firsthand experience with communism is a distinctive feature of contemporary post-Soviet states. Young people born in the post-communist period are on the cusp of becoming voting-age citizens, adding a new dimension to the dynamics of domestic politics. Compared to older generations, post-communist youth is more likely to press for democratic transformations and market reforms. Furthermore, young people are more likely to challenge the authorities and participate in protest events if their rights are violated. Given the political significance of the younger generation, it is important to understand how young citizens view political phenomena and envision their role in society. Yet the study of pre-adults is largely neglected in post-communist literature.

Addressing this oversight, this book has examined the political attitudes of adolescents in three Russian and three Ukrainian cities. While the analysis cannot be generalized to the whole adolescent population, this study provides some insights into the worldview of young citizens in the selected states. A cross-country comparison registers a split within the post-Soviet generation. In particular, Russian and Ukrainian adolescents differ in their attitudes toward the dissolution of the Soviet Union. Furthermore, the analysis finds within-country variations in the political attitudes of adolescents.

The empirical evidence presented in this book supports the argument that political attitudes of Russian and Ukrainian adolescents diverge. The results indicate that high-school students in autocracy-leaning Russia tend to place more trust in the incumbent president than their peers in politically unstable Ukraine. Moreover, adolescents in the core of the Soviet Union (Russia) tend to harbor more Soviet nostalgia than adolescents in the periphery of the USSR (Ukraine). When Ukrainian adolescents endorse the dissolution of the Soviet Union, they are more likely to exhibit a high level of national pride. Most Russian adolescents, on the contrary, do not see a conflict between attachment to the old political community (the Soviet Union) and love of the newly independent state (Russia).

Furthermore, the empirical analysis demonstrates the presence of intra-country attitudinal differences. In Russia, Moscow adolescents appear to be more content with the status quo than those in the provinces. Students from Tula and Rostov-on-the-Don turn out to be more supportive of democracy than their peers from the capital city. The magnitude of regional differences is even more pronounced in Ukraine. Lviv adolescents tend to report greater support for democracy, display more national pride, and regret less the dissolution of the Soviet Union than their compatriots in Donetsk. This empirical evidence points to the formation of two generation units in post-communist Ukraine, with young people in different parts of the country subscribing to opposite political views.

To account for observed attitudinal differences, this study has explored the role of such agents of political socialization as parents, the mass media, and schools. In particular, this book argues that patriotic education contributes to cross-country attitudinal differences. Moreover, the analysis demonstrates that regional cleavages have an impact on the political attitudes of adolescents. This chapter concludes by considering the implications of this research for the survival of non-democracies in the selected states and the development of Russian–Ukrainian relations in the near future.

Sources of attitudinal differences

Adolescents learn about politics from various sources. From childhood onward, young citizens become exposed to politically relevant information at home. As young people go through the educational system, they acquire knowledge of political concepts and national historical narratives. Furthermore, the mass media supplies adolescents with a steady flow of political news. These multiple agents of political socialization leave an imprint on adolescents' political attitudes.

The empirical analysis indicates that parents in the post-Soviet states regularly speak about politics with their children. According to the survey results, approximately one third of Russian adolescents and half of Ukrainian ones daily discuss political issues with their parents. Those adolescents who frequently engage in political conversations with their parents tend to report higher levels of support for democracy. Yet parents' recollections about the Soviet period have divergent effects on adolescents' attitudes toward the Soviet demise. In Russia, the more adolescents speak with parents about politics, the more they disapprove of the dissolution of the Soviet Union. In Ukraine, on the contrary, frequent political conversations with parents are associated with a decline in the level of Soviet nostalgia.

Next, the empirical analysis suggests that the role of the mass media in shaping adolescents' attitudes differs, depending upon the national context and the media type. It appears that the mainstream media tend to present different interpretations of Soviet history in the post-Soviet states. The more Russian adolescents watch national TV channels, the more they regret the dissolution of the Soviet Union. This relationship holds even if one controls for the level of adolescents' trust in the mass media. In contrast, exposure to news on national TV channels is negatively correlated with Soviet nostalgia among Ukrainian adolescents. In addition, the analysis indicates that contemporary adolescents rely more on online publications than offline newspapers to keep track of current events. According to the survey results, those who use the Internet to obtain political news tend to place less trust in the incumbent president than others. This finding supports the argument that the Internet fulfills an important role in non-democracies by providing citizens with a broad spectrum of political news inaccessible via the mainstream media.

Finally, the analysis indicates that a significant proportion of teachers ventures to bring up politics in their interactions with students. Ukrainian teachers from the selected schools appear to devote more time to political discussions with their students than Russian ones. Still, in both countries, student–teacher discussions of current events tend to be associated with greater support for democracy and greater trust in the incumbent president. Furthermore, conversations with Ukrainian teachers tend to foster approval of the Soviet demise, while this trend is largely absent in Russia.

The importance of patriotic education

Patriotic education is vital to promoting a sense of national unity, building a strong state, and advancing democratic reforms. In non-democracies, however, patriotic education can be exploited as a tool for the consolidation of the non-democratic political regime. This study has focused on two cases of hybrid regimes falling somewhere between democracy and dictatorship. Incumbent governments in Russia and Ukraine adopted different approaches to patriotic education. In Russia, President Putin has devoted considerable attention to the patriotic education of young citizens in an effort to solidify his grip on power and secure the regime's survival. President Kuchma of Ukraine, on the contrary, downplayed the importance of patriotic education and focused on the short-term goal of winning elections. These policy choices, in part, contributed to the observed attitudinal differences in Russia and Ukraine.

History teaching can be considered a crucial component of patriotic education. Through the study of national historical narratives, young people are likely to develop a stronger sense of national identity and display greater attachment to the political community. Specifically, the content of history textbooks lays the groundwork for the acquisition of historic knowledge by the younger generation. This study examined two history textbooks to uncover cross-country differences in the construction of national history. Since the interpretation of Soviet history is a major point of contention in Russian–Ukrainian relations, the analysis focused on the textbook coverage of four historic events: (1) the formation of the Soviet Union, (2) the famine of 1932–33, (3) World War II, and (4) the dissolution of the Soviet Union. As expected, Russian and Ukrainian historians presented these events in a different light, fostering cross-country differences in adolescents' attitudes toward the Soviet Union and contemporary political processes.

The empirical inquiry demonstrates that Soviet-era historical myths seep into Zagladin's (2006) account of twentieth-century Russian history. The Russian textbook tends to disregard the failures of the communist system in domestic politics and emphasize the stellar performance of the Soviet Union in the international arena. As a prime example of Soviet superiority, the state-approved version of Soviet history attributes Soviet victory over Nazism to the extraordinary patriotism of ordinary citizens and the shrewd leadership of the Communist Party. Meanwhile, the Russian textbook downplays the negative consequences of forced collectivization and denies the targeting of ethnic Ukrainians during the famine of 1932–33. In addition, Zagladin *et al.* (2006) present ethnic mobilization against communism in the late 1980s as isolated acts of "extremists." Overall, Zagladin's textbook reflects the elite belief that scathing criticism of the communist state is unjustified and inappropriate.

In contrast, the Ukrainian textbook on twentieth-century history treats Nazism and communism as two evils that obstructed Ukraine's path to independence. Turchenko and his colleagues (2001) challenge key tenets of Soviet historiography in several ways. First, the Ukrainian textbook dispels the Soviet myth that the formation of the Soviet Union was a product of the voluntary union of independent states. Second, Ukrainian historians detail how two resistance movements – Soviet partisans and the Organization of Ukrainian Nationalists – waged guerilla fighting during World War II. High-school students learn that some Ukrainians put up resistance to the communist regime well into the 1950s. Third, the Ukrainian textbook devotes considerable attention to the Holodomor. Ukrainian students become aware of the gross disparity between Soviet propaganda about universal prosperity and the staggering starvation in the villages. Finally, Turchenko *et al.* (2001) pay tribute to the mobilization of Ukrainians against communism in the late 1980s and the early 1990s. The textbook, for example, discusses the hunger strike of Ukrainian students in October 1990, known as the Granite Revolution. In sum, the Ukrainian textbook provides a narrative of the nation's struggle for independence and hails the collapse of communism.

The cross-country differences in the textbook coverage of Soviet history contribute to stark variations in adolescents' attitudes toward the dissolution of the Soviet Union. Since state-sanctioned Russian textbooks emphasize the accomplishments of the communist state, it is not surprising that Russian adolescents tend to look upon the demise of the Soviet Union with regret. Ukrainian textbooks, on the contrary, foster positive attitudes toward the dissolution of the communist state by documenting gross human rights violations against ethnic Ukrainians and tracing the long-term struggle for national independence. Outside schools, family, the mass media, and popular culture reinforce attitudinal differences among adolescents in post-Soviet Russia and Ukraine.

The persistence of regional cleavages

The analysis of adolescents' political attitudes in Donetsk and Lviv confirms the salience of regional cleavages in Ukrainian society. Notwithstanding the fact that high-school students in eastern and western parts of the country have grown up during the same period and study national history with the help of the same state-approved textbooks, Donetsk and Lviv adolescents tend to hold divergent views about political processes in the country and interpret Soviet history in different ways. It would appear that the local social context has a strong impact on the formation of political attitudes among young people.

The presence of the east–west regional cleavage can be attributed, in part, to the enduring effects of historical legacies. Specifically, the length of communist rule varies across regions. The Lviv region was incorporated into the Soviet Union almost 20 years later than the Donetsk region. As a result, Ukrainians in the western part of the country lived one generation less under the communist rule and preserved better memories of life before the imposition of communism. Furthermore, Ukrainian politicians frequently fuel existing regional cleavages in the country. Rather than addressing the urgent political and socioeconomic problems that cripple the country's development, many politicians find it convenient to dwell on divisive identity-related issues and shirk accountability for the failures of the national government to deliver public goods.

Implications for the survival of the non-democratic regime

In mature democracies and non-democracies alike, young people tend to be a driving force behind political change. In the 1960s, American students protested against US involvement in the Vietnam War. More recently, many young voters cast their ballot for Barack Obama to bring about change in the way politics is done in Washington, DC. Likewise, it is often youth who summon the courage to challenge the status quo in repressive political regimes. In 1989, Chinese students risked their lives to push for concessions from the Communist Party. Another anti-communist protest turned into a massacre of Azerbaijani students by Soviet troops on 20 January 1990. Since the fall of the Berlin Wall, struggle for political liberalization is far from over in the post-Soviet region. There is a plethora of hybrid regimes falling somewhere between democracy and dictatorship. Under these circumstances, young people can play an important role in swaying the odds of the regime's survival.

On 25 March 2007, the youth group *Nashi* (Ours) organized a rally of more than 15,000 people to celebrate the seventh anniversary of Putin's election as president (Azar 2007a, 2007b). Russian youngsters adorned in white jackets and red baseball hats gathered in downtown Moscow to mobilize support for the incumbent president. Marching along Sakharov Boulevard (named after the famous Soviet dissident Aleksandr Sakharov), young people carried enormous placards embellished with images of the incumbent president and cell phones. The political slogan on the placards read, "The Putin Generation, Forward!" (*Pokolenie Putina, Vpered!*). As a part of the street action, *Nashi* activists stopped pedestrians and asked them to send SMS messages to President Putin. A huge TV screen was installed near the Kremlin to showcase written samples of public sympathy with the beloved politician. Furthermore, *Nashi* activists collected phone numbers of citizens who agreed with the statement that the threat of "the orange-brown plague" was present in Russia. The presence of home-grown anarchists was considered a source of domestic instability, while the "orange plague" concept originated from post-Orange Revolution Ukraine.[1]

In the fall of 2004, thousands of young Ukrainians gathered in Maidan, Kyiv's main square, to protest against electoral fraud and demand political change (Chivers 2004; Mite 2004). Many of them came to the capital city from other regions and stayed in the tent city until the annulment of fraudulent election results in December. Young people weathered harsh winter conditions and overcame the fear of police violence against peaceful protesters. A huge TV screen on Maidan showed field reports by Channel 5, covering protest rallies across the country. Furthermore, the ringing of cell phones was constantly heard in the tent city, as protesters coordinated their actions, disseminated information about happenings in the city, and communicated with friends and relatives. While *Nashi* served the cause of safeguarding the status quo in Russia, the technologically savvy, orange-clad youth were harbingers of change in Ukrainian society.

These two examples of youth mobilization suggest that contemporary youth perceive and respond to authoritarian tendencies in the post-Soviet states in different ways. At least, Russian youth appears to resign itself to the idea of living in a non-democratic political regime. Most young Russians are trying to survive and succeed within the confines of the current regime. In Ukraine, however, young people are more likely to reject Soviet-era methods of social control and challenge authority. Unlike the Putin generation, a large number of young Ukrainians mobilized in the fall of 2004 to defend their right to elect a national leader, delivering a serious blow to the strength of the hybrid regime.

These attitudinal and behavioral differences have some implications for the survival of non-democratic regimes in Russia and Ukraine. Putin's political regime is immune to political change in the foreseeable future. At least, the challenge to the current regime is unlikely to emanate from the entry of the post-Soviet generation onto the political scene. Although opposition political leaders have made numerous attempts to galvanize mass support for political change, a relatively small number of young people participated in anti-government protest events. To date, most young Russians passively observe the consolidation of power in the hands of Putin's close allies. Ukraine's political regime, on the contrary, is vulnerable to political change. Under Kuchma's presidency, hundreds of young people participated in anti-incumbent protests and built a network of citizens concerned about the rise of authoritarian tendencies in the country. Furthermore, like the adult population, young Ukrainians are divided along regional lines, hampering the nationwide acceptance of a political regime. The presence of a divided titular nation slows down any type of political transformation in the country.

Implications for Russian–Ukrainian relations

Over the past several years, Russian–Ukrainian relations have deteriorated.[2] The contestation of Soviet history has become one source of acrimonious exchanges between the incumbent governments in Russia and Ukraine. While Putin praised the alleged accomplishments of the Soviet Union, Yushchenko denounced the communist regime. In particular, Russia's refusal to recognize the Holodomor as genocide against ethnic Ukrainians caused tensions in bilateral relations. In parallel with the debate over Soviet history, the incumbent governments in Russia and Ukraine disagreed over the interpretation of current political developments in the post-Soviet region. The Orange Revolution signifying the loss of the pro-Russian presidential candidate was a wake-up call for Russian policymakers (Torbakov 2004). The Kremlin launched a powerful propaganda machine to discredit the Ukrainian government and condemn Ukraine's drift out of Russia's sphere of influence.

Opinion polls indicate that the Kremlin succeeded in changing public opinion toward Ukraine among the Russian population. The Levada Center (2009b) finds that the share of Russians who view Ukraine positively has dropped by 30 percent within the past decade, going from 71 percent in July 2001 to 41 percent in March 2009.[3] Almost half of the surveyed Russians reported negative attitudes toward the former Soviet republic. When prompted to describe Russian–Ukrainian relations, more than two-thirds of Russians chose adjectives with a negative undertone: intense (48 percent), lukewarm (20 percent), or hostile (19 percent) (see Levada Center 2009a).[4] Notably, negative attitudes toward Ukraine prevail among Russians of all ages. In September 2009, 54 percent of 18–24-year-olds, along with 52 percent of 40–54-year-olds and 51 percent of 55-year-olds and older respondents reported negative attitudes toward Ukraine (Levada Center 2009c).[5] These findings suggest that the younger generation in Putin's Russia is growing up with the perception of Ukraine as a cardinal enemy, a sell-out to the West.

In Putin's Russia, Ukraine was perceived as the least friendly former Soviet republic, with the exception of Georgia. Like the post-Orange Revolution Ukraine, the post-Rose Revolution Georgia triggered a spike in Russia's animosity when the Western-oriented government headed by Mikheil Saakashvili came to power in 2003. Though Georgia was not particularly popular among Russians prior to Saakashvili's election, negative attitudes toward the former Soviet republic jumped from 40 percent in October 2001 to 60 percent in March 2009 (Levada Center 2009b). For comparison, Belarus, often labeled Europe's last dictatorship by the Western media, has steadily maintained a positive image in Russia. Throughout the decade, positive attitudes toward Belarus hovered at over 70 percent.

While unfavorable attitudes toward Ukraine prevail in Russia, Ukrainians view Russia with much less hostility. The opinion poll conducted by the Kyiv International Institute of Sociology (KIIS) in March 2009 indicates that a whopping 90 percent of Ukrainians hold positive attitudes toward their powerful neighbor (KIIS 2009).[6] The Ukrainian sociologist Valery Khmelko contends that cross-country variations in the perception of each other can be attributed, in part, to the role of the mainstream mass media in Russia (*Den'* 2008). The news coverage on state-controlled Russian TV channels is inundated with negative reports about Ukraine, while Ukrainian TV channels tend to air less antagonistic reports of Russian–Ukrainian relations. Cross-country differences in media framing are likely to affect citizens' criteria for determining the dynamics of cross-border relations. Given the intense politicization of Ukraine's image in the Russian media, Russian respondents tend to draw a close link between Ukraine and its pro-Western government. At the same time, Khmelko contends that the plurality of Ukrainians think about ordinary citizens, rather than Putin and Medvedev, when reporting their attitudes toward Russia. In particular, most Ukrainians in eastern and southern parts of Ukraine tend to associate Russia with the homeland of their relatives and friends. Some analysts might raise questions about the validity of the KIIS survey results.[7] The reported level of positive attitudes toward Russia is extraordinarily high. Still, it is indisputable that Ukraine's population tends to report more tolerance for ethnic Russians than Russia's citizens for ethnic Ukrainians. Shortly after the 2004 presidential election marred by Putin's blatant support for Yanukovych and the conspicuous presence of Russian political technologists in Kyiv, only 2 percent of Ukrainians reported that they wouldn't let ethnic Russians into the country if it were in their power (Panina 2005: 63).[8]

In light of the available empirical evidence, it is safe to conclude that Russian and Ukrainian adolescents on the opposite sides of the border drift apart from one another. The Kremlin's promotion of Soviet-era historical myths, coupled with Russia's belligerent foreign policy, hampers the establishment of an open dialogue between young Russians and young Ukrainians.

Appendix A

Questionnaire wording

Variable	Question wording and coding
Support for democracy	To what extent do you agree with the following statement: Democracy is the best form of government for my home country. 1 – strongly disagree, 2 – disagree, 3 – agree, 4 – strongly agree, 99 – difficult to answer
Evaluation of democracy	How would you grade the level of democratic development in your home country? 1 – unsatisfactory, 2 – satisfactory, 3 – good, 4 – excellent, 99 – difficult to answer
Trust in authorities	How much do you trust the following: the president, parliamentarians, political parties, the army, police, and judges? 1 – not at all, 2 – not much, 3 – quite a lot, 4 – a great deal, 99 – difficult to answer
National pride	How proud are you to be a citizen of your home country? 1 – not at all, 2 – not much, 3 – quite a lot, 4 – a great deal, 99 – difficult to answer
Soviet nostalgia	Do you think that the dissolution of the Soviet Union was a positive or a negative thing in your country's history? 0 – negative, 1 – positive
Political discussions	How frequently do you obtain political news by speaking with parents? speaking with teachers? 1 – never, 2 – less than once a week, 3 – 1-2 times a week, 4 – 3-4 times a week, 5 – daily, 99 – difficult to answer
Media news consumption	How frequently do you obtain political news by watching TV? reading newspapers? using the Internet? 1 – never, 2 – less than once a week, 3 – 1-2 times a week, 4 – 3-4 times a week, 5 – daily, 99 – difficult to answer
Parental education	Please indicate the level of your mother and your father's education: 1 – incomplete secondary, 2 – secondary, 3 – incomplete higher, 4 – higher, 99 – difficult to answer

Variable	Question wording and coding
Ethnicity	[In Russia] Please indicate your ethnicity [In Ukraine] Please indicate the ethnicity of your mother and your father 1 – Russian, 2 – Ukrainian, 3 – other (please specify) 99 – difficult to answer
Gender	0 – female, 1 – male
Age	Self-identified age (in years)
Grade	Self-identified

Descriptive statistics

Variable	Russia Mean	Standard Deviation	Ukraine Mean	Standard Deviation
Support for democracy	2.98	(0.80)	3.19	(0.82)
Evaluation of democracy	1.62	(1.06)	1.90	(1.30)
Trust in authorities				
President	2.96	(0.89)	2.23	(1.05)
Parliamentarians	1.76	(0.78)	1.92	(0.83)
Political parties (Russia)	1.88	(0.78)	—	—
Pro-president political parties (U)	—	—	2.08	(0.92)
Anti-president political parties (U)	—	—	2.12	(0.96)
Army	2.66	(1.04)	2.73	(0.96)
Police	2.15	(0.98)	2.16	(0.98)
Judges	2.63	(0.94)	2.45	(0.99)
National pride	3.33	(0.78)	3.37	(0.78)
Soviet nostalgia	0.63	(0.48)	0.38	(0.48)
Political discussions				
Speaking with parents	3.25	(1.37)	3.89	(1.27)
Speaking with teachers	2.48	(1.24)	2.92	(1.37)
Media news consumption				
Watching TV	4.15	(1.11)	4.09	(1.06)
Reading newspapers	2.66	(1.20)	2.75	(1.22)
Using the Internet	2.40	(1.48)	2.33	(1.47)
Parental education				
Father's education	3.44	(0.85)	3.28	(0.88)
Mother's education	3.47	(0.83)	3.37	(0.85)
Ethnicity				
Ethnicity: Russian (R)	0.90	(0.30)	—	—
Father's ethnicity (U)	—	—	0.20	—
Mother's ethnicity (U)	—	—	—	(0.40)
Gender (male)	0.49	(0.51)	0.49	(0.51)
Age	14.6	(0.92)	14.5	(0.64)
Grade 10	0.31	(0.46)	0.45	(0.50)

Appendix B

List of participants in semi-structured interviews

Moscow, Russia (N = 17)

Alex, 10th grade (cadet), 16, male
Andrei, 10th grade, 16, male
Artem, 10th grade (cadet), 15, male
Liuda, 10th grade, 16, female
Masha, 9th grade, 15, female
Maksim, 9th grade, 14, male
Max, 9th grade, 14, male
Milana, 9th grade, 15, female
Nastia, 10th grade, 16, female
Roman, 9th grade, 15, male
Sasha, 10th grade (cadet), 16, male
Stas, 10th grade (cadet), 16, male
Sveta, 9th grade, 15, female
Vlad, 10th grade, 16, male
Yana, 9th grade, 15, female
Zhenia, 9th grade, 14, female
Zhora, 9th grade, 15, male

Tula, Russia (N = 15)

Ania, 9th grade, 15, female
Ania, 10th grade, 16, female
Denis, 10th grade, 15, male
Dima, 10th grade, 16, male
Elena, 9th grade, 15, female
Kirill, 9th grade, 14, male
Lesha, 10th grade, 16, male
Liuda, 10th grade, 15, female
Misha, 9th grade, 14, male
Natasha, 9th grade, 14, female
Oleg, 10th grade, 15, male
Roman, 9th grade, 15, male
Sasha, 9th grade, 15, male
Sveta, 9th grade, 15, female
Zhenia, 10th grade, 16, male

Rostov-on-the-Don, Russia (N = 8)

Artur, 9th grade, 15, male
Grisha, 9th grade, 14, male
Liuda, 9th grade, 14, female
Masha, 9th grade, 15, female
Olga, 10th grade, 16, female
Olia, 10th grade, 16, female
Sergei, 10th grade, 16, male
Viacheslav, 10th grade, 16, male

Kyiv, Ukraine (N = 12)

Anzhelika, 9th grade, 14, female
Ihor, 9th grade, 14, male
Ihor, 10th grade, 15, male
Julia, 9th grade, 14, female
Julia (D), 9th grade, 14, female
Julia, 10th grade, 15, female
Kolia, 10th grade, 15, male
Larysa, 9th grade, 14, female
Nastia, 10th grade, 15, female
Oleh, 9th grade, 14, male
Oleh (D), 9th grade, 14, male
Stas, 9th grade, 15, male

Donetsk, Ukraine (N = 13)

Aniuta, 10th grade, 15, female
Anton, 9th grade, 13, male
Bohdan, 9th grade, 14, male
Ilona, 9th grade, 14, female
Katia, 10th grade, 15, female
Kolia, 10th grade, 16, male
Lesha, 10th grade, 16, male
Liuda, 9th grade, 14, female
Natasha, 10th grade, 15, female
Rostik, 10th grade, 15, male
Sasha, 10th grade, 15, male
Vika, 10th grade, 15, female
Yura, 10th grade, 15, male

Lviv, Ukraine (N = 11)

Andrii, 10th grade, 15, male
Iryna, 10th grade, 15, female
Olena, 10th grade, 14, female
Olha, 9th grade, 14, female
Pavlo, 8th grade, 13, male
Petro, 9th grade, 14, male
Uliana, 8th grade, 13, female
Volodymyr, 9th grade, 14, male
Volodymyr, 10th grade, 15, male
Yurko, 10th grade, 15, male
Zhenia, 9th grade, 14, female

Notes

Chapter 1

1. On the methodology of regime classification, see Freedom House (2005).
2. For a full list, see the Committee to Protect Journalists (2001).
3. Samuel Huntington (1991: 266–67) contends that a new democracy must undergo two peaceful turnovers of power to become consolidated. The same logic can be applied to evaluate the extent to which a non-democratic regime has consolidated.
4. On this point, see Zarakhovich (2007).
5. For the full text of the address, see Kuchma (2002).
6. Even citizens in mature democracies are not immune to excesses of patriotism. On this point, see Miller (2007).
7. On the ideology of the youth organization, visit the website http://www.brsm.by.
8. The full text of the programs is available (in Russian) on the website of the Federal Agency of Education at http://www.ed.gov.ru. For an in-depth analysis of the program, see Blum (2006).
9. Vladislav Surkov, deputy chief of presidential staff and chief Kremlin ideologist, spelled out the government's vision of political development by coining the phrase "sovereign democracy." It implies that Russia will adopt its own version of democracy that takes into account peculiarities of Russian culture and its current stage of economic development.
10. The full text of the document is available (in Ukrainian) on the website of Verkhovna Rada, Ukraine's national parliament, at http://zakon.rada.gov.ua.
11. On 10 January 2002, the Cabinet of Ministers of Ukraine issued a decree that annulled a series of government decrees, including the 1999 decree on patriotic education.
12. In particular, the communist parties in Russia and Ukraine frequently play the history card to mobilize the electorate. Since the electoral success of the Communist Party depends, to a large degree, upon the positive image of the Soviet Union, the party tends to campaign for the continued celebration of Soviet holidays and an extensive study of the Great Patriotic War in school textbooks.
13. On census results, visit the websites http://www.perepis2002.ru (Russia, 2002) and http://www.ukrcensus.gov.ua (Ukraine, 2001).
14. The results from the nationwide opinion poll conducted by the Levada Center in November 2005 reveal that only one quarter of those surveyed disapproved of the idea that Russia is for ethnic Russians (*Rossiia dlia russkikh*). Fifty-three percent of respondents supported this idea. An additional 24 percent reported either difficulty answering the question or lack of interest in this issue. See http://www.levada.ru.
15. As a result of the 2007 parliamentary election, only four parties entered the Duma, the lower house of the national parliament. United Russia received 70 percent of seats, the Communist Party of the Russian Federation came a distant

second with 13 percent of seats. The rest of the seats were almost equally split between the two pro-Kremlin parties: Just Russia and the Liberal Democratic Party of Russia (whose party program is neither liberal nor democratic).
16 For a detailed discussion of political competition in Ukraine, see Birch (2000b).
17 A total of 28 states participated in the survey, including the following 11 post-communist states: Bulgaria, the Czech Republic, Estonia, Hungary, Latvia, Lithuania, Poland, Romania, Russia, Slovakia, and Slovenia. By 2008, all of them, except Russia, had joined the European Union and consolidated democratic institutions. For an in-depth discussion of the survey results, see Torney-Purta *et al.* (2001).
18 Furthermore, Easton distinguishes between diffuse and specific support. This distinction, however, is tenuous in post-communist societies because the newly formed political and social institutions have yet to build a reservoir of unwavering popular support.
19 On the conceptualization of triple or quadruple transitions, see Kuzio (2001), Offe and Pierre (1991).
20 There is an ongoing debate in political science literature on how to specify and measure attributes of democracy. See Collier and Levitsky (1997), Munck and Verkuilen (2002).
21 The control of extraneous variance means that the influences of independent variables extraneous to the purposes of the study are minimized, nullified, or isolated.
22 For a comprehensive discussion of Ukraine's history, see Magosci (1996).
23 The opinion poll based upon the national representative sample was conducted by the Levada Center; N = 1,603. For more information, visit the website http://www.russiavotes.org.
24 The Institute of Sociology, National Academy of Sciences of Ukraine conducted the opinion poll in 2004. Respondents were prompted to evaluate incumbent job performance on a scale from 1, worst, to 10, best. The plurality of Ukrainians (28 percent) gave President Kuchma the lowest possible mark. Less than 2 percent assigned his job performance the highest score; N = 1,800. For further details about the survey, see Panina (2005).
25 For the official results of the 2002 population census, see the website http://www.perepis2002.ru.
26 The word "Cossack" comes from the Turkish word "qazaq," which means "free man." In the fourteenth and fifteenth centuries, peasants fled serfdom and settled in the valleys of the Dnieper, Don, and Ural rivers. Subsequently, the Russian tsars used Cossacks to protect the empire's frontiers and wage wars for the expansion of the Russian empire. Upon the overthrow of the Russian tsar Nicholas II, many Cossacks fought against the installment of communist rule. In the post-Soviet period, Cossacks began to revive their traditions. See BBC (2007).
27 For the regional distribution of votes, visit the website of the Central Election Commission of Ukraine at http://www.cvk.gov.ua.
28 For the 2001 census, visit the website http://www.ukrcensus.gov.ua.

Chapter 2

1 The transcript of the 2005 Annual Address is available at http://www.akorda.kz. In contrast to the official rhetoric, the level of political openness in Kazakhstan has been deteriorating. See *Economist* (2002), Radio Free Europe/Radio Liberty (2009).
2 On how the notion of stability was salient during Kuchma's election campaign in 1999, see Nikolayenko (2004).
3 According to the Life in Transition Survey, 65.4 percent of Russians, compared to 77.8 percent of Ukrainians, agreed with the statement that an independent

press was important for their home country. When asked to assess the importance of strong political opposition, 55.8 percent of Russians and 66.8 percent of Ukrainians agreed with this statement.
4 The questionnaire provided free space for respondents to say how they understand the word "democracy." Technically, the literature distinguishes between "don't know," the choice of reporting difficulty with answering the question, and item non-response, the refusal to answer a survey item. See Francis and Busch (1975); Gilljam and Granberg (1993). But the "don't know" option was not included for the open-ended question. Thus the residual category combines don't knows and non-responses. Students resorted to a variety of strategies to decline a substantive answer. Many respondents placed a dash (–) to signal difficulty with answering the question. An alternative strategy was to write down "I don't know." Finally, some respondents left the space blank. Nonetheless, it is reasonable to assume that a high percentage of respondents in the residual category do not have a clear idea of what democracy stands for.
5 The Ukrainian questionnaire included a survey item measuring the level of adolescents' interest in politics. The question wording was, "How interested are you in politics: not at all, not much, quite a lot, very much?" The bivariate cross-tab analysis reveals statistically insignificant differences between boys and girls: 56.5 percent of girls and 59.7 percent of boys report "high" or "very high" level of interest in politics.
6 In 2000, the OECD Program for International Student Assessment (PISA) conducted an international assessment of reading, mathematical, and scientific literacy among 15-year-old students in 43 countries. The results indicate that female students in Russia reach higher levels of reading literacy and spend more time reading for pleasure than male students. In addition, Russian females display a better performance in science than male students. See OECD/UNESCO (2003).
7 Prior to the administration of the survey in one of the classes, the school principal warned me that the selected students came from dysfunctional families and had below-average academic attainments.

Chapter 3

1 In Russia, compulsory military service was reduced to 18 months in 2007 and 12 months in 2008. See Feifer (2002).
2 According to the 2005 survey by the Levada Center, 67 percent of Russians object to the military conscription of their close relatives. The question wording was: "Would you like your son, brother, husband, or another immediate family member to serve in the army? If not, why." Those who opposed conscription referred to the following problems in the army: hazing – 36 percent; the military conflict in Chechnya – 33 percent; discrimination and harassment of conscripts – 19 percent; unbearable living conditions – 18 percent; moral degradation, alcoholism, and drug-addiction – 12 percent. The survey was conducted in January 2005, N = 1,800. See Levada Center (2005). On human rights violations in the army, see the website of the Union of the Committees of Soldiers' Mothers of Russia at http://www.ucsmr.ru.
3 On the firing of Prime Minister Julia Tymoshenko in September 2005, see CNN Online (2005); Klussmann (2005).
4 United Russia, the party of power, has a majority in Russia's parliament. Sergei Mironov set up Just Russia as an alternative pro-Putin political party. The real opposition parties, including Yabloko and the Union of Right Forces, experienced a string of problems in registering for the 2007 municipal elections. On the establishment of the two-party system in Russia, see *PravdaRu* (2004); Myers (2007b).

5 On the Supreme Court's ruling, see CNN Online (2004); BBC (2004).
6 The Ukrainian questionnaire included two survey items measuring adolescents' attitudes toward political parties. The question wording was: "How much do you trust political parties that support Yushchenko and political parties that are in opposition to Yushchenko?"
7 See Democratic Initiatives/Kyiv International Institute of Sociology (2005).
8 See the website http://www.russiavotes.org.
9 National representative surveys were conducted on 29 April–19May 2000 (N = 2,407) and 8–11 February 2008 (N = 1,600).
10 The opinion poll was conducted on 5–6 November 2005; N = 1,500. See Public Opinion Foundation (2005).
11 The national government initiated the abolishment of the national traffic police (DAI) and the creation of a new state road patrol in 2005. See *Moscow News* (2005).
12 The IEA Civic Education survey measured trust in government-related institutions by asking: "How much of the time can you trust each of the following institutions?" The list included national government, parliament, political parties, courts, and police. Responses were coded on a four-point scale, ranging from 1, never, to 4, always. The survey was conducted in April–May 1999; N = 2,129.
13 The question wording was as follows, "I am going to name a number of organizations. For each one, could you tell me how much confidence you have in them: is it a great deal of confidence (1), quite a lot of confidence (2), not very much confidence (3), or none at all (4)?" N = 2,500.
14 On methodology, visit the website of Transparency International at http://ww1.transparency.org/cpi/2005/cpi2005_infocus.html (accessed November 2006).
15 Another theoretical perspective posits that social trust leads to greater trust in government. See Putnam (1993).
16 The survey item measuring interpersonal trust among adolescents replicates the question wording from the World Values Survey to perform a cross-age comparison. Respondents are prompted to report whether one can trust most people or whether one needs to be careful in dealing with people.
17 The question wording was: "How much of the time can you trust people who live in your home country? 1 – never; 2 – only some of the time; 3 – most of the time; 4 – always." The combined percentages from the last two response categories are reported in the text; N = 3,167 (Hungary) and 3,376 (Poland).
18 Interpersonal trust was measured with the help of a four-point scale ranging from 1, not at all, to 4, quite a lot. The question wording was: "How much do you trust your fellow citizens?" See Panina (2005).
19 On alcoholism in Russia, see Rodriguez (2005); *PravdaRu* (2006).
20 The controversy surrounding the re-privatization of the steel mill Krivorozhstal' received a lot of media attention during the field-work period. Viktor Pinchuk, the son-in-law of President Kuchma, and Rinat Akhmetov, a wealthy Ukrainian oligarch, initially bought the plant from the state for a fraction of the real price. In 2005, the government annulled the deal and organized a new public bid for ownership of the plant. As a result, Arcelor Mittal, the world's largest steel company, purchased the Ukrainian steel mill. On the re-privatization, see *Kommersant* (2006).
21 One of the hallmarks of the anti-Yushchenko PR campaign was a billboard portraying Ukraine as a country divided into three parts based upon the alleged quality of people. Allegedly, first-class citizens resided in western Ukraine, second-class citizens were from central Ukraine. Finally, third-class citizens came from eastern Ukraine. The tagline read, "Yes! That's what *their* Ukraine looks like."
22 Ample evidence documents the pervasiveness of human rights violations during the draft and military service in Eurasia. The civic coalition For Democratic

Alternative Civil Service (*Za demokraticheskuiu al'ternativnui grazhdanskuiu sluzhbu*) in collaboration with the Union of the Committees of Soldiers' Mothers of Russia (*Soiuz komitetov soldtaskikh materei*) publishes the annual report "Violations of Human Rights in the Context of Military Conscription and Draft in Russia." The English-language version of the 2005 report is available at http://ags.demokratia.ru/library/?content=book&id=96.
23 On the state of Russia's army, see Baev (1996); Herspring (2006); Lambeth (1995).
24 The Cadet Corps was set up as an elite educational institution in 1731 to provide military training for boys from upper-class Russian families. The Cadet Corps was abolished in the aftermath of the October Revolution (1917) and revived in the post-Soviet period. In addition to specialized post-secondary institutions (*kadetskie uchilishcha*), a number of Russian public schools opened cadet classes to prepare middle- and high-school students for entrance to a military school.

Chapter 4

1 The website of the Russian TV project, *Name of Russia*, is available at http://www.nameofrussia.ru/. The website of the Ukrainian TV project, *Great Ukrainians*, is available at http://greatukrainians.com.ua/.
2 In Russia, the list of finalists comprised 12 individuals: Aleksandr Nevsky, Piotr Stolypin, Stalin, Aleksandr Pushkin, Peter the Great, Lenin, Fyodor Dostoevsky, Aleksandr Suvorov, Dmitrii Mendeleev, Ivan the Terrible, Catherine II, and Aleksandr II. In Ukraine, the following top 10 public figures were shortlisted: Yaroslav the Great, Mykola Amosov, Stepan Bandera, Taras Shevchenko, Bohdan Khmelnytsky, Valery Lobanovsky, Viacheslav Chornovil, Hryhoriy Skovoroda, Lesia Ukrainka, and Ivan Franko.
3 Alexander Suvorov (1729–1800) was a Russian nobleman who served in the Russian army and gained fame for his military victories during the Russo-Turkish wars.
4 The question wording was: "Please give examples of which things from Russian history boost your sense of national pride." Forty-one percent of Russian adults named Soviet victory in the Great Patriotic War. The second most popular choice was Soviet accomplishments in the space industry.
5 In Russia, 7 November was labeled the Day of Accord and Reconciliation from 1992 to 2004. Since 2005, 7 November is no longer an official holiday, but the government of Russia introduced another national holiday – the Day of National Unity – to be celebrated on 4 November. The newly created holiday marks the expulsion of Polish garrisons from Moscow in 1612 and the end of the Time of Troubles. In Ukraine, the government abolished 7 November as a national holiday in 2002.
6 On attitudes of Russian youth toward 4 November, see http://4november.ru/narod.html.
7 Numerous opinion polls show that older generations have a more positive attitude toward Soviet holidays than youth. See Bychenko (2002); *RegnumRu* (2008).
8 The Levada Center conducted the opinion poll on 8–12 December 2006; N = 1,600. For more information, see http://www.levada.ru.
9 Yegor Gaidar (1993), for example, warned in 1993 that the deteriorating economic situation might facilitate the spread of the Weimar syndrome in Russia. On the emergence and implications of the Weimar syndrome in Germany, see Maier (1988).
10 The question wording was: "Could you say whether or not you regret the dissolution of the Soviet Union?" Russia's Public Opinion Foundation conducted the opinion polls in December 1992, January 1997, January 1999, March 2001,

134 *Notes*

December 2001, and December 2006. The sample size each time was 1,500 respondents.
11 An alternative explanation is that the unification treaty with Belarus has rekindled hopes for the resurrection of the Soviet Union in a new political form.
12 On Yeltsin's presidency, see Shevtsova (1999).
13 On the demographic situation is Russia, visit the website of Goskomstat, Russia's State Statistics Committee, at http://www.gks.ru/free_doc/new_site/population/demo/vita1_bd.htm (accessed 10 June 2009). On US population statistics, see the website of the Center for Disease Control and Prevention http://www.cdc.gov/nchs/deaths.htm (accessed 10 June 2009).
14 The survey was conducted on 12–22 December 2006; N = 4,998. For further details, see Institute of Politics (2007).
15 For more information on the activities of the organization, see http://www.memo.ru.
16 The Russian government continues to deny the Soviet occupation of the Baltic states. When the government of Estonia expressed its intention to remove the monument to Soviet soldiers from a central location in the capital city of Tallinn, Russia immediately issued a note of protest. On the dispute over Soviet-era monuments, see Myers (2007a).
17 The socialist system guaranteed each individual a job upon graduation from university and a stable income for life. Hardly any employee was fired regardless of his or her job performance. Though discouraging personal initiative and high productivity, such a labor policy fostered an extremely stable socioeconomic environment.

Chapter 5

1 On the history of *Maidan*, see Zubar (2005).
2 On press freedom violations in Russia, see the weekly "Authorities versus Media" bulletins published by the Moscow-based Centre for Journalism in Extreme Situations. These bulletins are available at http://www.cjes.ru.
3 The Public Opinion Foundation conducted the survey on 16–17 December 2005. Respondents were asked to report whether they had children or grandchildren aged 7–17 in their household. Twenty-eight percent of respondents who replied in the affirmative were then prompted to report the Internet habits of their offspring. A national representative sample was drawn; N = 1,500.
4 On this point, see Norris (2000).
5 On the revision of historic myths during the Yeltsin period, see Smith (2002).
6 The exact wording of the controversial assignment was as follows: "President Vladimir Putin is an authoritarian ruler bent on establishing a new dictatorship in Russia. President Vladimir Putin is a democrat at heart whose structural reforms are paving the way for Russia to emerge as a liberal democracy. Present your evidence and discuss."
7 See the full-text of the manifesto at http://www.nashi.su/manifest.
8 For a summary of *Nashi*'s activities, see http://nashi.su/projects.
9 On the importance of teachers, see Hahn (1999); Zeigler (1967).

Chapter 6

1 The opinion poll was conducted on 22 October 2002; N = 1,500.
2 The American sociologist James Loewen (1996) published a scathing critique of history teaching in the United States. He began his account by stating that "high school students hate history … *Bor-r-ring* is the word they apply to it."
3 On the Soviet use of force, see Helsinki Watch Committee (1991a, 1991b); Lieven (1994: 244–54).

Chapter 7

1. In 2004, Russia's mainstream media referred to the mass mobilization of Ukrainians against electoral fraud as "the orange plague" (*oranzhevaia chuma*).
2. This manuscript was completed before the 2010 presidential election in Ukraine. When Yanukovych was elected president of Ukraine, bilateral relations improved.
3. The survey was conducted on 20–23 March 2009; N = 1,602.
4. The survey was conducted on 23–27 January 2009; N = 1,600.
5. The survey was conducted on 12–15 September; N = 1,600.
6. The survey was conducted on 13–23 March 2009; N = 2,000.
7. Even ordinary citizens cast doubt on the survey results. See, for example, comments posted by readers of the online publication *Ukrainska Pravda* in response to its article of 27 February 2009. See *Ukrainska Pravda* (2009).
8. The question wording was: "Please choose one of the statements that describes best how far you would allow members of the following ethnic groups into your lives: (1) members of the family, (2) close friends, (3) neighbors, (4) colleagues at work, (5) residents of Ukraine, (6) visitors to Ukraine, or (7) I wouldn't let members of this ethnic group into Ukraine at all."

Bibliography

Adams, Gerald R. and Michael D. Berzonsky, eds. 2003. *Blackwell Handbook of Adolescence*. Malden, MA: Blackwell.
Adelson, Joseph and Robert O'Neil. 1966. "The Growth of Political Ideas in Adolescence: The Sense of Community." *Journal of Personality and Social Psychology* 4 (Sept.): 295–306.
Almond, Gabriel and Sidney Verba. 1963. *The Civic Culture: Political Attitudes and Democracy in Five Nations*. Princeton, NJ: Princeton University Press.
Arel, Dominique. 1995. "Language Policies in Independent Ukraine: Towards One or Two State Languages?" *Nationalities Papers* 23 (3): 597–622.
Asad, Alam, Mamta Murthi, Ruslan Yemtsov, Edmundo Murrugarra, Nora Dudwick, Ellen Hamilton, and Erwin Tiongson. 2005. *Growth, Poverty, and Inequality: Eastern Europe and the Former Soviet Union*. Washington, DC: World Bank.
Aslund, Anders and Michael McFaul, eds. 2006. *Revolution in Orange: The Origins of Ukraine's Democratic Breakthrough*. Washington, DC: Carnegie Endowment for International Peace.
Baev, Pavel. 1996. *The Russian Army in a Time of Troubles*. London: Sage.
Bahry, Donna. 1987. "Politics, Generation, and Change in the USSR." In *Politics, Work, and Daily Life in the USSR*, ed. James R. Millar. New York: Cambridge University Press, pp. 61–99.
Bahry, Donna, Cynthia Boaz, and Stacy Burnett Gordon. 1997. "Tolerance, Transition, and Support for Civil Liberties in Russia." *Comparative Political Studies* 30 (4): 484–510.
Barrington, Lowell W. and Eric S. Herron, 2004. "One Ukraine or Many?: Regionalism in Ukraine and Its Political Consequences." *Nationalities Papers* 32 (1): 53–86.
Bart-Tal, Daniel and Ervin Staub, eds. 1997. *Patriotism in the Lives of Individuals and Nations*. Chicago: Nelson Hall Publishers.
BBC. 2004. "Ukraine Court Ruling: Excerpts." BBC News Online, 3 December. Retrieved from <http://news.bbc.co.uk/2/hi/europe/4067269.stm> (accessed 10 January 2005).
BBC. 2006. "Gorbachev Invests in Major Paper." BBC News Online, 8 June. Retrieved from <http://news.bbc.co.uk/2/hi/europe/5059124.stm> (accessed 15 August 2006).
BBC. 2007. "Russia's Cossacks Rise Again." BBC News Online, 9 August. Retrieved from <http://news.bbc.co.uk/2/hi/europe/6937562.stm> (accessed 23 September 2007).

Beck, Adrian and Ruth Lee. 2002. "Attitudes to Corruption among Young Russian Police Officers and Trainees." *Crime, Law, and Social Change* 38 (4): 357–72.

Beck, Paul. 1977. "The Role of Agents in Political Socialization" In *Handbook of Political Socialization*, ed. Stanley Reshon. New York: Free Press, pp. 115–41.

Bennett, Lisa L.M. and Stephen Earl Bennett. 1989. "Enduring Gender Differences in Political Interest." *American Politics Research* 17 (1): 105–22.

Bennett, Stephen Earl. 1999. "The Past Need Not Be Prologue: Why Pessimism about Civic Education Is Premature." *PS: Political Science and Politics* 32 (4): 755–57.

Ben-Porath, Sigal. 2007. "Civic Virtue out of Necessity: Patriotism and Democratic Education." *Theory and Research in Education* 5 (1): 41–59.

Berelowitch, Wladimir. 2003. "Contemporary Russian Textbooks: Many-Faced Truth or Yet Another National Idea." *Eurozone*, 27 March. Retrieved from <http://www.eurozine.com/articles/2003-03-27-berelowitch-fr.html> (accessed 18 March 2006).

Bilinsky, Yaroslav. 1968. "Education of the Non-Russian Peoples in the USSR, 1917–1967: An Essay." *Slavic Review* 27: 411–37.

Birch, Sarah. 2000a. "Interpreting the Regional Effect in Ukrainian Politics." *Europe-Asia Studies* 52 (6): 1017–41.

Birch, Sarah. 2000b. *Elections and Democratization in Ukraine*. Basingstoke: Macmillan.

Blomfield, Adrian. 2006. "Envoy Demands Kremlin Calls Off Its Youth Gang." *Daily Telegraph*, 13 December. Retrieved from <http://www.telegraph.co.uk/news/worldnews/ 1536832/Envoy-demands-Kremlin-calls-off-its-youth-gang.html> (accessed 11 January 2007).

Blum, Douglas. 2006. "Official Patriotism in Russia: Its Essence and Implications." *Ponars Policy Memo* 420. Retrieved from <http://csis.org/publication/ponars-policy-memo-420-official-patriotism-russia-its-essence-and-implications> (accessed 18 March 2006).

Blum, Douglas. 2007. *Globalization, Identity, and State-Society Relations: Youth Socialization in Post-Soviet Eurasia*. New York: Cambridge University Press.

Bollen, Kenneth and Robert Jackman. 1989. "Democracy, Stability, and Dichotomies." *American Sociological Review* 54: 612–21.

Bransten, Jeremy. 2003. "Education Ministry Doesn't Like What It Learned about Free-Thinking Textbook." Radio Free Europe/Radio Liberty, 3 December. Retrieved from <http://www.rferl.org/content/article/1105228.html> (accessed 4 March 2004).

Brigg, Claire. 2006. "Brutal Hazing Incident Rocks Army." Radio Free Europe/Radio Liberty, 27 January. Retrieved from <http://www.rferl.org/content/article/1065152.html> (accessed 20 August 2006).

Bronfenbrenner, Urie. 1970. *Two Worlds of Childhood: US and USSR*. New York: Russell Sage.

Buerkle, Karen, Lisa Kammerud, and Rakesh Sharma. 2005. *Public Opinion in Ukraine after the Orange Revolution*. Washington, DC: IFES.

Bunce, Valerie J. and Sharon L. Wolchik. 2006. "Youth and Electoral Revolutions in Slovakia, Serbia, and Georgia." *SAIS Review* 26 (2): 55–65.

Bush, Jason. 2008. "The New Putin Generation." *Business Weekly*, 28 February. Retrieved from <http://www.businessweek.com/magazine/content/08_10/b4074026082666.htm> (accessed 1 April 2008).

Carnaghan, Ellen. 2001. "Thinking about Democracy: Interviews with Russian Citizens." *Slavic Review* 60 (2): 336–66.

Carnaghan, Ellen. 2008. *Out of Order: Russian Political Values in an Imperfect World*. University Park, PA: Pennsylvania State University Press.
Chivers, C. J. 2004. "Youth Movement Underlies the Opposition in Ukraine." *New York Times*, 28 November. Retrieved from <http://www.nytimes.com/2004/11/28/international/europe/28ukraine.html> (accessed 10 January 2005).
Ciobanu, Monica. 2008. "Teaching History and Building a Democratic Future: Reflections from Post-Communist Romania." *Democracy and Education* 17 (3): 58–62.
CNN Online. 1996. "Russian Communist Candidate Tells Americans Not to Worry," 26 May. Retrieved from <http://cnn.tv/WORLD/9605/26/russia.zyuganov/index.html> (accessed 10 January 2005).
CNN Online. 2004. "Ukraine Court Overturns Election," 3 December. Retrieved from <http://www.cnn.com/2004/WORLD/europe/12/03/ukraine.ruling/index.html> (accessed 10 January 2005).
CNN Online. 2005. "Yushchenko Fires Government," 8 September. Retrieved from <http://www.cnn.com/2005/WORLD/europe.yushchenko/index.html> (accessed 10 September 2005).
Coalson, Robert. 2008. "Does Putin, Like Lenin, See Film as 'Most Important of the Arts'?" Radio Free Europe/Radio Liberty, 20 December. Retrieved from <http://www.rferl.org/content/Putin_To_Head_Film_Council/1361814.html> (accessed 23 February 2009).
Collier, David and Robert Adcock. 1999. "Democracy and Dichotomies: A Pragmatic Approach to Choices about Concepts." *Annual Review of Political Science* 2: 537–65.
Collier, David and Steven Levitsky. 1997. "Democracy with Adjectives: Conceptual Innovation in Comparative Research." *World Politics* 49: 430–51.
Collin, Mathew. 2007. *The Time of the Rebels: Youth Resistance Movements and 21st Century Revolutions*. London: Serpent's Tail.
Colton, Timothy and Michael McFaul. 2003. *Popular Choice and Managed Democracy: The Russian Elections of 1999 and 2000*. Washington, DC: Brookings Institution Press.
Committee to Protect Journalists. 2001. "Enemies of the Press 2001." Retrieved from <http://cpj.org/reports/2001/05/enemies-01.php> (accessed 10 October 2004).
Committee to Protect Journalists. 2004. *Attacks on the Press*. New York: CPJ.
Corwin, Julie. 2005. "Analysis: Walking with Putin." Radio Free Europe/Radio Liberty, 2 March. Retrieved from <http://www.rferl.org/content/article/1057762.html> (accessed 9 July 2007).
Dahl, Robert A. 1971. *Polyarchy: Participation and Opposition*. New Haven, CT: Yale University Press.
D'Anieri, Paul. 2005. "The Last Hurrah: The 2004 Ukrainian Presidential Elections and the Limits of Machine Politics." *Communist and Post-Communist Studies* 38: 231–49.
D'Anieri, Paul. 2007. *Understanding Ukrainian Politics: Power, Politics, and Institutional Design*. Armonk, NY: M.E. Sharpe.
Darden, Keith. 2001. "Blackmail as a Tool of State Domination: Ukraine under Kuchma." *East European Constitutional Review* 10 (2/3): 67–71.
Dawson, Richard and Kenneth Prewitt. 1969. *Political Socialization*. Boston: Little, Brown.
de Figueiredo, Rui J. P. and Zachary Elkins. 2003. "Are Patriots Bigots? An Inquiry into the Vices of In-Group Pride." *American Journal of Political Science* 47 (1): 171–88.

Delli Carpini, Michael X. and Scott Keeter. 1991. "Stability and Change in the U.S. Public's Knowledge of Politics." *Public Opinion Quarterly* (Winter): 583–612.
Demes, Pavol and Joerg Forbig. 2005. "Pora – 'It's Time' for Democracy in Ukraine." In *Revolution in Orange: The Origins of Ukraine's Democratic Breakthrough*, ed. Anders Aslund and Michael McFaul. Washington, DC: Carnegie Endowment for International Peace, pp. 85–102.
Deutsch, Nancy and Jeffrey Jones. 2008. "'Show Me an Ounce of Respect': Respect and Authority in Adult–Youth Relationships in After-School Programs." *Journal of Adolescent Research* 23 (6): 667–88.
Diamond, Larry. 1994. "Toward Democratic Consolidation." *Journal of Democracy* 3: 4–17.
Diamond, Larry. 2002. "Thinking about the Hybrid Regimes." *Journal of Democracy* 13 (2): 21–35.
Diuk, Nadia. 2004. "The Next Generation." *Journal of Democracy* 15 (3): 59–66.
Dneprov, Edward, V. Lazarev, and V. Sobkin. 1993. "The State of Education in Russia Today." In *Democracy in the Russian School: The Reform Movement in Education Since 1984*, ed. Ben Eklof and Edward Dneprov. Boulder, CO: Westview Press, pp. 148–220.
Dowley, Kathleen M. and Brian D. Silver. 2005. "Crossnational Survey Research and Subnational Pluralism." *International Journal of Public Opinion Research* 17 (2): 226–38.
Dunstan, John. 1978. *Paths to Excellence and the Soviet School*. Windsor, UK: NFER Publishing Company.
Dyczok, Marta. 2003. "Ukraine's Media Landscape." In *Society in Transition: Social Change in Ukraine in Western Perspectives*, ed. Wsevolod W. Isajiw. Toronto: Scholar's Press, pp. 283–304.
Dyczok, Marta. 2005. "Breaking through the Information Blockade: Elections and Revolution in Ukraine 2004." *Canadian Slavonic Papers* 47 (3/4): 241–64.
Easterly, William and Ross Levine. 1997. "Africa's Growth Tragedy: Policies and Ethnic Divisions." *Quarterly Journal of Economics* (Nov.): 1203–50.
Easton, David. 1965. *A Systems Analysis of Political Life*. New York: John Wiley.
Easton, David. 1975. "A Re-Assessment of the Concept of Political Support." *British Journal of Political Science* 5 (4): 435–57.
Easton, David and Jack Dennis. 1969. *Children in the Political System: Origins of Political Legitimacy*. New York: McGraw-Hill.
Eckstein, Harry. 1998. "Congruence Theory Explained." In *Can Democracy Take Root in Post-Soviet Russia? Explorations in State-Society Relations*, ed. Harry Eckstein, Frederic Fleron, Erik Hoffman, and William Reisinger. Boulder, CO: Rowman and Littlefield, pp. 3–34.
Economist. 2002. "Authoritarian Kazakhstan: Silencing the Lambs." 16 November.
Elman, Michael and Sergei Maksudov. 1994. "Soviet Deaths in the Great Patriotic War: A Note." *Europe-Asia Studies* 46 (4): 671–80.
European Bank for Reconstruction and Development (EBRD). 2007. *Transition Report 2007*. London: EBRD.
European Institute for the Media (EIM). 2000. "Monitoring the Media Coverage of March 2000 Presidential Elections in Russia." Dusseldorf: EIM.
Evans, Geoffrey and Natalia Letki. 2006. "Understanding the Relationship between Social Capital and Political Disaffection in the New Post-Communist Democracies." In *Political Disaffection in Contemporary Democracies: Social*

Capital, Institutions, and Politics, ed. Mariano Torcal and Jose R. Montero. New York: Routledge, pp. 130–54.
Evans, Geoffrey and Stephen Whitefield. 1995. "The Politics and Economics of Democratic Commitment: Support for Democracy in Transition Societies." *British Journal of Political Science* 25 (4): 485–514.
Evans, M. D. R. and Jonathan Kelley. 2002. "National Pride in the Developed World: Survey Data from 24 Nations." *International Journal of Public Opinion Research* 14 (3): 303–38.
Feifer, Gregory. 2002. "Rights Group Criticizes Draft Practices." *CDI Russia Weekly*, 22 November. Retrieved from <http://www.cdi.org/russia/232-13.cfm> (accessed 20 August 2006).
Feldman, Shirley and Glen Elliot, eds. 1990. *At the Threshold: The Developing Adolescent*. Cambridge, MA: Harvard University Press.
Feshbach, Seymour. 1994. "Nationalism, Patriotism, and Aggression: A Clarification of Functional Differences." In *Aggressive Behavior: Current Perspectives*, ed. L. Husemann. New York: Putnam, pp. 275–91.
Finifter, Ada and Ellen Mickiewicz. 1992. "Redefining the Political System of the USSR: Mass Support for Political Change." *American Political Science Review* 86 (4): 857–74.
Finn, Peter. 2006. "Violent Bullying of Russian Conscripts Exposed." *Washington Post*, 30 January. Retrieved from <http://www.washingtonpost.com/wp-dyn/content/article/2006/01/30/AR2006013000699.html> (accessed 20 August 2006).
Fish, Steven. 2005. *Democracy Derailed in Russia: The Failure of Open Politics*. New York: Cambridge University Press.
Forbrig, Joerg and Pavol Demes, eds. 2007. *Reclaiming Democracy: Civil Society and Electoral Change in Central and Eastern Europe*. Washington, DC: German Marshall Fund of the United States.
Fournier, Anna. 2007. "Patriotism, Order, and Articulations of the Nation in Kyiv High Schools before and after the Orange Revolution." *Journal of Communist Studies and Transition Politics* 23 (1): 101–17.
Francis, Joe D. and Lawrence Busch. 1975. "What We Know about 'I Don't Knows.'" *Public Opinion Quarterly* 39 (2): 207–18.
Freedom House. 2005. *Freedom in the World Rankings*. New York: Freedom House.
Fukuyama, Francis. 1992. *The End of History and the Last Man*. New York: Free Press.
Gaidar, Yegor. 1993. "After Yeltsin's Victory, What Is Next for Reform?" Heritage Foundation Lecture, 26 July. Retrieved from <http://www.heritage.org/Research/Lecture/After-Yeltsins-Victory-What-Is-Next-for-Reform> (accessed 20 March 2006).
Gerber, Theodore. 2000. "Educational Stratification in Contemporary Russia: Stability and Change in the Face of Economic and Institutional Crisis." *Sociology of Education* 73 (4): 219–46.
Gibson, James, Raymond Duch, and Kent Tedin. 1992. "Democratic Values and the Transformation of the Soviet Union." *Journal of Politics* 54 (2): 329–71.
Gillespie, David. 2005. "Defense of the Realm: The 'New' Russian Patriotism on Screen." *Journal of Power Institutions in Post-Soviet Societies* issue 3. Retrieved from <http://pipss.revues.org/index369.html> (accessed 27 January 2006).
Gilljam, Mikael and Donald Granberg. 1993. "Should We Take Don't Know for an Answer?" *Public Opinion Quarterly* 57 (3): 348–57.

Goldstein, Joshua. 2007. "The Role of Digital Networked Technologies in the Ukrainian Orange Revolution." Berkman Research Center for Internet and Society at Harvard University, Research Publication no. 2007-14. Retrieved from <http://cyber.law.harvard.edu/publications> (accessed 23 February 2008).

Greenstein, Fred. 1965. *Children and Politics.* New Haven, CT: Yale University Press.

Grzymala-Busse, Anna. 2007. *Rebuilding Leviathan: Party Competition and State Exploitation in Post-Communist Democracies.* New York: Cambridge University Press.

Haerpfer, Christian. 2002. *Democracy and Enlargement in Post-Communist Europe: The Democratisation of the General Public in Fifteen Central and Eastern European Countries, 1991–1998.* London: Routledge.

Hahn, Carole L. 1999. "Citizenship Education: An Empirical Study of Policy, Practices, and Outcomes." *Oxford Review of Education* 25(1/2): 231–50.

Hahn, Carole and Theresa Alvair-Martin. 2008. "International Political Socialization Research." In *Handbook of Research in Social Studies Education*, ed. Linda Levstik and Cynthia Tyson. New York: Routledge, pp. 81–108.

Helsinki Watch Committee. 1990. *Conflict in the Soviet Union: The Untold Story of the Clashes in Kazakhstan* (Helsinki Watch Report). New York: Human Rights Watch.

Helsinki Watch Committee. 1991a. *Conflict in the Soviet Union: Black January in Azerbaijan* (Helsinki Watch Report). New York: Human Rights Watch.

Helsinki Watch Committee. 1991b. "Pattern of Violence: Lithuania is Latest Example of Soviet Army's Use of Lethal Force." *Helsinki Watch Newsletter*, 25 January.

Herspring, Dale. 2006. *The Kremlin and the High Command: Presidential Impact on the Russian Military from Gorbachev to Putin.* Lawrence: University of Kansas Press.

Hetherington, Marc. 1998. "The Political Relevance of Political Trust." *American Political Science Review* 92: 791–808.

Hibbing, John R. and Samuel Patterson. 1994. "Public Attitudes toward the New Parliaments of Central and Eastern Europe." *Political Studies* 42: 570–92.

Hibbing, John R. and Elizabeth Theiss-Morse. 1995. *Congress as Public Enemy: Public Attitudes toward American Political Institutions.* New York: Cambridge University Press.

Hibbing, John R. and Elizabeth Theiss-Morse, eds. 2001. *What Is It about Government that Americans Dislike?* New York: Cambridge University Press.

Hjerm, Mikael. 1998. "National Identities, National Pride, and Xenophobia: A Comparison of Four Western Countries." *Acta Sociologica* 41 (4): 335–47.

Holmes, Leslie. 2006. *Rotten States? Corruption, Post-Communism and Neoliberalism.* Durham, NC: Duke University Press.

Hughes, Donna and Tatyana Denisova. 2001. "The Transnational Political Criminal Nexus of Trafficking in Women from Ukraine." *Trends in Organized Crime* 6 (4): 43–67.

Huntington, Samuel. 1991. *The Third Wave: Democratization in the Twentieth Century.* Norman: University of Oklahoma Press.

Hyman, Herbert H. 1959. *Political Socialization.* New York: New Press.

International Foundation for Electoral Systems (IFES). 2006. *Public Views on Ukraine's Development, Election Law Changes, and Voter Education Needs: Findings from November 2006 Opinion Poll in Ukraine.* Washington, DC: IFES.

International Research and Exchange Board (IREX). 2007. *Media Sustainability Index 2006–2007: The Development of Independent and Sustainable Media in Europe and Eurasia.* Washington, DC: IREX.

Jacoby, Susan. 1974. *Inside Soviet Schools*. New York: Hill and Wang.
Janmaat, Jan G. 1999. "Language Politics in Education and the Response of the Russian in Ukraine." *Nationalities Papers* 27 (3): 475–501.
Janmaat, Jan G. 2005. "Ethnic and Civic Conceptions of the Nation in Ukraine's History Textbooks." *European Education* 37 (3): 20–37.
Janmaat, Jan G. 2006. "History and National Identity Construction: The Great Famine in Irish and Ukrainian History Textbooks." *History of Education* 35 (3): 345–68.
Jennings, Kent and Richard Niemi. 1974. *Political Character in Adolescence*. Princeton, NJ: Princeton University Press.
Jennings, Kent and Richard Niemi. 1981. *Generations and Politics*. Princeton, NJ: Princeton University Press.
Jones, Anthony, ed. 1994. *Education and Society in the New Russia*. Armonk, NY: M.E. Sharpe.
Kalashnikov, Vlad. 2008. "Moscow Richer than New York," *Exile*, 6 March. Retrieved from http://www.exile.ru/blog/detail.php?BLOG_ID=17472 (accessed 23 October 2010).
Kaplan, Vera. 2005. "History Teaching in Post-Soviet Russia." In *Educational Reform in Post-Soviet Russia: Legacies and Prospects*, ed. Ben Eklof, Larry E. Holmes, and Vera Kaplan. New York: Frank Cass, pp. 247–71.
Karatnycky, Adrian. 2003. "Liberty's Expansion in a Turbulent World: Thirty Years of the Survey of Freedom." In *Freedom in the World 2003: The Annual Survey of Political Rights and Civil Liberties*. New York: Freedom House.
Kaufman, Cathy C. 1994. "De-Sovietizing Educational Systems, Learning from Past Policy and Practice." *International Review of Education* 40 (2): 149–58.
Keating, Daniel. 2004. "Cognitive and Brain Development." In *Handbook of Adolescent Psychology* (2nd ed.), ed. Laurence Steinberg and Richard M. Lerner. New York: Wiley, pp. 159–87.
Kerr, Stephen T. 1990. "Will Glasnost Lead to Perestroika? Directions of Educational Reform in the USSR." *Educational Researcher* 19 (7): 26–31.
Kerr, Stephen T. 1991. "Beyond Dogma: Teacher Education in the USSR." *Journal of Teacher Education* 42 (5): 332–49.
Kisanne, Carolyn. 2005. "History Education in Transit: Where to for Kazakhstan?" *Comparative Education* 41 (1): 45–69.
Klingemann, Hans-Dieter and Dieter Fuchs, eds. 1995. *Citizens and the State*. Oxford: Oxford University Press.
Klussmann, Uwe. 2005. "Tymoshenko Unbraided: Ukraine's Orange Revolution under Strain." *Spiegel Online*, 15 September. Retrieved from <http://www.spiegel.de/international/spiegel/0,1518,374257,00.html> (accessed 10 October 2005).
Knack, Stephen and Philip Keefer. 1997. "Does Social Capital Have an Economic Pay-Off? A Cross-Country Investigation." *Quarterly Journal of Economics* 112 (4): 1251–88.
Kolasky, John. 1968. *Soviet Education in Ukraine*. Toronto: Peter Martin Associates.
Kommersant. 2006. "Krivorozhstal Gets a New Name," 13 January. Retrieved from <http://www.kommersant.com/page.asp?idr=529&id=-7933> (accessed 1 December 2006).
Koshiw, Jaroslav. 2003. *Beheaded: The Killing of a Journalist*. Reading, UK: Artemia Press.
Kubicek, Paul. 2000. "Regional Polarization in Ukraine: Public Opinion, Voting, and Legislative Behavior." *Europe-Asia Studies* 52 (2): 273–94.

Kulakova, Julia and Maria Cherkasova. 2006. "Buyer Found Kommersant." *Kommersant*, 31 August. Retrieved from <http://www.kommersant.com/page.asp?id=701360 > (accessed 15 August 2006).
Kuzio, Taras. 2001. "Transition in Post-Communist Societies: Triple or Quadruple?" *Politics* 21 (3): 169–78.
Kuzio, Taras. 2002. "History, Memory and Nation-Building in the Post-Soviet Colonial Space." *Nationalities Papers* 30 (2): 241–64.
Kuzio, Taras. 2005a. "Regime Type and Politics in Ukraine under Kuchma." *Communist and Post-Communist Studies* 38: 167–90.
Kuzio, Taras. 2005b. "Nation Building, History Writing and Competition over the Legacy of Kyiv Rus in Ukraine." *Nationalities Papers* 33 (1): 29–58.
Kuzio, Taras. 2006. "Civil Society, Youth and Societal Mobilization in Democratic Revolutions." *Communist and Postcommunist Studies* 39: 365–86.
Kuzio, Taras. 2007. "Praise and Condemnation of Stalin: Russia and Ukraine Go Their Separate Ways." *Eurasia Daily Monitor*, 30 November. Retrieved from <http://www.jamestown.org/single/?no_cache=1&tx_ttnews[tt_news]=33205> (accessed 5 December 2007).
Kuzio, Taras, ed. 2009. *Democratic Revolution in Ukraine: From Kuchmagate to Orange Revolution*. New York: Routledge.
Lambeth, Benjamin. 1995. "Russia's Wounded Military." *Foreign Affairs* 74 (2): 86–98.
Lambroschini, Sophie. 2004. "Is the Education Ministry Trying to Rewrite History?" Radio Free Europe/Radio Liberty, 30 January. Retrieved from <http://www.rferl.org/content/article/1051381.html> (accessed 3April 2006).
Lerner, Richard M. and Laurence Steinberg, eds. 2009. *Handbook of Adolescent Psychology*. Hoboken, NJ: John Wiley and Sons.
Levitsky, Steven and Lucan Way. 2002. "The Rise of Competitive Authoritarianism." *Journal of Democracy* 13 (1): 51–65.
Levy, Jack S. 2007. "Qualitative Methods and Cross-Method Dialogue in Political Science." *Comparative Political Studies* 40 (2): 196–214.
Lieven, Anatol. 1994. *The Baltic Revolution: Estonia, Latvia, Lithuania, and the Path to Independence*. New Haven, CT: Yale University Press.
Linz, Juan and Alfred Stepan. 1996. "Towards Consolidated Democracies." *Journal of Democracy* 7 (2): 14–33.
Lipman, Maria. 2005. *How Russia Is Not Ukraine: The Closing of Russian Civil Society*. Washington, DC: Carnegie Endowment for International Peace.
Lipman, Masha. 2006a. "Putin's 'Sovereign Democracy.'" *Washington Post*, 15 July. Retrieved from <http://www.washingtonpost.com/wp-dyn/content/article/2006/07/14/AR2006071401534.html> (accessed 19 November 2006).
Lipman, Masha. 2006b. "After Beslan, the Media in Shackles." *Washington Post*, 4 September. Retrieved from <http://www.washingtonpost.com/wp-dyn/content/article/2006/09/03/AR2006090300743.html> (accessed 5 September 2006).
Lipman, Masha and Michael McFaul. 2001. "Managed Democracy in Russia: Putin and the Press." *Harvard International Journal of Press/Politics* 6 (3): 117–27.
Lisovskaya, Elena and Vyacheslav Karpov. 1999. "New Ideologies in Postcommunist Russian Textbooks." *Comparative Education Review* 43 (4): 522–43.
Loewen, James.1996. *Lies My Teacher Told Me: Everything Your American History Textbook Got Wrong*. New York: New Press.
Lokshin, Michael and Ruslan Yemtsov. 2008. "Who Bears the Cost of Russia's Military Draft?" *Economics of Transition* 16 (3): 359–87.

Lower, Wendy Morgan. 2007. "From Berlin to Babi Yar: The Nazi War against the Jews, 1941–1944." *Journal of Religion and Society* 9: 1–14.

McCann, Kelly M. 2006. *Economic Autonomy and Democracy: Hybrid Regimes in Russia and Kyrgyzstan*. New York: Cambridge University Press.

McFaul, Michael, Nikolai Petrov, and Andrei Riabov, eds. 2004. *Between Dictatorship and Democracy: Russian Post-Communist Political Reform*. Washington, DC: Carnegie Endowment for International Peace.

Magosci, Paul. 1996. *A History of Ukraine*. Toronto: University of Toronto Press.

Maier, Charles S. 1988. *The Unmasterable Past: History, Holocaust, and the German National Identity*. Cambridge, MA: Harvard University Press.

Markowitz, Fran. 2000. *Coming of Age in Post-Soviet Russia*. Chicago: University of Illinois Press.

Marples, David. 2007. *Heroes and Villains: Creating National History in Contemporary Ukraine*. Budapest: Central European University Press.

Mees, Wim. 1988. "Adolescent Rebellion and Politics." *Youth and Society* 19 (4): 426–34.

Mendeloff, David. 1999. "Explaining the Persistence of Nationalist Mythmaking in Post-Soviet Russian History Education: The Annexation of the Baltic States and the 'Myth of 1939–40.'" In *The Teaching of History in Contemporary Russia: Trends and Perspectives*, ed. Vera Kaplan, Pinchas Agmon, and Liubov Ermolaeva. Tel Aviv: The Cummings Center for Russian and East European Studies, pp. 185–228.

Mendelson, Sarah E. and Theodore P. Gerber. 2005. "Soviet Nostalgia: An Impediment to Russian Democratization." *Washington Quarterly* 29 (1): 83–96.

Mendelson, Sarah E. and Theodore P. Gerber. 2006. "Failing the Stalin Test: Russians and Their Dictator." *Foreign Affairs* 85 (Jan./Feb.): 2–8.

Mendelson, Sarah E. and Theodore P. Gerber. 2008. "Us and Them: Anti-American Views of the Putin Generation." *Washington Quarterly* 31 (2): 131–50.

Mickiewicz, Ellen. 1999. *Changing Channels: Television and the Struggle for Power in Russia*. Durham, NC: Duke University Press.

Miller, Arthur H., Vicki L. Hesli, and William M. Reisinger. 1994. "Reassessing Mass Support for Political and Economic Change in the Former USSR." *American Political Science Review* 88: 399–411.

Miller, Arthur H., Vicki L. Hesli, and William Reisinger. 1997. "Conceptions of Democracy among Mass and Elite in Post-Soviet Societies." *British Journal of Political Science* 27: 157–90.

Miller, Richard. 2007. "Unlearning American Patriotism." *Theory and Research in Education* 5 (1): 7–21.

Mishler, William and Richard Rose. 1997. "Trust, Distrust, and Skepticism: Popular Evaluations of Civil and Political Institutions in Post-Communist Societies." *Journal of Politics* 59 (2): 418–51.

Mishler, William and Richard Rose. 2002. "Learning and Re-Learning Regime Support: The Dynamics of Post-Communist Societies." *European Journal of Political Research* 41: 5–36.

Mishler, William and Richard Rose. 2005. "What Are the Political Consequences of Trust? A Test of Cultural and Institutional Theories in Russia." *Comparative Political Studies* 38 (9): 1050–78.

Mite, Valentinas. 2004. "Youthful Protesters Find that 'Times Are Changing'." Radio Free Europe/Radio Liberty, 1 December. Retrieved from <http://www.rferl.org/content/article/1056167.html> (accessed 5 December 2004).

Mitra, Pradeep and Ruslan Yemtsov. 2006. *Increasing Inequality in Transition Economies: Is There More to Come?* World Bank Policy Research Working Paper 4007. Washington, DC: World Bank.

Moscow News. 2005. "President Yushchenko Abolishes Ukrainian Traffic Police for Corruption," 15 July. Retrieved from <http://www.mosnews.com/news/2005/07/18/ukrainegai.shtml> (accessed 10 September 2005).

Moses, Joel C. 2002. "Political-Economic Elites and Russian Regional Elections 1999–2000: Democratic Tendencies in Kaliningrad, Perm and Volgograd." *Europe-Asia Studies* 54 (6): 905–32.

Muckle, James. 1988. *A Guide to the Soviet Curriculum: What the Russian Child is Taught in School*. London: Croom Helm.

Munck, Gerardo and Jay Verkuilen. 2002. "Conceptualizing and Measuring Democracy: Evaluating Alternative Indices." *Comparative Political Studies* 35 (1): 5–34.

Murphy, Kim. 2006. "Charges of Brutal Hazing Put Russian Military on Defense." *Los Angeles Times*, 10 February. Retrieved from <http://articles.latimes.com/2006/feb/10/world/fg-hazing10> (accessed 20 August 2006).

Mutz, Diana C. and Byron Reeves. 2005. "The New Videomalaise: Effects of Televised Incivility on Political Trust." *American Political Science Review* 99 (1): 1–15.

Myers, Steven Lee. 2006. "The Hazing Trial Bares Dark Side of Russia's Military." *New York Times*, 13 August. Retrieved from <http://www.nytimes.com/2006/08/13/world/europe/13hazing.html> (accessed 20 August 2006).

Myers, Steven Lee. 2007a. "Estonia Sparks Outrage in Russia." *International Herald Tribune*, 24 January. Retrieved from <http://www.iht.com/articles/2007/01/24/news/journal.php> (accessed 17 February 2007).

Myers, Steven Lee. 2007b. "Russian Opposition Parties Feel the Chill." *International Herald Tribune*, February 15. Retrieved from <http://www.iht.com/articles/2007/02/15/news/russia.php> (accessed 17 February 2007).

Myers, Steven Lee. 2007c. "Youth Groups Created by Kremlin Serve Putin's Cause." *New York Times*, 8 July. Retrieved from <http://www.nytimes.com/2007/07/08/world/europe/08moscow.html> (accessed 9 July 2007).

Nathanson, Stephen. 1993. *Patriotism, Morality, and Peace*. Lanham, MD: Rowman and Littlefield.

Nie, Norman, Jane Junn, and Kenneth Stehlik-Barry. 1996. *Education and Democratic Citizenship in America*. Chicago: University of Chicago Press.

Niemi, Richard and M. Hepburn. 1995. "The Rebirth of Political Socialization." *Perspectives on Political Science* 24 (Winter): 7–16.

Niemi, Richard and Jane Junn. 1998. *Civic Education: What Makes Students Learn*. New Haven: Yale University Press.

Nikandrov, Nikolai. 2008. "Upbringing and Socialization in Today's Russia." *Russian Education and Society* 50 (5): 56–75.

Nikolayenko, Olena. 2004. "Press Freedom during the 1994 and 1999 Presidential Elections in Ukraine: A Reverse Wave?" *Europe-Asia Studies* 56 (5): 661–86.

Nikolayenko, Olena. 2007. "The Revolt of the Post-Soviet Generation: Youth Movements in Serbia, Georgia, and Ukraine." *Comparative Politics* 39 (2): 169–88.

Nikolayenko, Olena. 2008. "Contextual Effects on Historical Memory: Soviet Nostalgia among Post-Soviet Adolescents." *Communist and Post-Communist Studies* 41 (2): 243–59.

Norris, Pippa, ed. 1999. *Critical Citizens: Global Support for Democratic Governance*. Oxford: Oxford University Press.

Norris, Pippa. 2000. *A Virtuous Cycle: Political Communication in Post-Industrialized Societies*. New York: Cambridge University Press.

Oates, Sarah. 2006. *Television, Elections and Democracy in Russia*. London: Routledge.

OECD/UNESCO. 2003. "Gender Differences and Similarities in Achievement." In *Literacy Skills for the World of Tomorrow: Further Results from PISA 2000*. France: OECD Publishing.

Offe, Claus and Adler Pierre. 1991. "Capitalism by Democratic Design? Theory Facing the Triple Transition in East Central Europe." *Social Research* 58 (Winter): 865–81.

Organization for Security and Cooperation in Europe (OSCE). 2004. "Report on the Media Coverage of the Beslan Tragedy: Access to Information and Journalists' Working Conditions." Special report prepared by the Representative on the Freedom of the Media. Retrieved from <www.osce.org/documents/rfm/2004/09/3586_en.pdf> (accessed 7 March 2006).

Orlov, Dmitry. 2008. "The New Russian Age and Sovereign Democracy." *Russian Politics and Law* 46 (5): 72–76.

Osborne, Kenneth. 2003. "Teaching History in Schools: A Canadian Debate." *Journal of Curriculum Studies* 35 (5): 585–626.

Ottaway, Marina. 2003. *Democracy Challenged: The Rise of Semi-Authoritarianism*. Washington, DC: Carnegie Endowment for International Peace.

Pannier, Bruce. 2006. "Zheltoqsan Protest Marked Twenty Years Later." Radio Free Europe/Radio Liberty, 16 December. Retrieved from <http://www.rferl.org/content/article/1073453.html> (accessed 4 March 2006).

Pearson, Tamara. 2008. "Youth Wing of United Socialist Party of Venezuela Born." *Venezuelan Analysis*, 15 September. Retrieved from <http://www.venezuelananalysis. com/news/3798> (accessed 19 October 2008).

Petrov, Nikolai. 2005. "From Managed Democracy to Sovereign Democracy: Putin's Regime Evolution in 2005." *PONARS Policy Memo* 396. Retrieved from <http://csis.org/files/media/csis/pubs/pm_0396.pdf> (accessed 4 March 2006).

Pietilainen, Jukka. 2008. "Media Use in Putin's Russia." *Journal of Communist Studies and Transition Politics* 24 (3): 365–85.

Pilkington, Hilary. 1994. *Russia's Youth and Its Culture*. London: Routledge.

Pilkington, Hilary, ed. 1996. *Gender, Generation, and Identity in Contemporary Russia*. London: Routledge.

Pilkington, Hilary, Elena Omel'chenko, Mona Flynn, and Uliana Bliudina. 2002. *Looking West?: Cultural Globalization and Russian Youth Culture*. University Park, PA: Pennsylvania State University Press.

Popson, Nancy. 2001. "The Ukrainian History Textbook: Introducing Children to the 'Ukrainian Nation.'" *Nationalities Papers* 29 (2): 325–50.

PravdaRu. 2004. "Russia Considers Opportunity to Set Up Two-Party Political System," 2 October. Retrieved from <http://english.pravda.ru/russia/politics/7139-parties-0> (accessed 10 October 2004).

PravdaRu. 2006. "Each of Seven Million Russian Alcoholics Drinks 27 Liters of Alcohol a Year," 9 November. Retrieved from <http://english.pravda.ru/society/stories/85432-alcoholism-0> (accessed 12 November 2006).

Prytula, Olena. 2006. "The Ukrainian Media Rebellion." In *Revolution in Orange: The Origins of Ukraine's Democratic Breakthrough*, ed. Anders Aslund and

Michael McFaul. Washington, DC: Carnegie Endowment for International Peace, pp. 103–24.

Przeworski, Adam. 1991. *Democracy and the Market*. Cambridge: Cambridge University Press.

Public Opinion Foundation. 2001. "The Treaty of Belovezhsk: Ten Years After." *FOM Online*, 6 December. Retrieved from <http://bd.fom.ru/report/cat/societas/image /collapse_FSU/belovezh/d014607> (accessed 20 January 2006).

Putin, Vladimir. 2005. Annual Address to the Federal Assembly of the Russian Federation, 25 April. Retrieved from http://archive.kremlin.ru/eng/speeches/2005/04/25/2031_type70029type82912_87086.shtml (accessed 1 May 2005).

Putnam, Robert. 1993. *Making Democracy Work: Civic Traditions in Italy*. Princeton, NJ: Princeton University Press.

Radio Free Europe/Radio Liberty. 2006. "When Bread Is Better Than Freedom." Poland, Ukraine, and Belarus Report, 26 February. Retrieved from <http://www.rferl.org/content/article/1343877.html > (accessed 19 November 2006).

Radio Free Europe/Radio Liberty. 2009. "Kazakh Students Protest 'Personality Cult'," 3 February. Retrieved from <http://www.rferl.org/content/Kazakh_President_Stars_In_New_Cartoon/1378650.html> (accessed 5 February 2009).

Ram, Haggay. 2000. "The Immemorial Iranian Nation? School Textbooks and Historical Memory in Post-Revolutionary Iran." *Nations and Nationalism* 6 (1): 67–90.

Reisinger, William, Arthur Miller, Vicki Hesli, and Kristen Hill Maher. 1993. "Political Values in Russia, Ukraine, and Lithuania: Sources and Implications for Democracy." *British Journal of Political Science* 24 (2): 183–223.

Roberts, Ken, S. C. Clark, C. Fagan, and J. Tholen, eds. 2000. *Surviving Post-Communism: Young People in the Former Soviet Union*. Cheltenham, UK: Edward Elgar.

Rodriguez, Alex. 2005. "Alcohol Destroying Rural Russia." *Moscow News*, 15 December. Retrieved from <http://www.mosnews.com/commentary/2005/12/15/alcoholism.shtml> (accessed 20 January 2006).

Roper, Steven D. 2005. "The Politicization of Education: Identity Formation in Moldova and Transnistria." *Communist and Post-Communist Studies* 38: 501–14.

Rose, Richard. 1995. "Freedom as a Fundamental Value." *International Social Science Journal* 145: 457–71.

Rose, Richard, William Mishler, and Christian Haerpfer. 1998. *Democracy and Its Alternatives: Understanding Post-Communist Societies*. Baltimore, MD: The John Hopkins University Press.

Rustow, Dankwurt. 1970. "Transitions to Democracy: Toward a Dynamic Model." *Comparative Politics* 2(3): 337–63.

Ryzhkov, Vladimir. 2005. "Sovereign Democracy and Usurper State." *Moscow Times*, 16 August. Retrieved from <http://www.themoscowtimes.com/stories/2005/08/16/006.html> (accessed 19 November 2006).

Saar, Ellu. 1997. "Transitions to Tertiary Education in Belarus and the Baltic Countries." *European Sociological Review* 13 (2): 139–58.

Sakwa, Richard. 1995. "Subjectivity, Politics, and Order in Russian Political Evolution." *Slavic Review* 54 (4): 943–64.

Sakwa, Richard, ed. 2009. *Power and Policy in Putin's Russia*. London: Routledge Press.

Sapiro, Virginia. 2004. "Not Your Parents' Political Socialization: Introduction for a New Generation." *Annual Review of Political Science* 7: 1–23.

Schumpeter, Joseph. 1942. *Capitalism, Socialism, and Democracy*. London: George Allen and Unwin.
Semetko, Holli A. and Natalya Krasnoboka. 2003. "The Political Role of the Internet in Societies in Transition: Russia and Ukraine Compared." *Party Politics* 9 (1): 77–104.
Shelley, Louise I. 2000. "Corruption in Post-Yeltsin Russia." *East European Constitutional Review* 9 (2): 70–74.
Shevtsova, Lilia. 1999. *Yeltsin's Russia: Myths and Reality*. Washington, DC: Carnegie Endowment for International Peace.
Shevyrev, Alexander. 2005. "Rewriting the National Past: New Images of Russia in History Textbooks of the 1990s." In *Educational Reform in Post-Soviet Russia: Legacies and Prospects*, ed. Ben Eklof, Larry E. Holmes, and Vera Kaplan. London: Frank Cass, pp. 272–90.
Silver, Brian. 1974. "The Status of National Minority Languages in Soviet Education: An Assessment of Recent Changes." *Soviet Studies* 26: 28–40.
Silver, Brian. 1987. "Political Beliefs of the Soviet Citizen: Sources of Support for Regime Norms" In *Politics, Work, and Daily Life in the USSR*, ed. James R. Millar. New York: Cambridge University Press, 100–41.
Simon, Janos. 1998. "Popular Conceptions of Democracy in Postcommunist Europe." In *The Postcommunist Citizen*, ed. Samuel H. Barnes and Janos Simon. Budapest: Erasmus Foundation, pp. 79–116.
Simons, Greg and Dmitry Strovsky. 2006. "Censorship in Contemporary Russian Journalism in the Age of War against Terrorism." *European Journal of Communication* 21 (2): 189–211.
Smith, Kathleen. 2002. *Mythmaking in the New Russia: Politics and Memory during the Yeltsin Era*. Ithaca, NY: Cornell University Press.
Smith, Tom and Lars Jarkko. 1998. "National Pride: A Cross-National Analysis." *GSS Cross-National Report*, no. 19. Chicago: National Opinion Research Center/University of Chicago. Retrieved from <http://www.norc.uchicago.edu/new/patriot.htm> (accessed 3 March 2006).
Solomon, Peter H. and Todd S. Foglesong. 2000. "The Two Faces of Crime in Post-Soviet Ukraine." *East European Constitutional Review* 9 (3): 72–76.
Stepanenko, Viktor. 1999. *The Construction of Identity and School Policy in Ukraine*. New York: Nova Science.
Sugimura, Kazumi, Mizuki Yamazaki, Jean S. Phinney, and Kazuko Takeo. 2009. "Compliance, Negotiation, and Self-Assertion in Japanese Adolescents' Disagreements with Parents." *International Journal of Behavioral Development* 33 (1): 77–87.
Sun, Yan. 1999. "Reform, State, and Corruption: Is Corruption Less Destructive in China Than in Russia?" *Comparative Politics* 32 (2): 1–20.
Szekely, Beatrice Beach. 1986. "The New Soviet Educational Reform." *Comparative Education Review* 30 (3): 321–43.
Torbakov, Igor. 2004. "Russian Analysts Ponder Orange Revolution's Implications for Kremlin Dominance in CIS." *Eurasia Daily Monitor* 1 (145), 13 December. Retrieved from <http://www.jamestown.org> (accessed 20 January 2005).
Torney-Purta, Judith. 2002. "The School's Role in Developing Civic Engagement: A Study of Adolescents in Twenty-Eight Countries." *Applied Developmental Science* 6 (4): 203–12.
Torney-Purta, Judith. 2004. "Adolescents' Political Socialization in Changing Contexts: An International Study in the Spirit of Nevitt Sanford." *Political Psychology* 25 (3): 465–78.

Torney-Purta, Judith, Carolyn Henry Barber, and Wendy Klandl Richardson. 2004. "Trust in Government-Related Institutions and Political Engagement among Adolescents in Six Countries." *Acta Politica* 39 (4): 380–406.

Torney-Purta, Judith, Rainer Lehmann, Hans Oswald, and Wolfram Schultz. 2001. *Citizenship and Education in Twenty-Eight Countries: Civic Knowledge and Engagement at Age Fourteen*. Amsterdam: International Association for the Evaluation of Educational Achievement.

Torney-Purta, Judith, Abraham Oppenheim, and Russell Farnen. 1975. *Civic Education in Ten Countries: An Empirical Study*. New York: Wiley.

Tucker, Joshua. 2005. *Regional Economic Voting: Russia, Poland, Hungary, Slovakia, and the Czech Republic, 1990–1999*. New York: Cambridge University Press.

United Nations Economic Commission for Europe (UNECE). 2005. *Trends in Europe and North America 2005*. Geneva: UNECE.

Varese, Federico. 2005. *The Russian Mafia: Private Protection in a New Market Economy*. Oxford: Oxford University Press.

Vovk, Elena. 2006. "The Treaty of Belovezhsk: Fifteen Years After." *FOM Online*, December. Retrieved from <http://bd.fom.ru/report/cat/societas/image/collapse_FSU/ belovezh/d064926> (accessed 12 January 2007).

Vyugin, Michael. 2006. "Victim of Hazing Andrei Sychev Becomes Symbol of Russian Military Corruption." *PravdaRu*, 9 February. Retrieved from <http://english.pravda.ru/russia/politics/09-02-2006/75688-sychev-0> (accessed 20 August 2006).

Walsh, Nick Paton. 2004. "A Police State without the Police." *Guardian*, 23 September. Retrieved from <http://www.guardian.co.uk/comment/story/0,,1310472,00.html> (accessed 3 March 2006).

Wanner, Catherine. 1998. *Burden of Dreams: History and Identity in Post-Soviet Ukraine*. University Park, PA: Pennsylvania State University Press.

Webber, Stephen L. 2000. *School, Reform and Society in the New Russia*. London: Macmillan.

White, Stephen, ed. 2008a. *Politics and the Ruling Group in Putin's Russia*. New York: Palgrave Macmillan.

White, Stephen, ed. 2008b. *Media, Culture, and Society in Putin's Russia*. New York: Palgrave Macmillan.

White, Stephen and Olga Kryshtanovskaya. 2003. "Putin's Militocracy." *Post-Soviet Affairs* 19(4): 289–306.

White, Stephen and Ian McAllister. 2008. "'It's the Economy, Comrade!' Parties and Voters in the 2007 Russian Duma Election." *Europe-Asia Studies* 60 (6): 931–57.

Whitefield, Stephen and Geoffrey Evans. 1999. "Political Culture versus Rational Choice: Explaining Responses to Transition in the Czech Republic and Slovakia." *British Journal of Political Science* 29: 129–55.

Wilson, Andrew. 2005a. *Virtual Politics: Faking Democracy in the Post-Soviet World*. New Haven, CT: Yale University Press.

Wilson, Andrew. 2005b. *Ukraine's Orange Revolution*. New Haven, CT: Yale University Press.

Xi, Jieying, Yunxiao Sun, and Jing Jian Xiao, eds. 2006. *Chinese Youth in Transition*. Farnham, UK: Ashgate.

Yakusheva, Tatiana. 2001. *The Treaty of Belovezhsk: Ten Years Later*. Moscow: Public Opinion Foundation, 12 December. Retrieved from <http://bd.english.fom.ru/report/ map/yakusheva/ed014624> (accessed 12 January 2007).

Yariv, Eliezer. 2009. "Students' Attitudes on the Boundaries of Teachers' Authority." *School Psychology International* 30 (1): 92–111.
Zarakhovich, Yuri. 2007. "Why Putin Loves WWII." *Time Online*, 8 May. Retrieved from <http://www.time.com/time/world/article/0,8599,1618531,00.html> (accessed 10 May 2007).
Zassourski, Ivan. 2004. *Media and Power in Post-Soviet Russia*. Armonk, NY: M.E. Sharpe.
Zeigler, Harmon. 1967. *The Political Life of American Teachers*. Englewood Cliffs, NJ: Prentice-Hall.
Zhao, Suisheng. 1998. "A State-Led Nationalism: The Patriotic Education Campaign in Post-Tiananmen China." *Communist and Post-Communist Studies* 31 (3): 287–302.
Zubar, Natalka. 2005. "In the Beginning Was the Word, and the Word Was …" *Maidan*, 10 December. Retrieved from <http://eng.maidanua.org/node/459> (accessed 19 December 2005).

Russian-language sources

Azar, Ilia. 2007a. "Zapishite telefon Putina" [Write down Putin's phone number]. *GazetaRu*, 21 March. Retrieved from <http://www.gazeta.ru/2007 /03/20/oa_234398.shtml> (accessed 27 March 2007).
Azar, Ilia. 2007b. "Putin za shest' tsentov bez NDS" [Putin for six cents without VAT]. *GazetaRu*, 26 March. Retrieved from <http://www.gazeta.ru/2007/03/26/oa_234852.shtml> (accessed 27 March 2007).
Bychenko, Andrei. 2002. "Den' sed'mogo noiabria – krasnyi den' kalendaria" [7 November is the red day on the calendar]. *Zerkalo Nedeli*, 15 November. Retrieved from <http://www.zn.kiev.ua/3000/3050/36675/> (accessed 8 September 2006).
Chuprov, Vladimir. 1992. *Molodezh' Rossii: Sotsial'noe razvitie* [Russian youth: social development]. Moscow: Nauka.
Demoscope Weekly. 2006. "Transformatsiia brachnoi modeli v sovremennoi Rossii: Tikhaia revoluitsia 90-kh" [Transformation of the marriage model in contemporary Russia: the quiet revolution in the 1990s], 16–19 October. Retrieved from <http://demoscope.ru/weekly/2006/0261/tema04.php> (accessed 5 May 2007).
Demoscope Weekly. 2007. "Brachno-semeinye protsessy: Evropeiskie tendentsii i ukrainskaia spetsifika" [Marital and family processes: European tendencies and Ukrainian peculiarities], 26–29 April. Retrieved from <http://demoscope.ru/weekly/2007/0285/tema01.php> (accessed 5 May 2007).
Diagilev, Anatolii. 2007. "Segodnia SMRU – samaia populiarnaia molodezhnaia organizatsia v Ukraine" [Today SMRU is the most popular youth organization in Ukraine]. *Fraza*, 30 July. Retrieved from <http://fraza.ua/interview/30.07.07/40159.html> (accessed 10 September 2007).
Dneprov, Edward, ed. 2002. *Modernizatsiia rossiiskogo obrazovaniia: dokumenty i materialy* [Modernization of Russian education: documents and proceedings]. Moscow: Gosudartsvennyi universitet-Vysshaia shkola ekonomiki.
Elvisti. 2004. "Zavershaetsia prizyvnaia kompania osen'-2004" [The fall 2004 call-up campaign is coming to an end], 22 November. Retrieved from <http://elvisti.com/node/47764> (accessed 20 November 2006).
Government of Russia. 2001. *Gosudarstvennaia programma "Patrioticheskoe vospitanie grazhdan Rossiiskoi Federatsii na 2001–2005 gody."* [National program "Patriotic Education of Citizens of Russian Federation 2001–2005"]. Decree

of 16 February. Retrieved from <http://www.ed.gov.ru> (accessed 8 September 2004).
Government of Russia. 2005. *Gosudarstvennaia programma "Patrioticheskoe vospitanie grazhdan Rossiiskoi Federatsii na 2006–2010 gody."* [National program "Patriotic Education of Citizens of Russian Federation 2006–2010"]. Decree of 11 July. Retrieved from <http://www.ed.gov.ru> (accessed 18 September 2006).
Kertman, Grigoriy. 2006. "Mezhlichnostnoe doverie v Rossii" [Interpersonal trust in Russia]. *Sotsial'naia real'nost'* 4: 7–24.
Kirillova, Svetlana. 2004. "Esli v konkurse pobedili deviat' uchebnikov, to pobeditelei skol'ko?" [If nine textbooks won the competition, how many winners are there?]. *Pervoe Sentiabria*, 6 March. Retrieved from <http://ps.1september.ru/article.php?ID=200401702> (accessed 12 March 2004).
Levada Center. 2005. "Rossiane ne khotiat, chtoby ikh blizkikh prizyvali v armiiu" [Citizens of Russia don't want their relatives to be drafted], 9 February. Retrieved from <http://www.levada.ru/press/2005020902.html> (accessed 12 April 2005).
Levada Center. 2007. *Obschestvennoe mnenie 2007: Ezhegodnik* [Public opinion 2007: annual report]. Moscow: Levada Center.
Levada Center. 2009a. "Otnoshenie rossian k SSHA, ES, Ukraine, i Gruzii (ianvar')" [Attitudes of Russians toward the USA, EU, Ukraine, and Georgia (January)], 30 January. Retrieved from <http://www.levada.ru/press/2009013001.html> (accessed 19 April 2009).
Levada Center. 2009b. "Otnoshenie rossian k SSHA,ES, Ukraine, Gruzii, i Belarusi (mart)" [Attitudes of Russians toward the USA, EU, Ukraine, Republic of Georgia, and Belarus (March)], April 1. Retrieved from <http://www.levada.ru/press/2009040102.html> (accessed 19 April 2009).
Levada Center. 2009c. "Rezkoe ukhudshenie otnoshenia rossiian k SSHA, ES, Ukraine, i Gruzii" [A steep decline in Russians' attitudes toward the USA, EU, Ukraine, and Georgia], 25 September. Retrieved from <http://www.levada.ru/press/2008092501.html> (accessed 1 November 2009).
Lisovskii, Vladimir, ed. 1996. *Sotsiologiia molodezhi* [Sociology of youth]. St. Petersburg, Russia: St. Petersburg University Press.
Lokshin, Aleksandr. 2008. *Istoria evreev Rossii v sovremennykh uchebnikah dlia srednei shkoly Rossii* [History of Russian Jews in contemporary textbooks for secondary schools in Russia]. Moscow: Russian Jewish Congress. Retrieved from <http://www.rjc.ru/files/RJC_Lokshin_summary.doc> (accessed 14 December 2008).
Malinin, S. A. and A. S. Pashkov. 1978. "O pravakh cheloveka i ikh prepodavanii" [About human rights and their teaching]. *Pravovedenie* 2: 3–11.
Newsru.Ua. 2008. "Akhmetov zanialsia sozdaniem izdatelskogo holdinga" [Akhmetov turned to the creation of a publishing holding], 28 January. Retrieved from <http://rus.newsru.ua/finance/29jan2008/axmetov.html> (accessed 30 January 2009).
Petrova, A. S. 2002. "Shkol'nye znania – poleznye i bespoleznye" [School knowledge – useful and useless]. Public Opinion Foundation Report. Retrieved from <http://bd.fom.ru/report/map/of024104> (accessed 1 March 2008).
Public Opinion Foundation. 2002. "Chem gordimsia, chego stydimsia?" [What do we take pride in, what are we ashamed of?]. *FOM Online*, 14 February. Retrieved from <http://bd.fom.ru/report/cat/man/patriotizm/d020608> (accessed 16 October 2006).
Public Opinion Foundation. 2005. "Militsiia i ee reputatsiia" [The militia and its reputation]. *FOM Online*, 10 November. Retrieved from <http://bd.fom.ru/

report/map/projects/dominant/dominan2005/dom0545/domt0545_3/d054513> (accessed 16 October 2006).
RegnumRu. 2008. "VtSIOM: Bolee poloviny rossian otmechat' 7 noiabria ne planiruiut" [VtSIOM: more than half of Russians are not planning to celebrate 7 November]. Retrieved from <http://www.regnum.ru/news/1077449.html> (accessed 24 January 2009).
Rzhevskii, V. A. and N. S. Bondar. 1982. "Mirovozrencheskaia napravlennost' uchebnogo kursa 'Osnovy sovetskogo prava'" [The ideological approach of the school course "Principles of Soviet Law"]. *Pravovedenie* 6: 68–75.
Sobkin, Samuil. 1997. *Starsheklassnik v mire politiki: Empiricheskoe issledovanie* [High-school students in the world of politics: an empirical investigation]. Moscow: Center for the Sociology of Education, Russian Academy of Sciences.
Turchenko, Fedir, Petro Panchenko, and Serhiy Timchenko. 2001. *Noveishaia istoria Ukrainy 1914–2001* [Modern history of Ukraine], trans. from Ukrainian, V. Hirich. Kyiv: Geneza.
Vzgliad. 2008. "Ozvucheno 'Imia Rossii'" [Name of Russia is articulated], 28 December. Retrieved from <http://www.vz.ru/society/2008/12/29/242897.html> (accessed 24 January 2009).
Zagladin, Nikita, Sergey Kozlenko, Sergey Minakov, and Yuriy Petrov. 2006. *Istoria Otechestva XX vek* [History of the fatherland: 20th century]. Moscow: Russkoe slovo.
Zhizn. 2004. "U Souiza molodezhi regionov Ukrainy popolnenie" [The Union of Youth from the Regions of Ukraine is expanding], 29 May.
Zubok, Julia. 1998. *Sotsial'naia integratsia molodezhi v usloviakh nestabil'nogo obshchestva* [Social integration of youth under the conditions of societal instability]. Moscow: Nauka.

Ukrainian-language sources

Amchuk, Leonid. 2005. "Andriy Yushchenko – Syn Boga?" [Andrew Yushchenko – Son of God?]. *Ukrainska Pravda*, 19 July. Retrieved from <http://pravda.com.ua/news/2005/7/22/6431.htm> (accessed 20 July 2005).
Cabinet of Ministers of Ukraine. 1999. *Pro zatverdzhennia Natsional'noi programy patriotychnogo vykhovannia naselennia, formuvannia zdorovogo sposobu zhuttia, rozvytku dukhovnosti ta zmitsnennia moral'nykh zasad suspil'stva* [On adopting the national program on patriotic education of the population, the promotion of healthy lifestyle, spiritual development, and the strengthening of moral values in society]. Decree of 15 September. Retrieved from <http://zakon.rada.gov.ua> (accessed 20 August 2004).
Cabinet of Ministers of Ukraine. 2002. *Pro likvidatsiiu deiakykh konstul'tatyvnykh, doradchukh ta inshykh organiv, utvorenykh Kabinetom Ministriv Ukrainy, ta vyznannia takymy, shcho vtratyly chunnist', deiakykh aktiv Kabinetu Ministriv Ukrainy* [On the liquidation of several consulting, advisory, and other organs created by the Cabinet of Ministers of Ukraine and the annulment of several decrees passed by the Cabinet of the Ministers of Ukraine]. Decree of 10 January. Retrieved from <http://zakon.rada.gov.ua> (accessed 20 August 2004).
Democratic Initiatives/Kyiv International Institute of Sociology (KIIS). 2005. "Dumky i pogliadu naselennia Ukrainy – veresen' 2005" [Thoughts and opinions of Ukraine's population – September 2005]. Press release of 28 September. Retrieved from <http://www.dif.org.ua> (accessed 1 November 2005).

Den'. 2008. "Chy vynni ZMI?" [Is the mass media to blame?], 2 October. Retrieved from <http://www.day.kiev.ua/254412/> (accessed 17 August 2009).

Institute of Politics. 2007. "Materialy do pres-konferentsii: 'Geroi, tsinnosti ta mifu suchasnoi Ukrainu'" [Material for the press conference "Heroes, values, and myths in contemporary Ukraine"], 10 January. Retrieved from <http://www.tomenko.kiev.ua/cgi/redir.cgi?url=nov107.html> (accessed 17 August 2009).

Kennan Institute. 2002. *Vitchyzniana istoriia v shkolakh i vuzakh Ukrainy: Ostannie desiaterichchia* [National history in Ukrainian schools and universities: the past decade]. Seminar proceedings. Kennan Institute: Kyiv.

Khmelko, Valery. 2006. "Cherez shcho politykam vdaietsia rozkoliuvatu Ukrainu" [Why politicians succeed in splitting Ukraine]. *Dzerkalo Tyzhnia* 24–30 June. Retrieved from <http://www.zn.kiev.ua/ie/show/603/53764/> (accessed 1 July 2006).

Kuchma, Leonid. 2002. *Zvernennia Prezydenta Ukrainy Leonida Kuchmy do ukrainskogo narodu u zv'iazku z Dnem pam'iati zhertv Holodomoru ta politychnykh represii* [The address of the president of Ukraine Leonid Kuchma to the Ukrainian people on the occasion of the day commemorating victims of the Holodomor and political repressions], 22 November. Retrieved from <http://memorial.kiev.ua/content/view/184/67/> (accessed 20 August 2005).

Kuchma, Leonid. 2004. *Zvernennia Prezydenta Ukrainy Leonida Kuchmy do ukrainskogo narodu u zv'iazku z vyboramy* [The address of the president of Ukraine Leonid Kuchma to the Ukrainian people concerning the presidential elections], 29 October. Retrieved from <http://www.elections.ukrinform.com/article.php?a=0727> (accessed 2 November 2004).

Kyiv International Institute of Sociology (KIIS). 2009. "Stavlennia naselennia Ukrainy ta Rosii do ukrains'ko-rosiis'kykh vidnosyn" [Attitudes of Ukrainian and Russian population toward Ukrainian–Russian relations]. Press release. Retrieved from <http://www.kiis.com.ua> (accessed 10 April 2009).

Panina, Natalia. 2005. *Ukrains'ke suspil'stvo 1994–2005: Sotsiologichnyi monitoring* [Ukrainian society 1994–2005: sociological monitoring]. Kyiv: Sophia Publishing House.

ProUa. 2005. "V Ukraini zavershylasia pryzovna kompania vesna-2005" [The spring 2005 call-up campaign is over in Ukraine], 31 May. Retrieved from <http://ua.proua.com/news/2005/05/31/115256.html> (accessed 20 January 2006).

Shkil, Andriy. 2004. *Proekt postanovy pro nepryiniatist proektu zakonu Ukrainy pro zagalnoderzhavnu programu patriotychnogo vykhovannia molodi na 2004–2008 roky (N 4593)* [Draft decree proposing the blockage of the draft law of Ukraine about the national program on patriotic education of youth in 2004–2008 (N 4593)], 21 September. Retrieved from <http://zakon.rada.gov.ua> (accessed 29 September 2004).

Telekrytyka. 2008. "Vakhgtang Kirpiani: Yaroslav Mudrui peremih u 'Velykykh ukraintsiakh' zavdiaku manipuliatsiam" [Vakhtang Kirpiani: Yaroslav the Wise won the Greatest Ukrainian title because of manipulation]. 15 May. Retrieved from <http://www.telekritika.ua/news/2008-05-18/38443> (accessed 10 June 2008).

Ukrainska Pravda. 2004. "Pomaranchesva Revoluitsia zmusyla ity v Internet" [The Orange Revolution made people go online], 14 December. Retrieved from <http://main.pravda.com.ua/news/2004/12/14/14841.htm> (accessed 16 December 2004).

Ukrainska Pravda. 2009. "Rosiianu ne liubliat' ukraintsiv nezvazhaiuchy na nashu liubov" [Russians don't love Ukrainians despite our love], 27 February. Retrieved from <http://www.pravda.com.ua/news/2009/2/27/90436.htm> (accessed 10 April 2009).

Verkhovna Rada. 2003. *Pro pryiniatta za osnovu proektu zakonu Ukrainy pro zagalnoderzhavnu programu patriotychnogo vykhovannia molodi na 2004–2008 roky (N 2033)* [Decree: using the draft as the basis for the law of Ukraine concerning the national program of patriotic education of youth in 2004–2008 (N 2033)], 22 September. Retrieved from <http://zakon.rada.gov.ua> (accessed 29 September 2004).

Verkhovna Rada. 2006. *Pro zniattia z rozgliadu proektu zakonu Ukrainy pro zagalnoderzhavnu programu patriotychnogo vykhovannia molodi na 2004–2008 roky (N 467)* [Decree: taking off the agenda the draft law of Ukraine concerning the national program of patriotic education of youth in 2004–2008 (N 467)], 14 December. Retrieved from <http://zakon.rada.gov.ua> (accessed 20 December 2006).

Index

adolescence 1, 8-10, 19, 35
case selection: countries 1-2, 11-12; cities 12-14
corruption 16, 28, 35, 39-40, 46, 48-50, 77, 79
democracy 1, 9, 11, 17, 90; attitudes toward 3, 10, 15-24, 45, 58, 75-6, 84-5, 94-5, 116-18; conceptions of 24-33; sovereign democracy 5, 17-18
family 73-5, 95, 102
Holodomor: official statements on 2, 122; in textbooks 97-8, 106-8, 110-11, 113-14, 119
hybrid regime 1-2, 11, 19, 33, 118, 120-1
IEA Civic Education Study 8-9, 35, 39-40
Kuchma, Leonid 1-2, 4-5, 7, 11-13, 18, 62, 79, 92, 118, 121; Kuchmagate 27, 79; "Ukraine without Kuchma" movement 73, 79
Life in Transition Survey 22-3, 38-40
mass media 1-2, 18-19, 29, 31, 34, 73, 75-81, 106, 117-19, 122-3; trust in the media 82-84, and political support 16, 84-5
Nashi 90, 120-1
national pride 3, 16, 52-61, 70-2, 75, 116-17
Orange Revolution 2, 12, 16-17, 36, 43-4, 52, 68, 73, 76, 92-93, 121-2; and political support 26, 28-32, 40, 49, 53, 55
patriotic education 3-8, 117-18
political support 10-11, 14, 75-6, 84-5, 94
Public Opinion Foundation 55, 63-4, 78, 96
Putin, Vladimir 1-2, 4-5, 7, 11-12,16, 18, 21, 30, 36-9, 41-2, 52, 62, 77-8, 89-91, 118, 120-3
schools 4, 22, 66, 69, 73, 97; Soviet educational system 86-9; educational reforms in the post-Soviet period 89-92; and political support 92-5, 117-18
Soviet nostalgia 3, 16, 62-72, 75, 84, 116-17; *see* the Soviet Union
Soviet Union 1-4, 8, 11, 15-16, 26, 29, 35, 40, 52, 55-8, 60-71, 84, 87, 116-22; in textbooks 96-115
textbooks 3-4, 6, 16, 55, 69, 86-7, 89-91, 96-115
trust in authorities 34-50; and interpersonal trust 40-1
World Values Survey 22-3, 39, 52-4
World War II 9, 13, 59, 69, 91, 97-8, 102-6, 108-15, 118-19
Yanukovych, Viktor 2, 5, 7, 12-14, 20, 29,31, 37, 43, 52, 74, 80, 83, 123
Yushchenko, Viktor 2, 7, 13, 29, 36-7, 42-4, 50, 55, 58, 62, 79-80, 83, 122